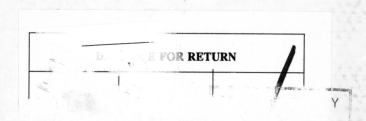

LANGUAGE, DISCOURSE, SOCIETY
General Editors: Stephen Heath, Colin MacCabe and Denise Riley

Published titles

Politics and Culture:

Working Hypotheses for a Post-Revolutionary Society

Michael Ryan

Associate Professor of English
Northeastern University

MACMILLAN

341966

First published 1989

Published by
THE MACMILLAN PRESS LTD
Houndmills, Basingstoke, Hampshire RG21 2XS
and London
Companies and representatives
throughout the world

Printed in the People's Republic of China

British Library Cataloguing in Publication Data

Ryan, Michael
Politics and culture: working hypotheses
for a post-revolutionary society —
(Language, discourse, society series).
1. Culture. Political aspects
I. Title II. Series
306

ISBN 0–333–36295–0

Series Standing Order

If you would like to receive future titles in this series as they are
published, you can make use of our standing order facility. To place a
standing order please contact your bookseller or, in case of difficulty,
write to us at the address below with your name and address and the
name of the series. Please state with which title you wish to begin your
standing order. (If you live outside the United Kingdom we may not
have the rights for your area, in which case we will forward your order
to the publisher concerned.)

Customer Services Department, Macmillan Distribution Ltd
Houndmills, Basingstoke, Hampshire, RG21 2XS, England.

To the memory of my parents –
Sean Ryan (1919–68) and Kathleen O'Neill (1918–69)
and
for my brother Donal (1945–87)

Contents

Acknowledgements

I wish to thank Jay Clayton, Tom Dumm, Nancy Fraser, Doug Kellner, Martha Minow, Fred Pfeil, and Julie Rivkin for their help in revising the manuscript. Stephen Heath's editorial criticisms were invaluable. Without Eric Halpern's prodding, I probably never would have finished. And to the anonymous reader, many thanks for your suggestions.

'I think that that's the origin of violence. They want something that's theirs. A possession. . . . I was like saying it was all right for you to hit me. Because I'm going to take it. I'm not going to leave.'
                            – 'Corie' on the Ophrah Winfry Show

'I'm sorry. Whenever I hear the term "alternative spaces" I think of safety valves for the dissatisfactions of people within our culture. I'd rather see those spaces as revolutionary planning committees.'
                            – 'Audience', DIA Art Foundation,
                            Discussions in Contemporary Culture,

'I mean that supposing the real chances of making a different kind of future are fifty-fifty, they are still usually fifty-fifty after the most detailed restatement of the problems. Indeed, sometimes, in one kind of detailed restatement, there is even an adverse tilt. It is only in a shared belief and insistence that there are practical alternatives that the balance of forces and chances begin to alter. Once the inevitabilities are challenged, we begin gathering our resources for a journey of hope.'
                            – Raymond Williams, *The Year 2000*

'I' th' commonwealth I would by contraries
Execute all things. For no kind of traffic
Would I admit; no name of magistrate;
Letters should not be known; riches, poverty,
And use of service, none; contract, succession,
Bourn, bound of land, tilth, vineyard, none;
No use of metal, corn, or wine, or oil;
No occupation; all men idle, all;
And women too . . .
No sovereignty.'
                            – W. Shakespeare, *The Tempest*

Introduction

The essays in this book were written between 1977 and 1988, and their alignment is necessarily autobiographical, staking out as much a personal development as an intellectual one.[1] They concern my feelings about certain ideas and the people who hold them as much as the ideas themselves. Anyone familiar with current debates at the intersection of French post-structuralism and German critical theory, the point of departure for this book, is aware that strong emotions are in play. Animosity and resentment, as much as loyalty and defiance, are evident in recent writing (and conferencing) on left cultural and social theory. It is all reminiscent of an old Kingston Trio song: 'The French hate the Germans, and the Germans hate the Dutch, and I don't like anybody very much'. I don't cite these lines as advertising a position, either intellectual or emotional. They do strike me, however, as reminders of the extent to which our intellectual positions are always contoured by the social worlds in which we think and the context of personal relationships in which we move. Post-structuralism configures a fundamental historical shift away from objectivist and rationalist cognitive paradigms and toward such a social and material understanding of the situatedness of what we have till now called reason. And it is perhaps because of this shift that it has inspired such animosity among neo-rationalists like Jurgen Habermas.

Once, at a conference of habermassians, I ventured a defence of the French against the accusation that they are 'young conservatives'. Afterwards, one of the speakers came up to me and mentioned my 'soft spot' for Derrida, implying that my position was therefore understandable. Soft spot? I think the statement was meant to suggest that one was supposed to have hard ideas, not soft spots. I felt appropriately situated in relation to the rigours of reason. And yet the thought, or is it a feeling?, well, let's just say the mental representation lingers that the distinction between hard ideas and soft spots could do well to be refigured. One goal of all our work, it seems to me, must be to show convincingly that the hard thinking of so-called 'mainstream discourse', which justifies economic injustice and the fine art of missile pointing, is not the rational science it claims it is, but instead a violent rhetorical reduction of complexity to simplicity, of differential relations to firm identities, of metonymic interconnections to metaphoric idealizations, of diffusely textured situations to tightly boundaried

1

containers, of webs of feeling to numbing objectifications, and of a potentially disturbing and disordering proliferation of democratic possibilities to a self-reproducing system of social domination.

The French description of this is accurate, and German rationalists like Habermas are wrong to dismiss it. But I have also come to feel that we who work on the French side would be wrong to ignore the insistent point the German thinkers make: that the measures of reason are necessary instruments for attaining a good society. A progressive politics based in the material energies of need and desire does not have to stand opposed to rationality altogether. Indeed, a scientific ordering of priorities according to principles of equality and equity would seem to be crucial to a politics that claims to be both democratic and just without lapsing into a romantic populism.

Neither the French materialist nor the German rationalist position is convincing in its own right. Rationalism has done too much damage in the world to be taken seriously in the even relatively modified communicative form in which the reformed Frankfurt School offers it to us, but counter-rationalism, for all its critical power, has so far offered little in the way of working hypotheses for a reconstructed society other than the ideal of a deleuzian rampage of libidinal nomadism, or the sectoral liberal reformism of the heideggerian-nietzschean left, or the mystical populism of the post-modernists. German thinking will only mature when it relinquishes its frightening authoritarianism and learns to take seriously the French insights into the constructive power of representation and the democratic power of need and desire, and the French will not overcome their combination of politically passive cynicism and sexy libertarianism until they once again reground their critical insights in a socially reconstructive project of the sort German critical theory attempts to outline.

This book takes that problem as its point of departure. I have sought in these pages to work beyond the impasse of critical theory and post-structuralism. As in my book *Marxism and Deconstruction*,[2] I argue for a political understanding of deconstruction particularly, and I attempt to develop the lessons of post-structuralism into strategies of ideological critique with political ramifications. My goal has been to bring the deconstructive critique of knowledge and representation to bear on the issue of modelling and formulating a post-revolutionary society. In so doing, I have sought to forge links between marxist autonomy theory, deconstruction, cultural studies, and object-relations psychoanalysis. Such divergent strands of thought are defined as much by incommensurability as by compatibility, and I have not sought to bring them into a unity. The necessity of combining diverse strategies of analysis suggests that the theoretical as well as the practical goal is a complex one to which notions of unity bear little relation. Indeed, to the degree that the practical goal might be summed up as difference within equality, the theoretical approach is necessarily multiple. It begins with certain dilemmas or differences of position that are not taken as problems to be processed into unities, but rather as measuring points for projecting new conceptualizations. The work is one as much of bringing something new into being as of naming an existing reality.

Easily the most serious of these dilemmas or differences is the one that separates materialism and rationalism. This is simply another name for the difference between French post-structuralism and German critical theory. By materialism here, I do not only mean the extra-cultural realm of nature. Materialism in the sense in which I am using it also includes all those things that constitute the practical, lived dimension of life, from language and cityscapes to cultural practices and libidinal desire. By rationalism, I mean the position that holds that the operations of reason should be the basis of a just society. In as much as post-structuralism is a critique of the logocentric tradition in philosophy – the position that holds that ideas transcend the representations that bear them, that reason can gain full access to the world and to its own operations without an unassimilable remainder or alterity made up of the very representational instruments that allow it to exist, and that reason is immunized to its institutional and historical setting – it stands at odds with such rationalism. The road to justice must, it argues, be as much concerned with the road itself as with the idea of justice.

Rationalism, on the other hand, which rightfully claims that there would be no road worth travelling if we could not together agree on a rational idea of justice (one characterized by a meta-empirical universality), must repel the materialist position, for in its most radical forms, that position precludes the purely rational formulation of universal principles independent of the contingencies of concrete situation or of worldly differences of power. If the materialist position cannot justify itself without recourse to a reason that seems reliant on processes that stand outside materiality, the rationalist position cannot address the material world without engaging contingencies that oblige it to sacrifice the very principles of universality and ideality that lend it efficacy.

One solution to the aporia of rationalism and materialism is to speak from a rationalist position while accepting the indeterminacies of materialism. I will suggest the possibility of a different approach that builds from the post-structuralist materialist position and seeks to incorporate a situated and contextualized reason to its agenda.

The major connection between materialism and rationalism is the idea of <u>form</u>. Form is at once a rational and a material concept. It stands between materiality and ideality, the objective world of things and the mental world of thoughts and ideas. Form gives empirical shape to mental entities; as words or acts or representations, form embodies thought materially. In a similar way, the material world can be said to exist only in so much as it assumes form or has certain shapes and patterns. There is no such thing as a formless substance or a materiality without shape, and this is particularly true of the materiality of social life.

Thoughts and ideas exist in the realm of sense through rhetoric, the tropes or figures that give ideas certain shapes, and through representation, that 'exteriority' of images or acts or words that renders the 'interiority' of mental experience sensible for others. Without form, rhetoric, or representation in general, there could be no thought and no communication. Habermas accurately points to the necessary inherence of reasoning in communication, but he does not push the insight far enough: thought also inheres in the tropes and forms of representation. Contained in the idea of a communicative rationality must be a description of the way thought assumes material shape (tropic forms) and thereby becomes communicable.

The post-structuralist position is that reason is inseparable from the realm of representation, a realm defined as much by relations that are contingent and indeterminate as it is by structuring rules of order or logic. Form is necessary to reason but as form, reason loses some of its transcendental power; it is forced to acknowledge its materiality and indeterminacy, its dependence on a democratic openness at odds with the necessitarian imperative of logic. It is obliged to accept that the construction of its ideals in the world can only occur through the instruments of representation and rhetoric (through education, political debate, advertising, acculturation, and so on).

Even the most rational idea of a just society will not be realized in the world until enough people are convinced by it to disempower those whose material interests oblige them to resist that idea. And the new institutions, beliefs, and attitudes that must necessarily accompany that idea as its personal and interpersonal correlates will be experienced and will operate as new representations of the world and of oneself. New kinds of cultural imagery, and schools, and family structures, and interpersonal scenarios are as important in this endeavour as the development of right concepts. Reason may reside in the mind's capacity to generate binding non-empirical universals, but it can only become operational as unbound, empirically contingent words, images, actions, feelings, and institutions.

Form also pertains to materiality. Social life is shaped and determined by forms that are inseparable from it; indeed, there is no content of social life outside that shaping or forming process. We exist and have being or content as social entities in the forms of behaviour we practice, the modes of interaction we engage in, the formal patterns of speech and communication we undertake, the styles of work we assume, and so forth. Social life consists of certain ways of doing things and of arranging institutions, of patterning behaviour in everything from marriages to bureaucratic organizations. It is a formal process to the extent that it entails shaping the material world in certain conventional ways – in a political form that is authoritarian or one that is libertarian, for example, or in a sexual form that is restricted and heterocentric or one that is expansive and polyvalent.

Form also extends into extra-social material existence. Our basic material needs are satisfied by agriculture not by agrinature, and the role of imagination, modelling, and technique in making agriculture its most productive need hardly be asserted. Form is also bodily and emotional. Human bodily life is shaped by nutrition into different possible forms, and human psychology is notoriously vulnerable to contouring according to levels of environmental nurturance. Our emotional life patterns take the form of stories whose scripts are not entirely idiosyncratic; they are often the translation into individual terms of general cultural narratives. And they are shaped by the institutional forms of the patriarchal family with its various representational strategies of care and abuse.

We frequently do not see the materiality of social life as a formal process because the stabilization of the current formal arrangement of life operates an effacement of its rhetorical basis and of its contingent origins. As a result, effects are taken to be grounds or substances when they are in fact patterns or shapes that themselves produce that very sense of substance. Such forms and procedures of social life as the market ideal, the superior individual succeeding on his own, the inevitability of unequal distribution, the naturalness of certain career results, and so on all seem to have a content that determines the particular forms of action, feeling, or thought people engage in, but the order of priority or causality can easily be reversed. It is the arrangement of terms, the disposition of forms, that generates the illusion of content, of a substance that somehow lies under the forms our lives assume, determining them. The seemingly objective rules of social arrangements are effects of those very arrangements of elements, and they have no substantive or natural objectivity outside of those arrangements.

Figures construct the semblance of a pre-figural social reality by projecting an appearance of literality where none exists. The relations between such social figures as 'the executive', 'the career woman', and 'the renegade' themselves create a semblance of reality that reduces the visibility of the figures. Similarly, such narratives as 'going for a piece of the action', 'equality of opportunity', and 'defending the national interest' work together to create a sense of a lived reality that appears to be merely named by these story outlines. Such rhetorical equations as the part-for-whole or synechdochic acceptance of entertainment as a substitute for self-fulfilment, the metonymic or contiguously connected displacement of sexual desire onto consumer fetishes, the litotic or doubly negated relation of constrained aspiration to constraining social context create as one effect of their operation a tautology that posits the reason for the necessity of certain social rules in the effects of those rules.

Form is thus a bridge concept between rationalism and materialism, between the realm of thought, in as much as it can only exist in the form of representations, and materiality, in as much as it can only exist in certain forms of being. Form is a plastic medium that is not a simple conductor of forces of determination from one realm to the other, from materiality to thought, as in traditional materialism, or from thought to materiality, as in traditional rationalism. Rather, it designates the necessary materiality of everything, as well as its supreme figurality and malleability.

Form is a crucial concept in one other way. It underscores the importance of boundaries both in the constitution of identities and in their undoing. Form exists along the boundary that separates an inside from an outside, the supposedly ideal interiority of thought, say, from the exteriority of material representation in language. It externalizes, and in so doing, it undoes the identity or interiority it safeguards. It is therefore a radical principle that emphasizes how ideological identities might be undermined while also supplying a principle for the construction of alternatives. A focus on form draws attention to the procedures that secure rational and social identities by establishing boundaries

that separate insides from outsides, selves from others, and social
realities like capitalist individualism from communitarian relations
that are supposedly outside them altogether. But it also draws
attention to the ways in which contextual outsides inhere in such things
as personal interiority, or to how differential relations between people
constitute the social figure of individuality.

If boundaries are essential to the illusion of a social reality exempt
from rhetorical shaping and relational determination, they are also key
in the maintenance of the illusion of the identity of concepts and
universals like 'freedom' as things separable from such specific and
contingent material determinants as economic context. The universal
form of the idea of freedom assures its identity as a unique and general
concept, but that form must also distinguish universal freedom from
mere empirical contingencies of economic situation, and in that
institutional act of boundary distinction, the identity of the concept is
impugned. Its form determines it as much by what it keeps at bay as by
what it includes as its own.

The formal dimension of boundaries is also evident in the very
patterns of action in daily life, which are boundaried in certain ways
spatially and temporally (the eight-hour day or monogamous sexuality), and these exist in a continuum with the prevailing patterns of
rationality in society. The acceptance of work discipline can occur only
when accompanied by a rationale that establishes a boundary between
the virtuous endurance of pain and the rewards of leisure enjoyment.
The formal shaping of life itself follows a pattern of displacement,
whereby leisure substitutes for a more general enjoyment throughout
the day, and desire is deferred or displaced onto cultural fetishes
whose isolation testifies to the relations and larger wholes that are
deflected. These formal shapes would not be possible without an
accompanying rational representation or narrative that gives sense to
pain and sublimates it into the compensatory pleasure of meaning.
One endures by being the hero of the narrative, and meeting the
company deadline becomes an adventure story. Thus, one can say that
life itself has genres that establish the boundaries of social meaning,
from the melodrama of socialized domesticity to the pathological epic
of militarism, all of which themselves concern issues of boundaries.

As in thought, in social life, form is a boundary concept that belies
the identities it seems to assure. The forms of life that designate a
boundaried identity of 'labour' have meaning only in distinction from
other possible forms to which they are connected and to which they
refer. Rather than an identity, what one is confronted with is a

differential of relational terms – jeans not silk, Toyota not Lamborghini, Amway not Fabergé – each of which has meaning only in constellation with the others. Similarly, institutions like corporations exist as forms of behaviour that undo their identity even as they constitute it. The life of a corporation is determined at the boundary it has with consumers and with other corporations. To be 'itself', it must always be 'other', always somehow directed outward and away from itself. Its identity is plausible only through differential relations that deprive it of a self-sufficient identity.

The concept of form thus draws attention to issues of identity in reason and in society that can be useful in the project of social reconstruction. By studying form, one notices processes of undoing at the boundaries designated by form and one sees the interconnections between social reason and the forms of social life. What seems selfsame comes undone, and the identities proclaimed by ideology are shown to be denials, negations that affirm differential or relational realities that they attempt to disavow. The ideological quality of such figures as freedom (conceived as a universal idea detached from material situations) or the entrepreneur (conceived as an individual whose actions are not inherently social) stands forth, but so also does a halo at the boundary where such figures are formed as identities, a halo of relations, differences, and contingent connections that suggest an alternative way of formulating those putative identities.

On the basis of the concept of form, then, the project of social reconstruction can be more specified as a refiguration of the rhetoric of thought and as a reformulation of the formal arrangements that shape social existence in certain ways. As a result, rationalism is refigured by emphasizing the dependence of reason on the shapes of rhetoric and the processes of representation in general. And traditional materialism is refigured by showing how the supposed substantive content of social life is dependent on formal arrangements of terms, on rhetorics of relation between elements.[3]

Another name for that boundary between reason and materiality that I have described as form might be culture since culture generally is applied to everything that falls on the social and historical side of materiality, and it can also be a name for everything that falls on the rhetorical and representational side of reason. Culture includes the domains of rhetoric and representation, as well as the domains of lived experience, of institutions, and of social life patterns. This emphasis on culture draws attention to the political character of reason as of social reality, to the way force operates rhetorically in such putatively

FORCE NOT POWER

rational universals as 'freedom' and to the way force shapes such supposedly non-rhetorical realities as personal life into certain formal patterns.

I suggest the concept of force as a replacement for the concept of power that is now used in work of this sort for several reasons. Force names the interaction between different kinds of social energy that establishes the shape of social forms. When capitalists exercise force against subordinated groups (non-whites, workers, women, and such like) in response to the force of resistance those groups exercise or to the instability of difference their activities inject into the supposedly unitary and self-identical social system, capitalists thereby determine the shape and form of the lives of those groups. And the expansion or contraction of the rights and powers of those subordinated people – their form of life – will in part be determined by what counter-forces they can muster against the force exercised against them.

The advantage of this description is that it draws attention to the mobile and flexible character of this interchange. While the concept of power suggests a stabilization of domination, the concept of force permits a description of the flows of tension within unequal social arrangements. Those arrangements necessarily give rise to forces that contend with each other and that ultimately move structures founded on tense inequalities toward greater equality as structural tension moves toward release, a running down of the energy consumed in maintaining the tense and unequal stasis. But though the necessity of a certain direction in the movement of those forces is stressed here, the possibility of contingency and indeterminacy of direction is still left open. The 'greatest number' are still capable of choosing the imposed order of facism, especially in capitalist contexts, although it must be understood that such choices are always structured as limited options by the determining context. In a situation where a powerful group only permits a choice between pain and fantasies of power, the results seem scarcely surprising.

* The possibility that culture might be determining of materiality is alien to orthodox marxism, whose defining trope in relation to capitalist liberal idealism is the positing of a material world external to the human subject's 'freedom'. Yet marxism as a political project requires an ideal of a world where culture would subsume materiality. In such a world, the issue of the form of life would become primary and would be something determinable in a democratic and participatory fashion. Marxist theories of culture – especially the work of Raymond Williams and the works produced by the Birmingham Centre for

Contemporary Cultural Studies – display how problematic that
political goal becomes if too heavy an emphasis is placed on the
exteriority of materiality to culture. I will review the theory of culture
and then look more closely at Williams' work and that of the Centre.

The relationship between culture and materiality, or culture and
social structure, has been described in a number of different, even
contending ways. At one extreme are those like Marvin Harris who
emphasize the determining force of materiality in relation to culture.
At the opposite extreme are theorists like Jean Baudrillard for whom
culture has become determining of materiality, so that media simulation now shapes reality more so than material determinants. On the
spectrum between these two stand thinkers as diverse as Pierre
Bourdieu, Clifford Geertz, Victor Turner, Louis Althusser, Antonio
Gramsci, Juri Lotman, and Tetsuo Kogawa.

According to Harris's 'cultural materialism', culture is the 'learned
repertory of thoughts and actions exhibited by the members of social
groups'.[4] In other words, culture is a rather narrow ribbon of patterned
behaviour that does not extend into social institutions and that is
external to a very powerfully determining set of material constraints
and forces. For Bourdieu, especially in his two books *Reproduction*
and *Distinction*, culture both expresses and maintains class differences. Access to different kinds of cultural capital is determined by
one's class position and one's educational status, and differentiations
in culture operate to reproduce these social inequalities. The process
of cultural differentiation, whereby working class people are allocated
technical education and popular culture, while upper class people have
access by virtue of their social position to élite schools and high culture,
works to maintain differences in social power.[5]

The liberal alternative to these material determinist marxist
approaches conceives of culture as an autonomous realm that acts
independently of material conditions to give shape and meaning to
social life. The tensions and contradictions as well as the founding
values of a society are negotiated and resolved or projected and
reaffirmed through culture's rituals, symbols, and narratives. Anthro-
pologists like Clifford Geertz and Victor Turner represent this position
most clearly.[6]

In between the expressive and the reflective positions stands the
work deriving from cultural marxists like Louis Althusser. From this
perspective, culture does not simply express and directly reproduce
social power through a distribution of cultural capital, nor does it
simply project and negotiate social values in a general sense,

independently of class politics. Culture is the arena in which the contradictions that arise within a capitalist society are resolved in ways that assure the continuation of a ruling group's hegemony. This position, which owes much to Claude Levi-Strauss, combines the ideas of reproduction and negotiation, expression and reflection that characterize the other two positions. The althusserian theory of culture marks an advance on the liberal anthropological one in that it sees culture more accurately as a function of power, and it broadens the concept of social reproduction in that it assumes culture is something more than an expressive medium for extra-cultural social structures. Culture also generates social subjects and distributes subject positions.[7]

The althusserian theory of culture is limited, however, in that it sees culture as reproducing power but not contesting it. The possibility that seemingly ideological cultural artifacts might be sites of important political tensions or that their ideology might itself be symptomatic of incipient struggles or that they might be antidotes to threatening popular potentials is not granted within the althusserian framework. The theory of cultural politics associated with the ideas of Antonio Gramsci, especially the idea of hegemony, tends on the whole to cede more importance to the exercise of political resistance on the popular level through culture. Most of this work, however, also assumes an althusserian and lacanian stance; consequently, popular culture especially is pictured as consisting of 'imaginary' resolutions to extra-cultural social contradictions.[8]

At the opposite extreme from these positions stand the theories of Juri Lotman, Tetsuo Kogawa, and Jean Baudrillard. Lotman's theory of culture accords more power to culture as a force capable of reshaping social life. In his semiotic theory, culture consists of 'a hierarchy of semiotic systems' the purpose of which is 'structurally organizing the world around man'. In his work on Russian cultural history, Lotman places even more emphasis on culture as a shaping procedure. The adoption of western European ideals and models by the Russian aristocratic class in the middle of the nineteenth century led to an entire refashioning of modes of behaviour, speech, and dress.[9] The Japanese cultural theorist, Tetsuo Kogawa, makes an even stronger claim for cultural determination. He has developed a theory of how what is called the 'Emperor System' in contemporary Japanese society reshaped social and bodily life along western capitalist lines in the late nineteenth century. The emperor was installed deliberately during the Meiji Restoration, a period of great modernization and industrialization, as a cultural symbol that would help inculcate certain attitudes of discipline, respect, and obedience that were necessary to the process of modernization. At the same time, a 'samurization' of Japanese society occurred that consisted of the imposition of certain highly formal patterns on bodily comportment, patterns and gestures designed to instill a sense of rank and deference. The materiality of the body was itself reshaped by cultural designs.[10]

Kogawa's post-modern theory of Japanese culture is similar to one that develops out of post-structuralism in the work of Jean Baudrillard. Derrida's deconstructive description of the impossibility of a referent outside of signification and representation becomes in Baudrillard's theory of culture a negative metaphysic in which reality is transformed by capitalism into simulations that have no backing. I will argue against Baudrillard's negative use of post-structuralism in more detail in chapter 4. Here, I will offer a more politically enabling post-structuralist account of culture.

In the post-structuralist perspective, culture inhabits materiality as the forms of social life, from the family to the workday to our very psychological dispositions.[11] The forms and representational patterns of culture are not simply added onto an already constituted substance of social existence. The supplement of cultural form is that without which no sociality could be possible; decultured sociality would be a diffusion of formless and boundless energy or matter. Consequently, in this perspective, the politics of culture comes down not to a choice between repressive culture and a good, extra-cultulral world of free or natural materiality. It comes down to a choice of cultures.

In the post-structuralist framework, materiality clearly recedes in power or value as a purely extra-cultural determinant. Materiality is still what is outside human will, but it ceases to be entirely outside. And human culture ceases to be entirely artificial and acquires a power of refabrication that extends into social and natural materiality – as, for example, the narratives of national identity in history writing or education that fashion nationalist subjects out of otherwise undistinguished peoples. The cultural discourse of liberalism in seventeenth and eighteenth century England, for example, was not the expression of a particular group's social power; it was, rather, inseparably part of the production of that power through the creation of institutions and ideologies, patterns of legal formulation and theories of the self, post-mercantilist economic forms and modes of class cultural differentiation. Locke's constitutional theory is as much a cultural as a political document in that it establishes the dominant tropes of liberal political culture. The rhetoric of legal action that will eventually congeal in Blackstone's *Commentaries* is part of the same process of rhetorical construction that will appear artistically in Defoe's *Crusoe*, which does not so much reflect a social current as inflect its constituting rhetoric and disseminate it further.[12]

The cultural and rhetorical components were not secondary to the process of establishing a post-authoritarian economic and political arrrangement. Without them, that arrangement could not have come into existence. Even the crucial extra-cultural element of that arrangement – the incipient industrial revolution with its shift to steam engine-based loom production – was itself dependent on cultural factors – the emergence of an educational system that created the literacy and the national language that were the preconditions for invention, the formation of an academy that promoted experiment, and the invention of experimentation itself in Bacon's new science, itself made possible by a court culture that fostered intellectual life.

Similarly, in the US between 1978 and 1988, right-wing economic power asserted itself as the institutionalization of brutality, but it was clear as well that the new right-wing culture arose around certain dominant discursive motifs, metaphors such as the ideal of 'freedom' or synecdoches such as the displacement of all social frustration onto 'big government'. This rhetoric informed the shaping of economic and political as well as cultural institutions and values. The frontier ideal of the unconstrained male individual was telescoped into an economic programme hostile to governmental regulation of business and into a political programme that brooked no restraint on even illegal actions in the name of turning back a metaphorized threat to economic freedom – communism. This cultural mobilization was carried out through popular cultural modes such as film, which transcoded the social metaphors into images of identification that aided the enactment of the economic and political programmes.

The post-structuralist theory of culture breaks down the boundary between the traditional concept of culture, conceived roughly as the arts, the media, and symbolic social relations, and the supposedly extra-cultural realm of materiality, economics, social reality, and so forth. Such concerns as economic planning and the spatial design of the built environment become part of a broader realm of rhetorically-shaped social construction. The shape or form of the built environment from this perspective becomes a cultural and a rhetorical question in that it concerns what the formal arrangement of things will be. That formal arrangement is crucially a matter of economic distribution, of the allocation of pleasures dependent on economic power. But that power cannot in this view be considered the emblem of a material necessity immune to cultural or rhetorical reconstruction; rather it is seen as the sign of a sign system that is itself cultural and by that token remakeable. Capitalist urban design does not simply refer to an extra-cultural reality of economic power. Rather, it inflects the rhetoric of capitalist culture in general, as that manifests itself in such institutions and practices as corporate management, popular entertainment, and city life. It is the sign of a code, the rhetorical troping of a system which consists of other materialized tropes, other conventional and contingent social forms.

Along with breaking down the boundary between the cultural and the extra-cultural, then, the post-structuralist theory also dissolves the structure of reference whereby what was seen as extra-cultural was conceived as a non-rhetorical ground that put an end to further referentiality, further troping or rhetorical signification. According to this theory, whenever one encounters such a ground, be it as a theory of economic necessity, or as a theory of the self, or as a theory of nature, one has in fact merely come across the dead residue of a rhetorical process, the historical remains of another social construction, another shape or form. The stakes of this reconstruction of the theory of culture are thus explicitly political. By locating simulation where others find grounds of truth or nature or necessity, the theory insinuates an element of indeterminacy and contingency into what ideological thinking would prefer to see remain determinate, necessary, and extra-cultural, which is to say natural, absolute, and true.

I will look at two recent marxist theories of culture in this light – the work of Raymond Williams and the Birmingham School of Cultural Studies. In his book, *The Sociology of Culture*, Williams defines culture narrowly as a 'realized signifying system'. Although he does argue that 'a signifying system is intrinsic to any economic system, any political system, any generational system, and, most generally to any social system', he nonetheless maintains that culture 'in practice [is] distinguishable as a system in itself: as a language, most evidently ; as a system of thought or of consciousness, or, to use that difficult alternate term, an ideology; and again as a body of specially signifying works of art and thought. Moreover, all these exist not only as institutions and works, and not only as systems, but necessarily as active practices and states of mind'. Williams acknowledges that the broader anthropological definition of culture as a way of life is a powerful weapon 'against the habits of separated analysis, historically developed within the

CULTURE
| → BOUNDARY IS DECONSTRUCTED

MATERIALITY

" INHERENCE OF CULTURE IN
MATERIALITY "

Introduction   15

capitalist social order, which assume in theory and practice, an "economic side of life", a "political side", a "private side", a "spiritual side", a "leisure side", and so on'. Nevertheless, for Williams, there is an area of material and social interaction and organization which lies beyond culture defined as a realized signifying system, a domain that cannot be subsumed by culture. Williams offers as examples currency and dwellings. Currency, he argues, is a sign system, but 'there is no real doubt that in any genuine currency the needs and actions of trade and payment are dominant, and the signifying factor, though intrinsic, is in this sense dissolved'. Similarly, dwellings may with time become art forms, but they are essentially a 'solution to socially developed primary needs which are always at one level dominant'.[13]

From the post-structuralist perspective, the line demarcating culture from materiality appears more tenuous. And the concept of technology – of shaping, forming, and fabricating – allows the boundary between the two to be crossed. If we define culture as technology broadly conceived, that is, as a process of fabrication, of making based on modelling, then it becomes difficult to separate out such 'materialities' as trade and dwellings from culture. Trade can only occur through the mediation of certain forms or procedures that give shape to, while enabling, exchange. The value of goods is relational, a matter of construction, and beyond direct barter, it assumes the form of a metaphoric substitute – money. Moreover, trade develops usually in sites where survival needs have already been satisfied and a surplus occurs; trade is therefore not the token of a basic survival need, since if those needs could not be met in a society, there would be no trade, as there would be no society/ Rather, trade is the sign of a post-survival economy, of the insertion of culture, understood as the use of technology and imagination to reshape one's physical conditions, into materiality.

Similarly, dwellings are formal arrangements that enact the distribution of symbolic as well as material power in a community. They signify prestige, and they divide up the natural environment according to social hierarchies whose form is as much cultural as material. Bourdieu argues for a symbolic understanding of habitation along these lines.[14] Rather than suggest the independence of culture from materiality, however, this understanding of dwelling signals the inherence of culture in materiality. The development of forms of dwelling that provide not only shelter but also symbolic meanings, which reflect and help reproduce divisions of power and labour, transforms the simple, unarticulated need for a boundary between oneself and the elements into an articulated, relational, and referential system. Unless one is alone in the woods in a putative 'state of nature', there is no such thing as a simple roof over one's head; there are only politically meaningful roofs.

Even hunger, that defining line where the human and the extra-human or natural world intersect as a norm of material necessity, never exists simply as such, outside certain shapes or forms that it is given by human action. The modern famine is a political event, as much as a natural one, and hunger in New York City is as much a social metonym, shaped by cultural forces and connected to social policies, as is an Independence Day Parade. Nevertheless, one could argue, hunger may be culturally produced, but it is itself a material event of deprivation that is mute and unarticulated. The point of the post-structuralist theory of culture is not to eliminate that concept of materiality. Rather it resituates it both historically and contextually.

What materiality is at the end of the twentieth century is quite different from what it was at the end of the nineteenth. There is no singular materiality outside history, which is to say as well, outside culture. Materiality changes shape, and as it does so, it also becomes more and more subsumed to human control and increasingly vulnerable to human activity. (Even the ecological ideal of leaving 'nature' outside human interference becomes dependent on a human political decision.) As this subsumption takes place, supposedly material and natural or extra-cultural events like hunger also change. They cease to be describable as events outside human reach, and they increasingly acquire a meaning that is discursive or relational rather than singular or detached. As such, hunger cannot be understood as a mute and unarticulated natural event, a sign of a materiality or a necessity that stands apart from human culture. It becomes rather the sign of a failure of that culture. At a point in historical time when hunger no longer is a natural necessity, when it no longer needs to exist, it takes on the character of an indictment levelled at its cultural context.

If things that apparently were extra-cultural can be included under the rubric of culture, then they must also be understood as falling within the realm of politics. Though material and need-orientated, the specific shape they assume is determined by the relations of force, the patterns of human interaction, that prevail in a society. Moreover, if such things as habitation are assigned to materiality rather than culture, to the realm of need or necessity rather than freedom or creativity, then the risk is run that they cease to be on the agenda of a reconstructive politics. They cease to be subject to a technological or cultural remaking and remodelling – something we can all mull over in our block houses whose social content is given by a purely material need-fulfilment exempt from considerations of form or aesthetics.

The point, therefore, of emphasizing the culturality or rhetoricity of such things as trade and dwellings is to underscore both their role in the elaboration of political power and their plasticity as social forms that can change shape and acquire new contents. If trade is a form of domination and a source of power, it can also be a mode of equal distribution. And if dwellings communicate power and exclude those without status, they also provide a lexicon for constructing less exclusionary habitational modes that would be the practical form of a non-status society. Ultimately, then, materiality and culture, needs and politics, the realms of necessity and of aesthetics, have to be understood as part of the same field of interrelated endeavours. And for this reason, an expansive, rather than a restricted concept of culture is, I would argue, more enabling for a marxist politics.[15]

Some of the most fruitful work in cultural theory was done during the 1970s at the Birmingham Centre for Contemporary Cultural Studies. Stuart Hall, the former head of the centre, in his account of its work, describes the way their definition of culture shifted from a narrow one to a broad one. 'Culture no longer meant a set of texts and artefacts. Even less did it mean the "selective tradition" in which those texts and artefacts had been arranged and studied and appreciated.' Hall goes on to describe two moves involved in this shift of emphasis: 'First, the move to an anthropological definition of culture – as cultural practices; second, the move to a more historical definition of cultural practices: questioning the anthropological meaning and interrogating its universality by means of the concepts of social formation, cultural power, domination and regulation, resistance and struggle. These moves did not exclude the analysis of texts, but it treated them as archives, decentering their assumed privileged status – one kind of evidence, among others'.[16]

My critique of the Birmingham School's work will focus on two things – the conceptual or theoretical models they use and the implied political assumptions of those models.

The Birmingham School is concerned with the study of culture, not with the development of political strategies. Nevertheless, certain of their key concepts are extracted from the works of political theorists, and they imply political attitudes. Gramsci's notion of hegemony, for example, which names domination by consensus rather than by coercion, through culture rather than through the exercise of force, is a crucial concept for cultural studies in that it opens a space for analyzing the role of the media, of religion, and of educational institutions in maintaining domination. The older economistic model, whereby all cultural phenomena were referred back to their economic determinants, was thus successfully superseded. But at a price. For although Stuart Hall especially is careful to point out that hegemony is never stable but instead is constantly negotiated through struggle, the concept nonetheless implies that the primary agent of cultural activity is the dominant class. The dominant class exercises its hegemony through culture, and the subordinate class, sex, and race are placed in a secondary position in relation to that hegemony. All they can do is resist a more primary vector of domination, which is accorded a determining priority. Hence, the title of the Birmingham volume, *Resistance Through Rituals*.

In addition, almost all the resistances that are studied are judged unsuccessful. As one researcher puts it, there are no subcultural careers. This pessimism regarding the efficacy of popular-based alternative cultural activity is congruent with the leninist underpinnings of the concept of hegemony. If the primary social vector is the exercise of domination as hegemony, then the unavoidable implication is that the only feasible political alternative is a counter-hegemonic bloc capable of matching the force and the power of domination. This political programme is not made explicit in the Birmingham work, though Hall has suggested as much while teaching, and it is implicit in the very concept of hegemony.[17]

A different concept of social power would result in a different theory of culture. One could argue, for example, that hegemony is in fact itself a kind of resistance, a means of securing the identities of property and of political power against very real internal threats that are always potentially active in a system of economic subordination founded on a radical difference or inequality. Hegemony is the attempt by the holders of power to keep those threats stabilized and pacified by constraining the potentially very disruptive energies of that rather large mass of people that constitutes, through its various productive and reproductive activities, the material substance of society. The biggest threat, of course, is quite simply that anyone who is subordinated might reverse the line of force that maintains subordination. Pressure down on people, as hegemony, always contains within itself a counter-pressure that pushes in the other direction. In this conception, hegemony would not be needed in the first place if there were not a fairly powerful antithetical force that calls hegemony forth as a response or resistance to its threatening potential. Social stasis is always a stand-off between equal forces rather than a univocal exercise of power. Such stasis is therefore precarious, no matter how pacified the social system appears, and hegemony has to be understood as the containment of a force that bears the potential of tipping the balance of power.

Thus, what we understand as domination consists of an actual position or site of power, but it also consists of a deflection of threats that constitute an altogether different kind. And this second dimension of domination is reconceptualized within the post-structuralist framework as being itself a form of resistance, an attempt to deflect and waylay structural tendencies toward the erosion of hegemony that are endemic to any inegalitarian system.

In this frame, hegemony shifts out of its determining position and is seen as part of a dynamic antinomy, an interplay of forces. It stands in relation to the power of those outside hegemony who, by virtue of their position, push against it and whose force determines the shape and content of hegemony. Rather than being the singular vector of social action, hegemony instead appears as a response to the potential threat to domination posed by those under subordination, and the threat is precisely that they represent a potentially much more powerful force. There is no single primary vector, then; culture is a differential of forces, and hegemony a structure of containment. Power is power precisely because it is always threatened, always matched by a real counter-force which is a potential counter-power. And the two forces form an oscillating differential devoid of identity.

The post-structuralist approach to culture thus places a much more positive emphasis on popular forces and on the potential of popular struggles. And it can be extended to the cultural sphere. Rather than being understood simply as an instrument of hegemony, cultural forms can be read as sites of political difference, where domination and resistance, the resistance to the positive power of the dispossessed that is domination and the counter-power, the threat of reversed domination, that is the potential force of the dispossessed, meet. In so-called 'cultural hegemony', therefore, the marks of potential threats to power must be deciphered. Indeed, the presence of such exercises in hegemony is itself a testament to something that must be deflected and contained. As in psychoanalysis, the strongest denials are usually metaphors that deflect the most powerful affirmations.

Using the post-structuralist model, one can reinterpret the Birmingham School reading of subcultural practices as imaginary resolutions of contradictions between such things as parent culture puritanism and consumer culture hedonism. For example, kids engage in hedonistic activities like consumerism and hanging out as a reaction to the repression of desire that is enforced in their parents' working class culture. The contradiction between the call to consume in modern capitalist culture and the denial of pleasure in the more traditional culture of the parents spurs the young practitioners of sub-cultural style to imaginarily resolve the dilemma by having fun but within a context and in a manner that assures the reproduction of the working class world, since such imaginary cultural solutions do not challenge the structuring assumptions that shape their lives.

The post-structuralist model permits one to see sub-cultural practices as representing a more positive potential – the potential to produce cultural and social possibilities over and beyond the limits and boundaries that capitalist culture requires. From this perspective, the reason there are no sub-cultural careers may simply be that a capitalist culture that requires work discipline cannot afford to allow the possibility that youth might on a mass basis choose to be artists, or musicians, or dancers, or do-nothings. Such a possibility is counterproductive in a literal economic sense. But more crucially, and more dangerously, it represents a potential on the popular level that must be curtailed if capitalism is to survive. And it could not survive if the freedom, available in sub-cultural arenas, to refuse work discipline for the sake of everyday aesthetics or play were available on a mass scale.

Thus, rather than being nothing more than an imaginary resolution, sub-cultural styles might also be seen as representing a potential and as prefiguring a possibility. What they exemplify is the creative power of cultural production, and what they sketch is the outline of a world in which rhetoric, the creative play of cultural forms, rather than the logic of work discipline, would shape the materiality of social life.

Like Williams, the Birmingham School operates within a concept of culture that could be modified in terms of the post-structuralist contribution to cultural theory. They define culture as 'that level at which social groups develop distinct patterns of life and give expressive form to their social and material life experiences . . . Culture is the practice which realizes or objectivates group life in meaningful shape or form . . . the distinctive shapes in which this material and social organisation expresses itself'. They also define culture as containing 'maps of meaning' that organise life and as being a reservoir of meanings for life that is passed on. Elsewhere, they speak of homologies between cultural expressions or style and group life. To

IS ANYTHING PRIOR TO
DISCOURSE ?

sum up, one could say that culture is an expressive form that is homologous with group life.[18]

The question posed by the post-culturalist theory of culture would go something like this: is culture a secondary representation or embodiment of a group life substance that is assumed to be prior and that is expressed through culture, or does culture, defined as shape, form, representation, embodiment, and objectification play a more primary constitutive role in the making of group life? Prior to the cultural representation, is there a pre-representational life that delegates itself into representation, leaving its substantive presence temporarily, or is that life itself structured by representations? When one analyzes culture in relation to society, does one move from culture to life substance or does one move from culture to culture? Can group life even be said to be at all possible prior to cultural embodiment or form?

The post-structuralist answer to these questions is that people don't live materially and then add culture; they live and have culture at the same time. And although one can say that theoretically or logically, one comes before the other in regard to what one can do without and still survive, it is nonetheless the case that there is no such thing as a group life or a material existence of a community that is not simultaneously and necessarily accompanied by what we call culture in the narrow sense, by forms of interaction and structures of meaning.

The very manner of conducting material life – something as raw as growing food or gathering it – is a matter of form, of what models or representations exist in the culture for carrying out such activities (whether women or men are deemed 'appropriate' for doing it, for example). A group without a model of agriculture, some image of how to do it, will survive by some other sense of how to get food, usually by gathering. A group of agricultural people survives from year to year, harvest to harvest, by imitating what it did the previous year, by remembering, bearing in its mind images or representations of what the group did before in order to survive.[19] At the very moment of material survival, in other words, representations are at work, and as human life has progressed, those representations and forms have acquired greater and greater significance in the conduct of that life. For this reason, both historically and logically, it is difficult if not impossible to locate a moment prior to culture that would not be constitutively infected by the characteristics of culture, that is, by representation, imaging, fabrication, technology, and form.

The post-structuralist position questions the metaphysical opposi-

tion that places the substance of group life before cultural representation, and it precludes defining culture as something that begins, as the
Birmingham theorists argue, at a certain point of group life. Prior to
that moment, culture is already at work, constituting the life of the
group and permitting it to come into being, which is to say, to assume
form. The working class communities of English sub-cultures, for
example, never did and never could exist outside a general process of
culturation, a shaping of their lives by such images as that of the self-
abnegating Jesus in Christianity or a forming of their existence by such
industrial models as the division of labour. The narratives of their lives
are determined and shaped by the stories of life they inherited and
internalized, limiting their possibilities and enforcing obedience to an
industrial scheme or arrangement that is itself a way of narrating life,
of forming it into continuous patterns of repitition, alternation, and
simultaneity. In a very real sense, such life is the product of
technology, of a process of fabrication or making. Its substance is not
natural, nor is it pre-cultural.[20]

Once again, this post-structuralist argument is not merely a matter
of philosophical manoeuvre. The reconceptualization it promotes has
political consequences. Without it, culture can seem to be a play of
forms or representations posed against a more substantive or material
ground of social life or of class society, one whose presence is pre-
representational and non-cultural, and one that is more politically
important, the one true target of radical reconstruction that comes
before such supplementary things as the way psychologies and bodies
are shaped by representations or the way interpersonal domination is
established through symbolic interaction in families or social relationships. Sub-cultural practices can then be conceived of as merely
imaginary resolutions in relation to more real or more substantive
economic problems and solutions (economism by the back door), and
economic solutions can be offered that replicate some of the worst
features of a merely cultural understanding of symbolic interaction.

According to the post-structuralist argument, the best way to
deprive such seemingly substantial aspects of capitalist society as the
labour process and hierarchical management of their substance is to
see them as dimensions of culture, as forms that are contingent and
malleable. Deprived of the sense of substantiality and reality that the
term 'economy' usually implies when juxtaposed with 'culture', they
would instead be assigned the sense of constructedness and conventionality usually implied by culture.

The point of this argument is that the enforcement of labour discipline in the workplace, while it hinges crucially on the threat of material deprivation, must, increasingly in advanced capitalist settings at least, the sites where working class youth sub-cultures like the punks emerge, depend on the internalization of certain representations regarding one's status as a worker, of the prevailing myths of the nation, of the dominant narrative about workers' lives, of the reigning self-representations of capitalists, and so on. Even the acceptance of the use of police force against working class youth when those conventions break down requires an internalized sense of the legitimacy of state power when put to such uses. Part of that representational system includes the belief that their own practices are 'sub-cultural' in relation to a primary or parent culture. The mainstream culture must not be represented as merely one other sub-culture, one that has succeeded in universalizing itself.

The major political consequence of this argument is that supposedly pre-cultural economic forms and necessities must be deprived of any objective or natural status that might have accrued to them by virtue of being deemed a pre-cultural aspect of group life. And sub-cultural practices like doing nothing, hanging out, and wasting time must be seen as having an economic significance. They signify not only an alternate cultural practice, but also an alternate economic practice, that of refusing the discipline of work and the narrative of logic of the labour process that segregates 'leisure' into segments that are controllable and predictable. In so doing, they point out the possibility of an alternative group life, one in which work is no longer the paradigmatic narrative of social life, in which the capacity to script alternative life stories becomes a privileged goal rather than a marginal, merely cultural event.

The Birmingham School argument that there are no sub-cultural careers is thus very much to the point. The work world triumphs eventually; structural economic change is necessary to alleviate the conditions that produce such sub-cultures as the only way of finding social meaning. But it also misses the point that the refusal of the discipline of work, however temporarily and untheoretically, is a significant, prefigurative political phenomenon. The closing of the opening that this refusal represents indicates that it constitutes a threat to the system of work, and the threat is precisely the very unavailability of such sub-cultural practices to a career logic. They indicate that the dominant social narrative that aligns lives into careers is not the only possible one. The very failure of sub-cultural 'careers' is a token of the chance – indeed the threat – that they might succeed.

A critical examination of cultural theory from the perspective of the post-structuralist concept of culture thus suggests the extent to which social reality and social rhetoric are interwoven. The lives of working class kids are given shape and narrative form by the discourse in which they live, one whose privileged metaphor is the freedom of the white capitalist and whose most prevalent synecdoche is the part-for-whole lives to which the majority are reduced. And they won't change significantly, even under leninist tutelage, if the creative configurations of their lives are thought of as having meaning only in relation to more meaningful issues of social structure or as being ideological in relation to a science that perceives the truth of things in terms not computable in the figures of their experience. That very format of discussion, distinguishing between the hard science of socio-economic analysis and the soft ideology of empirical experience, replicates the boundary between materiality and culture that is at stake in this inquiry.

A radicalization of the concept of culture makes available for our work terrains usually thought to be outside the realm of representational action. We must begin to see that particular exclusion as ideological, a strategy for securing the mid-century construction of capitalist 'reality' that goes hand in hand with the ascendance of linguistic analysis in philosophy to the exclusion of critical thinking, with the reduction of economics to a non-normative 'science' of mathematical equilibria computation to the exclusion of 'utopian' marxism, with the limitation of literary criticism to non-substantive, non-historical, and non-sociological formal textual concerns to the exclusion of understanding the study of literature as the study of social life, with the limitation of political science to a positivist repetition of the facts of existence as the norms of existence to the exclusion of reconstructive ethico-political projects, to the definition of science as knowledge that does not submit its own social context to scientific analysis at the exclusion of an internalization of social reconstruction to the scientific endeavour, and so on.

If the social ideals projected in this critical description seem utopian, it is because that perception is itself symptomatic of what I am describing. The isolation of reality from reformulation conjoins with the isolation of culture in a realm secured from all impact on so-called reality. We will know that these kinds of ideological distinctions have been overcome when we can begin to think of social reality as a movie that we can shoot, cut, edit, and narrate at will. The positing of form as a catetgory that helps us move beyond the dilemma of materialism and rationalism is meant to open up this kind of possibility, as is the radicalizing of culture that I have proposed. If the making of a new society is our goal, then one way to begin is by making new categories. And we must think of this not as an indulgence in detached rational speculation, but rather as the building of models that function like theoretical hypotheses in experimental science. Only then will the forces whose most salient emblem is the powers that declare their non-existence begin to appear on the stage of a future history.

1 The Joker's Not Wild: Critical Theory and Social Policing

Jurgen Habermas' *Theory of Communicative Action* marks a right turn in the tradition of German Critical Theory.[1] Habermas rejects marxism and the radical materialist perspective in favour of an amalgam of liberal rationalism, conservative sociological theory, and mainstream language philosophy, and he puts aside the revolutionary goal of earlier Frankfurt School thinkers like Marcuse in favour of a social democratic accommodation with the 'rational' realities of capitalism. The ideal of social equality that has motivated so much leftist radicalism in the past century is replaced by a justification of the necessity of inequality. Sacrificing any attempt at an imaginative modelling of social reconstruction, Habermas engages instead in a conservative romanticism that offers spurious ideals of interiority as remedies for the excesses of social welfare bureaucracy. Seldom has so-called leftist social theory looked so indistinguishable from mainstream attempts to make power palatable and exploitation acceptable.

Habermas combines a theory of knowledge and a theory of society. He argues that social scientists and rational social agents, rather than locate some foundation that will guarantee truth from a supposedly transcendental position, should base their claims to truth in communicative action oriented toward mutual understanding and consensus. In such historically anchored dialogue, arguments are proposed, criticized, and either accepted or rejected depending on whether or not they are in accordance with standards of validity. Only those arguments prevail that everyone can recognize as valid. The goal of this process is consensus, the communal recognition and acceptance of unified truths. This communicative ideal is also a social ideal, since Habermas believes that the life world can be rationalized, that is, can be subsumed increasingly to the process of communicative interaction oriented toward a rational consensus, an ideal of semantic unity that is rendered practical as the process of social integration. Relying on the developmental psychology of Piaget, he identifies an increasing differentiation, formalization, and complexity with such rationalization.

The theory of knowledge justifies itself in terms of the theory of society, and the theory of society justifies itself in terms of the theory of knowledge. Both are modern; both privilege what is abstract. What is most rational is what has attained the highest stage of cognitive development, the capacity to engage in communicative interaction normed by validity and oriented toward consensus. And what is most modern socially is also what has attained the highest stage of cognitive development, the greatest capacity for differentiation of social sub-systems, formalization of laws, rightness of values, and efficiency of operations. The assumption at the outset in the theory of knowledge of an *Einheit* or unity of valid truth that would be recognizable in communicative interaction leads, therefore, to a necessary outcome in the theory of society of the importance of a goal of *Eineignung*, of unification or integration. Everyone will agree, and no one will stand outside the rational society, unless they are irrational.

Habermas attempts to reconcile the systemic and the phenomenological approaches to sociology by positing a separation between abstract reason and empirical experience. This is translated into his social theory as the distinction between systems such as money and power that steer society toward stabilization on the one hand and the life world on the other, which is a realm of common experience mediated by communication oriented toward social integration, a consensus of mutual understanding or agreement. Habermas locates his politics along the line separating systems from life world. The systems of money and power, which he describes as good, rational features of capitalist modernity (Marx's great failing was not to grasp this), are also partially pathological in that they intrude on the life world, colonizing the family, for example, which is subjected to too much legal supervision, and schools, which are too administered. This romantic metaphysics assumes there is a life world interiority that is separable from the exteriority of systems and that constitutes a virtuous realm outside power that should be protected from 'external' legal remedies. It is the great achievement of Habermas' mainstream rationalist method not to take into account the well-documented presence of power, violence, and functional domination in such sites as schools and families. But it is also a symptom of the pre-post-structuralist metaphysics in his work that the spuriousness of his ideal of a life world interiority free from force is not apparent to him. The family is not only a place where people dialogue in a rousseauist pastoral heaven; it is also a place where people are taught to consume, to work, to accept capitalist or state socialist social discipline, to assume power roles over others, and to be reconciled to the exercise of violence against them. The distinction between an external world of systems and an internal realm of life world communication is not sustainable.[2]

Equally unsustainable is Habermas' claim that so-called modern capitalism constitutes a higher form of social rationalization that marxists must learn to accept. The differentiation of systems like money and power from the everyday world they regulate is also a token of increased domination. Habermas is able to ignore the possible contingency of such supposedly rational and modern developments only by claiming that such steering systems as money have lost their class specificity. But he ignores sociologists who study how money and social power differentiations get translated into real political power in a self-reproducing class system. The defect is also due to Habermas' commitment to a conservative model of evolution. According to this way of conceptualizing history, any differentiation of a system into increasingly complex sub-systems must be seen as an advance in rational modernization. But if the entirety of modernity is seen as one large camp in which a majority are obliged to spend all their time working so that a much smaller minority can accumulate profit from their labour (a very simple version of the marxist description), then refinements in sub-systems are merely contingent responses to trouble in the system of domination, efforts at social policing of the kind necessary in domination systems founded on radically contingent premises, rather than signs of modernizing advance or of rational maturation.

Habermas' model of rational discussion is aimed at attaining the same kind of stability that he so cherishes in society. Its goal is to stabilize and integrate around a modern capitalist system whose pathologies can be remedied, and whose pathologies consist primarily of allowing necessary systems of power and money to intrude excessively into a romantically conceived life world. Stabilization occurs through the imposition of norms of validity (truthfulness, rightness, sincerity) on discussion – only valid statements will be deemed rational –, norms defined, like the life world itself, by purely internal rationalist criteria. They are not social, historical, contingent, or material. Once everyone has learned to behave in accordance with these norms (and in conformity with legitimate cultural standards), then the social system will become fully rationalized. It will be governed by agents who have learned to be rational and to see rationality in the world. And no doubt what they will see in the world

of capitalism will be what Habermas sees – a rational social system
rather than a camp whose defining value is legitimate violence. When
people get up in the morning and go to work for eight hours for
someone else so that he can be rich and they can be middle class, they
are simply behaving in accordance with the non-class-specific rationality of the social system, one that requires these kinds of differentiations
and these abstractions of one group over another. If one cannot accept
this rationale, one is not rational, and one is not making valid
statements.

The Theory of Communicative Action is thus as important for what it
overlooks as for what it brings into its field of vision. What it overlooks
most crucially is the radical contingency of the world and of social
institutions like capitalism, and what it fails as a result to project into its
field of vision is a radically democratic concept of social transformation. Faithful to an ideal of reason conceived as a non-negotiable norm
of social analysis and social reconstruction – the standard of validity
that is the gatekeeper of social debate – the theory of communicative
action constitutes a paternalist and potentially authoritarian model of
social science and of social reconstruction. The exclusion of the
deconstructive critique of meaning is symptomatic of that authoritarian potential because the implications of deconstruction for the
project of social reconstruction are cognitively as well as socially
democratic. It should not be surprising, then, that Habermas
denounces deconstruction in *The Philosophical Discourse of Modernity*, which is in some respects a companion piece to *The Theory of
Communicative Action*. To a certain extent, he must do so because the
post-structuralists not only suggest that the social institutions Habermas calls rational are contingent, pathological effects of power, but
they also take issue with the very standards Habermas uses – especially
rationality and validity – to justify such institutions.

Habermas' denunciation of Derrida is particularly remarkable and
symptomatic.[3] He rejects Derrida's critique of Husserl's attempt to
establish a realm of transcendental meaning (so that the intuitive
meaning of words in the mind would rise above signification, with its
relations of spatial and temporal difference that threaten to break up
ideational unities.) Habermas' target is significant because it bears on
the status of his own discourse in as much as it pretends to base itself in
rational norms like validity that are exempt from rhetoric and power.
Derrida argues that the husserlian ideal of transcendence is impossible
because thought must always occur in signification or relate to
representation as a possible mode of its being. Habermas must reject

this claim because it would be impossible for him to entertain it and still privilege reason over its representational instruments and over the empirical world it supposedly transcends, or social rationalization over the materialities of need and desire that must be sublated if capitalist domination is to be accepted as a form of rationalized modernity.

Without a transcendental point outside signification and outside the malleable empirical contingencies of social struggle, the rationalist cannot secure his desired vision of social order. That point is the theoretical equivalent of the social democratic ideal of an assumed political authority lodged in the legitimate governmental representatives of the populace, representatives who transcend the contingencies of malleable popular desires and needs and who therefore are more capable of determining what are the non-malleable criteria of social justice. If the post-structuralist argument is accepted, then communicative interaction must consist of debate over social forms like the distribution of resources, the allocation of pleasure, or the sharing of power instead of over the right conceptual content of 'what will count as rational'. And the criterion of judging what proposal is acceptable will not be its conformity with a transcendent norm like validity that is assumed to be authoritative, but rather its ability to address the needs and desires of the populace as they are constituted at any particular contingent moment of social history.

This alternative is likely to be more radically egalitarian, and it certainly is more radically democratic than what a republican social democrat like Habermas would be willing to accept as politically rational (that is, as in keeping with such cognitive standards as validity and authenticity, which is to say, with what would be isomorphic with the rationality of stability secured by necessary steering mechanisms like money and power). It would be more egalitarian in all likelihood because social rationalism invariably requires that some inequality be deemed acceptable, despite the feelings of those who must bear with it. Rationalism suffers this blindness because the subsumption of feeling to rationalization, the acceptance of the necessity of something despite how much it contradicts one's needs and desires, is the constitutive mechanism of social rationalism, the instrument of its authoritarian power. It imposes a social order that can contradict bodily and emotional feelings, and this is why it is always aligned with political ideals of republican governance by an élite of rationalist representatives who know better than the populace what the populace should want.

In one of his interviews, Habermas makes a statement that is symptomatic of the relation between rationalism and republicanism or managerial social democracy: 'Marxists . . . have to ask themselves whether socialism today, under present conditions, can still really mean a *total* democratic restructuration from top to bottom, and vice versa, of the economic system: that is a transformation of the capitalist economy according to models of self-management and council-based administration. I myself do not believe so. . . . I wonder – this is an empirical question which cannot be answered abstractly, but only through experimental practice – if we should not preserve part of today's complexity within the economic system, limiting the discursive formation of the collective will precisely to the decisive and central structures of political power: that is, apart from the labor process as such. . . . We must start from the fact that social systems as complex as highly developed capitalist societies would founder in chaos under any attempt to transform their fundamental structures overnight. . . . Such a path would . . . accomplish a prudent and long-term process of transformation. The task is a very difficult one, for which an extraordinarily intelligent party is necessary'.[4]

If one defines the labour process as a structure of domination in which a group defined by the work they perform is forced for the sake of survival to labour for another group of owners, then the retention of the labour process should be inimical to a democratic social system – if the workers themselves are given a voice in determining its shape. It is symptomatic of managerial social democracy that Habermas formulates the issue as one that should be decided by an intelligent party for those workers. This legitimation of inequality under social democratic party rationalism is made possible by the privileging of cognitive activities over physical ones or over emotional processes. In such an abstracted framework, in which reason has been made transcendent over the contingencies of materiality and the norm of social rationalization has been elevated over the material needs and desires of the populace, 'intelligent parties' can be legitimately proclaimed justifiable managers of an economic system that assumes labour exploitation as a necessary and rational feature of its operations. Indeed, the theory of social reason could lead to no other conclusion. Intelligent parties must subsume the material energies of exploited groups in the same way that reason must subsume the contingencies of material feelings like need and desire. There is implicit in social rationalism therefore a process of discipline whereby bodily feelings that diverge from the cognitive norms of reason must be controlled. The rationalist differentiation of higher cognitive powers from mere rhetorical forces that legitimates the assumption of a position of authority by a social democratic governing élite also legitimates the imposition of bodily discipline and the repression of emotion on those deemed incapable of rising to such transcendence.

The subsumption of the labouring proletariat to the managerial power of social democratic government representatives can thus be correlated with the move in rationalist discourse to annul the dependency of ideas on the signifying body of representation and to subsume the potentially indeterminate contingencies of social discussion to the authoritative norms of validity. The obviation of the contingencies of signification parallels the obviation of the contingency of the social institutions that social democratic management holds in place. Such institutions as the labour process are not seen by such rationalism as symptoms of social power, accidents of social domination that could be eliminated; rather, such contingent features of capitalism are seen as necessary and rational. Their rationality legitimates the authority of the managers, whose power rests on the claim that they are capable of knowing rationally the rationality that is implicit in the social system, and their higher knowledge is predicated on the greater virtue and difficulty of rationalist argumentation. Democracy can for this reason never consist of the simple expression of feelings or needs; it must be a cognitive discipline that requires logical arguments and good reasons.

At stake in Habermas' rationalist theory, therefore, is a vision of political order. To accept the method is to buy into a particular social world of capitalist modernization. It is a package deal, and the stakes of normal theoretical debate are raised accordingly. What interests me particularly is the relationship between the fear of deconstruction in the book on modernity and the implicit fears of radical democracy in the vision of political and communicative order in the book on social theory. Rationalism creates its own feared others, just as a desire for discipline automatically turns an otherwise harmless free-for-all into a 'lack of order'. What Habermas' social theory projects as its most feared other, that which would destroy the order his theory seeks to assure, is 'dedifferentiation'. It is feared because it threatens the separations between ideas and signs, reasons and emotions, system and life world that define order in Habermas' social universe. Differentiation is for Habermas a progressive process of greater and greater formalization (of laws, for example), which entails increased abstraction from material contingency, or increased division into structurally differentiated sub-systems, which bring ever more order to potentially disordered events. Differentiation is a means of control both socially and cognitively. This is why communicative reason, which Habermas wants to differentiate from the instrumental reason criticized by earlier, more radical proponents of Critical Theory, is itself ultimately a form of instrumental reason, the attempt by 'ego' to persuade 'alter' to accept his point of view. Its goal is identity, a singularity of perspective called consensus, and its method is integration and stabilization. In society, differentiation similarly is a means of attaining a unity, a greater rational integration of the social whole. Dedifferentiation is feared because it threatens the hierarchies and orders instituted by separating spheres such as economics from excessively democratic inputs. The intelligent party must maintain the labour process intact and not make the determination of its status a matter of democratic debate, direct and participatory, on the part of workers. If it did not, disorder might ensue.

In as much as it promotes a sense of differential relations between realms supposedly hermetically sealed from one another, so that law even at its most formal must be seen as a differentially constituted response to empirical events and contextual factors that threaten social order and that must be pacified, post-structuralism, like marxism, must be banished from the republic of reason. It promotes dedifferentiation by refusing to grant the separation of reason from the materialities of representation and context that founds the ideology of rationalism. In so doing, it calls into question the other boundaries of separation or differentiation that underlie rationalist order, and it implicitly troubles the vision of social order that rationalism supports by discrediting the rationalization of social hierarchy – intelligent party over non-rational workers who must accept the labour process. From this perspective, true social maturity consists not of ever increasing differentiation and formalization, but rather a full dedifferentiation of economics from direct democratic participation, for example, or of law from social action so that there are no more 'internal' realms like the family or the workplace that are declared immune to 'external' remedies. Using dedifferentiation as a norm, legal form and social substance ultimately become one as an ethical culture.

Habermas fears these possibilites, these crossings of boundaries, these confusions of identity, and these losses of control. The intelligent party would be out of work if the system of economic steering were collapsed into civil control and if society as a result became fully democratic and self-regulated. This explains his recourse to a rationalism that thrives on separations and subdifferentiations between varieties of reason and validity, for example. And it explains why validity is the criterion of determining who is rational enough to participate in such discussion and what will count as a rational reason in debate. It ensures that only those who already believe in such rationalism will be allowed to speak to issues of social control. They will already accept the necessity of separation and differentiation; otherwise, they would not be rational and could not take part. And they will only use reasons that are socially credited; they will not resort to emotional pleas that confuse the separation of reason from bodily feeling or rhetoric. 'Only responsible persons can behave rationally . . . Only those persons count as responsible who, as members of a communicative community, can orient their actions to intersubjectively recognised validity claims.' And further: 'Well-grounded assertions and efficient actions are certainly a sign of rationality'. In other words, only responsible rational persons who already believe in the results Habermas privileges – a perception of the rationality of capitalist modernization most importantly – can play in this particular rationalist game. One has already to belong to the party to be deemed intelligent enough to belong to the party.

Rationalism is thus an ideal form of social policing because its very method assures certain social results. To buy into the game is to already accept the rationality of capitalist abstraction, of republican representational forms of government, of legal formalization, and the like. The criterion of entry into social policy formulation is thus a gate of exclusion. Guided by the piagetian hierarchy that places abstract cognition over the expression of concrete material needs and desires, Habermas' criterion of access to communicative interaction necessarily leaves out the perspective of those (the exploited and the oppressed, to use an 'emotive' vocabulary) who for one reason or another can only voice their position in terms of need and desire. That perspective is constituted as concrete, emotional, and bound to contingency by the social structure of rationalized domination. And its exclusion is reinforced and justified by a social theory that claims that only those are rational who can transcend such contingencies.

The differentiation that lies at the heart of the rationalist enterprise is the one that separates ideas from representations and rational ideals like validity from the materiality of language and of social context. It has always supplied the managers of systems of domination based on exploitation, hierarchy, and privilege with a justifying ideology from the Greeks to the latter day capitalists, and it promises to supply social democratic managers with a similar legitimation. Without it, capitalist modernization, with its ever increasing separation of realms – finance capital from industrial capital, for example – could not legitimately be declared rational. It would appear rather to be what it is – sophisticated domination. That deconstruction is centrally a critique of this ideology should say something to us about the relevance of Habermas' denunciation of it to the theory of communicative action. I will now suggest some ways in which Habermas' theory is itself susceptible to a deconstructive critique. I will concentrate on showing how the differentiation of a realm of rational ideas from a shaping worldly context is impossible.

Rationalized social processes are precisely those that operate according to formal rules rather than to the contingencies of power or feeling. Yet like all formalism, such social rationalism merely addresses one feature of social reality. It pretends to substitute ideal standards and rules for the accidents of social interaction, but in fact it merely connects with one dimension of that interaction. The pretence to substitution creates an appearance of impartiality, but it also reveals a certain partiality. The formal rule forbidding insider trading on stock markets substitutes for the accidents of monetary power a rational standard of good behaviour, but it does not really address the deep context that gives rise to such features of capitalism as insider trading. Indeed, as many theorists have noted, such rules posit a normal, good, and fair brand of trading that is presumed to be exempt from the violence of structural unfairness.

In eliminating the more dysfunctional contingencies of feeling and force, such rationalism also legitimates the exclusion of many other more potentially disruptive feelings and forces from social policy decision-making that pretends to be geared toward social rationalization. Habermas lists law, power, and money as system steering mechanisms; he does not mention fear, anxiety, paranoid projection, identification, and emotional dependence. He does not because such feelings are not sufficiently abstract and formalized to constitute systems in their own right. And he does not mention the implicit violence of systemically coerced labour or of systemically imposed social roles such as child, student, or housewife. These things cannot really be seen by his theory, since they do not constitute formal rational categories.

The social system thus reproduces itself through theories that privilege the very operations that constitute the rationalized power of that very system. As the system discounts emotions such as fear in its computation of efficiency, so also does Habermas' theory. The efficiency of its conceptual computation of how modern or rationalized the social system is would be hampered by such an inclusion. Yet if the system is so thoroughly rationalized, Habermas cannot account for such things as the desire for revolution except as irrational pathologies. He cannot account for people who reject the rationale that divides rational acceptance from irrational rejection. The arena of emotion thus stands outside Habermas' theory, yet the social system of which it gives an account is crucially dependent on emotion. Feelings like fear are as much a part of the structuring glue of steering mechanisms like power as any functional mechanism. Sublimated pain cannot be a universally valid norm of the kind rationalism demands, yet no contemporary reasonable society, one founded on the rationalization and normalization of brutality as 'work', 'family life', and any number of other ideological platitudes, could survive without it.

If social rationalism cannot be divorced from feelings, neither can it be divorced from the exercise of force. Piaget's developmental psychology (which plots a progressive evolution in each person from rudimentary sensory-motor capacities that are bodily and emotional to supposedly higher cognitive powers that are characterized by greater autonomy, complexity, differentiation, abstractness, and formalization) privileges a cognitivist perspective that permits the refinement of processes of domination to be described as rationalization or modernization. But it also permits one to see such rationalization itself as a part of the process of domination. The differentiation of economic and political 'steering' systems from civil life occurs in response to the pressures exercised against domination by exploited groups. When exploited groups demand a greater say in such systems (a reduction of the differentiation of the systems from civil society), they sometimes force concessions out of the ruling groups (civil rights legislation for blacks in the US, for example). They often also force a greater assumption of authority on the part of corporations and the state for the sake of imposing formal criteria of efficiency and legal ordering (the conservative counter-revolutions in the anglophone countries in the 1980s). That process of reactive differentiation takes the form of greater and greater abstraction, the creation of stronger organizational and hierarchical boundaries between the empowered groups and those under exploitation. Such boundaries afford an ever greater distance of protection for those in power. Their abstraction permits greater manipulation of the material world of labour, as well as a greater detachment and consequent mobility in response to the pressures exerted on the safeguarded spheres of power from those who surround and are kept at bay by that power.

A privileging of cognitivism is appropriate to this republican power structure. Abstraction from the contingencies of materiality permits a substitution of representatives for popular self-determination and of representative rational ideals like efficiency for a purely self-determined economy, which is the implicit goal of all expressions of countervailing needs and desires against the efficiency-austerity requirements of capitalism. And rationalist social theory also reacts against material contingency by banishing need and desire from the republic of acceptable criteria of rationality. One can therefore understand Habermas' rationalism as a reaction-formation, a counter-force that consists of a flight to an opposite extreme that must be framed in terms of what it reacts against. It reacts against the possibility that those who are condemned to be exploited by those who live within the reasonably safeguarded realm of capitalist modernity will destroy the system by placing irrational material needs and desires before the rational austerity imperatives of that system. Those imperatives are secured by the eminently rational demand that need and desire give way to the greater force of a universal rationality that is formal and abstract, and those demands impose sacrifice on people who have no say in the rationalization of such systemic rules.

The contingencies of empirical feeling and force thus intrude in the supposedly purely formal realm of social rationalization. The same can be said of the theory of communicative reason. It presents itself as a set of rules of engagement for arriving at an inter-subjectively produced consensus that would have the binding power of objective standards. To do so, however, it must contradict its own premise of democratic participation. If to participate one has to meet the criteria of rationality, and if rationality is bound up with the shape of the modern social universe, then democracy begins to verge on a pledge of allegiance. Moreover, Habermas cannot really start with the contingency of social interaction in dialogue. He must hold in reserve a rationalist trump that assumes a transcendent moment outside the empirical event of debate. Yet even as he attempts to win the game in advance, he must lose it to contingency. Like all social theories, his must be a lesson in the overwhelming power of the material world, a power that dictates that in order to arrive at a rational world, one must begin outside reason.

Although he asserts that foundationalism has given way to the need to justify one's positions using reasons in dialogue with others,

Habermas nevertheless assumes as the standard regulating such dialogue a norm of validity (the truthfulness, rightness, and sincerity of utterances) that is never rationally justified. It is the trump in a deck in which nothing else is allowed to be wild. One would think that validity too should be submitted to democratic debate, to a process of communicative interaction that would determine whether or not it should be the standard guiding communicative interaction. Why is it not? Perhaps because an interrogation of the reasons justifying its use as a norm would disturb its function of permitting distinctions or boundaries between what and who is rational and what and who is not. Without some assumption like validity as a criterion of measure or judgement, we would be left with nothing more than the contingencies of our material historical situations to base our claims on, contingencies that do not permit purely rational distinctions and differentiations. Decisions would become matters of the contingencies of power rather than of rational justification. But are we always in the middle of such contingencies anyway, even when we claim to be most valid, most rationally transcendent of mere contingency?

Some indication of the validity of this point is given in Habermas' own text, though it occurs in marginal moments because it is a point he must suppress. In describing his ideal of a communicative interaction 'oriented to achieving . . . a consensus that rests on the intersubjective recognition of criticizable validity claims', he argues that 'the rationality of those who participate in this communicative practice is determined by whether, if necessary, they could, *under suitable circumstances*, provide reasons for their expressions' (I, 47; italics mine). The expression 'under suitable circumstances' suggests that the external contingencies of material context play a role in the ideal of communicative interaction normed by the supposedly purely rational or internal norm of validity, one whose truth value cannot be dependent on contingencies of context or situation.

Indeed, in actual situations of use, the meaning of validity is notoriously context-dependent and circumstantially variable. It is always tied into the material situation, the representational network, and the interpretive frame in which it is deployed. What counts as valid among black youth in urban ghettos will differ greatly from what counts as valid for white professionals. And this is so because validity is never merely a formal quality of utterances; it is always also a specific contingent content. 'We're not gonna take no more of this shit' and 'I think we should reinvest our mutual fund, dear' are both valid statements, yet their validities are not commensurate. They cannot be commensurate because their validity is a function of situation and of empirical content, of who is speaking and who is addressed. It is a matter of the materialities of the surrounding discursive frame, not simply a matter of a quality of truthfulness that is a formal and internal feature of utterance. The white professional utterance will not seem valid to the black ghetto youth because its referents are not shared, and its meaning consequently does not get communicated. Similarly, the black youth's utterance cannot be valid to the white professional because he is part of the shit that is at issue. Thus, the social and situational referents of valid utterances are essential to the quality of validity, and they determine whether or not the utterance will be communicated in a way that preserves its validity in the communication situation.

Moreover, differences over the meaning of such values as validity are derived from social differences. Those differences generally have to do with power differences and with inequalities of station that make people need to interpret what counts as valid in different ways. And the desire for validity, for a valid meaning of validity, must be understood as a response to such differences, as an attempt to occlude them in the name of a rationalized social order. Habermas places such differences and such material inequalities on the back burner when he exempts a concept like validity from debate and presumes it has a unified, non-differential, purely internal meaning that would be immune to the specificities of contingency and be universally binding. Yet his ideal of a validity-normed, rational consensus is called forth by those differences, since material social inequalities of resources and power motivate all dreams of consensual unity. Rather than being an externality in relation to the internally normed norm, context becomes inseparable from validity. We would not need to dream of a consensual utopia based on binding validity claims if we did not live in a dystopia of radically differentiated material possibilities. Those differences have a certain material priority, therefore, in relation to the ideal of a rational consensus normed by the standard of validity in that they motivate the desire for its attainment.

If the meaning of a formal concept like validity is variable between material contexts and across differences of power, then one can never arrive at a valid, that is, a singular, unified meaning of validity that we would all agree on until that variability is exorcised. This means that the removal of circumstantial and contextual variability is an internal presupposition both of valid meaning and of the meaning of validity. The supposedly purely internal and unified meaning of the criterion of validity, in other words, is in an essential way dependent on circum-stances that are external and material rather than internal or cognitive in character. And this implies that the removal of context variations in meaning comes to depend crucially on a rectification of material inequalities. This has to occur before the idea of validity can even be advanced as a norm of rectification. To a certain extent, society must be 'rationalized' – that is, made to be characterized by actual material equality – before the kind of rationalization Habermas envisions, one normed by purely cognitive criteria like validity, could even be conceived as a possibility. A commonality of material sites precedes a commonality of interpretation. This materialist conclusion stands opposed to the rationalist one, which presumes that a commonality of ideal meaning is possible despite material differences of site and situation.[5]

The usual habermassian response to this kind of argument is that Habermas is describing an ideal situation that presupposes the rectification of structures that distort communication. But if he did have such assumptions, he would begin his theory with prescriptions for rectifying the material conditions that now make validity a political rather than a philosophical concept. And one of those prescriptions would be the need for a democratic determination of what constitutes communicative normativity. Validity could no longer be offered as an unquestioned prenorm of debate that is given as the standard of what will be accepted as reasonable in such debate. In other words, such a materialist perspective would imply that an élite substitution of ideal representations like validity could no longer pre-empt a direct determination of communicative normativity by social subjects inde-pendent of all such prenorms. It would be for them to determine whether or not they wanted their discussions to be carried out according to such a standard as validity, or whether they wanted altogether different standards, or no standards at all (which would assume they trust each other well enough and exist in a sufficiently equal material situation in which power was neutralized to act together without feeling the need for rationalist cops).

One consequence of my argument so far is that one cannot speak any longer of reason alone as a criterion of what Habermas calls social rationalization. One also has to speak of such things as materialization or actualization, the making concrete of the promises of formal rationality not as secondary or derivative events (arrived at finally at the end of one's second volume where the 'real abstraction' of communicative reason is realized) but as preconditions of reason. If reason can never be merely ideal and formal, if it always has in its very constitution to be attached to the materiality of rhetorical form and material circumstance, the same is true of the rationalization of society. It too must be, immediately and indissociably, a materialization of rational imperatives as the creation of materially equal circumstances suitable to rational discussion. But as such, social rationalization cannot be a project of reason alone; it must also be a matter of need, desire, housing, food, sexuality, psychological health, family reconstruction, and the like (not at the end of the second volume, but before the first volume begins, before concepts like validity can even be advanced or assumed). Indeed, one can no longer speak of rationalization as a process with its own internal rules or self-sufficient values of validity without evoking these things. Validity is, so to speak, in the streets.

This reverses the order of priority Habermas' model establishes. Validity only has meaning as a rational norm in a social world that calls it forth, a social world that is lacking something such concepts supply in a compensatory fashion. What that world lacks are actual structures of self-worth guaranteed by social contexts that do not threaten harm, or rational social organizations that create a sense of secular meaning in the social universe, or an ethical culture that creates communities of understanding around realized material structures of equality, or the material preconditions of the cognitive standards associated with the idea of validity, such things as symmetry of distribution, commensurability of access and allocation, intersubstitutability of roles, transitivity of power, elimination of differences of station, and the like – all things that would remove the fear, insecurity, boundary anxiety, and object inconstancy that motivates the rationalists' need for paternal internalizations like an unquestionable norm of validity. And what this means, of course, is that the creation of a just, materially equal world might also create the conditions that would make validity no longer valid as the criterion of rationality. We might no longer have to worry so much about who's rational and who isn't.

The goal of such social reason would not be to know the world theoretically, but to engage with it in order to change it in ways that are materially normed (by need instead of validity, for example). Rather than conceiving of reason as extracted from circumstance, it would recognize its constitutive mediation and determination by its contexts. Such social reason would as much interact with its material environment as with others in communicative reasoning. And it would do so from a perspective of ego security that permits an elasticity of boundaries, an acceptance of the contingency of social existence, and a concomitant capacity to create new social possibilities. Such reason would not acquiesce in the authority of what one is able to formalize categorically as what is; rather it would take what exists as one possible formulation of a contingent and remakeable reality whose norm is not whether or not it is 'rationalized', but rather whether or not it is just and equal in a way that permits concepts like validity to be heard by everyone in society without semantic inequality. For this kind of reason to be imaginable, Piaget's hierarchy of lower emotive-material, sensory-motor capacities and higher cognitive capacities that are formal and abstract would need to be replaced by a more contextual model that sees value in formal cognition only in so much as it is practicable and relevant to the social world and in so much as it is supplemented by a sense of context-responsible participation in one's material environment. Application, interaction, responsibility, and creativity would in this perspective also be considered important features of rational 'maturity'.

This alternative concept of reason also assumes the creativity of possible permutations of meaning according to material circumstance. In this perspective, the semantic polyvalence of a category like validity according to situation and circumstance is not negative; rather, it provides a positive lever for the process of social reconstruction in that the instruments at our disposal are seen as having a rich well of semantic possibilities within them. The reality of semantic difference, whereby an identity of meaning always exists in relation to other possible meanings in other contexts, suggests an elastic expandability of those meaning identities, a polyvalence with potentially multiplicatory effects. Progressive possibilities reside in the metonymic contiguities of material relations. Authenticity and validity would seem thereby, through their material linguistic connections to other possible acceptations of their meaning, to contain the possibility of expanding toward social activities that might now seem to lie beyond their boundary, as inauthentic or invalid projects that cannot yet be deemed rational.

Habermas's inability to accept this radical opening testifies to the desire for control that motivates his theory. Ultimately, one has to see his theory itself as a symptom of a certain context, a certain material situation that is discursive, socio-historical, and psychological. It is discursive in that it emblematizes the tendency in liberal ideological discourse to use a euphemistic and metaphoric language of substitution that carries out linguistically what liberal governance accomplishes socially. That euphemistic language abstracts from actual conditions of inequality and power, and it replaces those conditions with formal rational terms like validity that make the stabilization of social violence seem normal. This tendency is evident in the way Habermas treats other theories that he finds threatening, and the rhetoric of euphemism is designed in part to waylay the threats – direct and emotional – that exploited groups pose to professional class groups that are willing to live with exploitation. He translates marxism, for example, into a scarcely recognizable parody that sounds more like leninism than marxism, and he quite literally renames it 'the philosophy of history', thus exorcising its political dimension (summed up in the usual description of marxism as concerned with 'class struggle'). Habermas' theory is socio-historically symptomatic in that it embodies the liberal ideas of the post war era, a time when earlier radical aspirations (especially associated with the early radicalism of the Frankfurt School itself) were discredited in favour of a complacent coming to terms with the rights of capital and a carping at the malfunctions of social welfare bureaucratism. That capitulation takes the theoretical form of reviving the long-discredited rationalism of the classic age of bourgeois stabilization (the eighteenth century, a time Habermas somewhat romantically idealizes as the era of a good bourgeois 'public sphere' of social discussion) and of denouncing the critical materialist philosophies of post-structuralism in favour of liberal mainstream descriptive philosophy, which expunges all criticism from the philosophical task. Finally, Habermas' theory is psychologically symptomatic in that it evinces a distinct fear of boundary crossing and of formlessness that testifies to an inability to live without authoritarian psychological internalizations. The most striking of those internalizations is reason, which constitutes an internal mental construct that permits one's own values to become grandiose and inflated. One's own contingent aspirations are transformed into norms others must obey. Thus the desire or need to control one's own psychological processes, to establish boundaries and to secure oneself against the threat of their loss, becomes a desire to control others. Social policing, the maintaining of a social order that is essential to one's psychological well-being, is one derivative of this psychology.[6]

The great conundrum of rationalism is that in order to achieve valid validity, one that would be universal, inclusive, and tolerant, not simply an excuse for social policing, it must be willing to accept as valid social possibilities that at first glance might seem invalid, or inauthentic, or untrue when measured against the standards of what we

construct as 'valid' in our particular social world. This is why
Habermas chooses neo-kantian rationalism, one that assumes from
the outset certain standards or norms like validity that are exempt from
debate, over a democratic and participatory social experimental
science. It protects against this conundrum by assuring certain results.
Ends are to a large degree preordained. Nothing is left up to chance.
The danger posed by contingency is neutralized, as is the danger of
democracy. But reason can prove its relevance to the world only by the
kinds of just worlds it permits us to model and build. For those worlds
to be democratic, reason itself must be participatory. And this means
that concepts like validity cannot be left off the docket or held in
reserve as trumps against democracy.[7]

2 The Theory of Autonomy

Marxist materialism and post-structuralist philosophy offer alternatives to the rationalism Habermas proposes. But marxist materialism, while it provides a philosophic basis for economic and political democracy that seems marginalized by the rationalist perspective, easily lapses into a metaphysics of substance and of subjectivity that would be dismantled from the post-structuralist perspective. And post-structuralism, while it provides a valuable perspective on the enabling and positive power of indeterminacy and difference, is caught politically between a radical reformism that prescribes work from within existing institutions and a philosophic utopianism that denies to the oppressed access to necessary instruments of struggle – ideals of identity most importantly. I will consider the politics of post-structuralism in the next chapter. Here I will discuss the evolution of a thinker, Antonio Negri, whose theory of autonomy connects a democratic revolutionary political model to a materialist philosophy and whose work offers one of the most sustained meditations on the necessity of democratic organization to marxist politics in the contemporary experience. Yet his work also relies on a model of an expressive subjectivity that owes much to liberalism and that marginalizes instrumental and contextual factors that I will argue are in fact crucial to both subjective life and to the formulation of post-liberal democracy.

I will first gloss the theory of 'autonomy' in his writings; then, I will suggest how his model of subjectivity needs to be reshaped if it is to be useful in the project of social reconstruction.[1]

From the late 1960s through the late 1970s, Italy witnessed an uprising on the part of industrial workers and intellectual radicals that far exceeded any of the dreams of the New Left. The struggles of the time were characterized by worker occupation of factories, industrial sabotage, work slow-downs, wildcat strikes, mass demonstrations, and the direct appropriation of food and public services. It was an era of tremendous worker and student militancy, but it was also the era of the Red Brigades, the urban guerrillas who succeeded eventually in bringing on a conservative counter-attack in favour of law and order in the late 1970s that effectively ended the period of struggle. Radical workers were fired *en masse*, and the intellectual leaders of the movement (including Negri) were imprisoned for alleged links to the

Brigades. The repression helped end the movement, but the movement also failed because it did not open itself to feminism, and at the last meeting of *Autonomia* in 1977, feminists, criticizing the masculinist practices of the movement, disrupted the organization.

Negri was a legal philosopher before he became a theorist of politics. His early work, *Stato e diritto nel giovane Hegel* [*State and Law in the Young Hegel*] (1958) and *Alle origini del formalismo giudico, Kant* [*The Origins of Legal Formalism, Kant*] (1962) especially, were concerned with legal theory from the point of view of an internal dialectical critique. After *Descartes politico o della ragionevole ideologia* [*Political Descartes or on Reasonable Ideology*] (1970), a critique of the relationship between rationalist philosophy and capitalist ideology, Negri's work became more explicitly political. In the early 1970s, he started writing essays dealing with issues of marxist economic politics, and he began to elaborate a theory of autonomy. Two important essays of this period are collected in *Operai e Stato* [*Workers and the State*] (1971). One of these – 'Marx on the Cycle and the Crisis' – is crucial for understanding Negri's later work.

The most important emphasis in this essay is on the active role played by workers' struggle (*lotta operaia*) in determining the way the capitalist economy develops and in bringing about a crisis in that economy. This is one of the most important ideas of the theory of autonomy. It assumes that workers are the moving force in a capitalist economy. Their 'autonomous' creative potential is the basis of capitalist wealth; their struggles for wages and other benefits – the assertion of their autonomy from capital – bring on crises in the capitalist system; and the vectors of their struggles oblige capital to recompose itself in response, changing its composition to meet the changing composition of workers' struggles (which, Negri argued, should be free from control by unions and the Communist Party). Workers are most powerful when they affirm their autonomy from capital.

Negri refuses to grant a separation between economics and politics of the sort that legitimates the leninist assumption that workers' economic struggles for such things as wages and time are pre-political and therefore in need of the political mediation only a party can provide. For Negri, economics and politics are inseparable because politics permeates the economy, which can no longer be seen as a mechanism for allocating goods and wealth, but must instead be seen as a dynamic relation of antagonistic political forces in constant struggle with each other. The state brings institutional politics to bear in order to enforce labour peace and to assure a stable climate for capitalist planning, but even prior to this institutionalized intervention, politics inheres in the encounter between labour and capital that is the defining condition of capitalism.

Thus, an apparently objective economic structure is the product of subjective activity as well as being the embodiment of a power relation, the attempt of one subject to subordinate another. The apparent equilibrium of the capitalist economy, its semblance of being a rationalizable, objective mechanism, covers over an antagonistic relation between contending subjects. Capitalist economic development (the creation of wealth, the building of industry, the manufacture of more commodities and more jobs) is therefore a problem and a project of capitalist political power, rather than being a matter of objective economic laws. It is the result of a particular configuration of the antagonism between capital and labour, more specifically of the excess of surplus value (the extra amount of value in commodities over the amount paid out as wages) over money used to sustain the workforce. The system necessarily enters crisis when that stasis or equilibrium is disturbed, and it is disturbed particularly when workers exercise their power over capital (without them, there can be no work, no production, no economic development) by striking and demanding higher wages, independently of the arranged or planned wage raises negotiated by unions. Those negotiated settlements preserve capitalist development and profitability while imposing austerity on workers. Thus, it is the 'autonomy' of workers, not some imbalance in its laws, that drives capitalism into disequilibrium.

Negri argues that the development of state intervention in the economy in the form of keynesian planning after the Great Depression sought to pacify that fundamental antinomy and to contain workers' autonomy. Capital made use of the crisis of the Depression to rearrange the fundamental relation of forces between capital and labour in favour of capital. In this way, an attempt was made to integrate the crisis into the cycle of a continuing capitalist development. Negri argues that for Marx capitalism's periodic cycles are necessarily marked by crises. Economic equilibrium is more of an accident than an essential feature of the system. 'Normal' development is merely the anormal possibility of crisis always present in the apparent smooth functioning of the machine.

More importantly for the theory of autonomy as Negri develops it, Marx attributes to the working class an active role in bringing crises about. Marx argues that wage pressure produces a falling rate of profit, and that this tendency is produced solely by competition between the classes. From this argument, Negri concludes that the crisis of the falling rate of profit is the result of a relation of forces, of the tendencies and counter-tendencies of subjects in struggle, not of an objective mechanism working out its logic independently of that basic antagonism. The working class raises the level of the necessary wage, and capital is constrained as a result to diminish the amount of living labour incorporated into production. Consequently, workers' struggles constitute an absolute limit on capitalist development. They cannot be incorporated into cycles or into a state plan. Even as capital uses crises like the Depression to rectify the imbalance in the antagonism between capital and labour, it cannot help but display the precariousness of that antagonism.

In another essay, Negri describes how Fordism (the massification of production – hence, the 'mass worker' that Negri sees as a crucial feature of the composition of the modern proletariat) was designed to neutralize Bolshevism, but such measures only relaunched the composition of the working class on a higher level. Consequently, a higher degree of control was needed so that workers' autonomy could be channelled to serve the interests of capital. This was accomplished through a merger of the economy and law that assumed as normative Keynes' ideal of equilibrium and that therefore characterized any working class action that disturbed equilibrium as illegal. The major result of this was that all of society was turned into a factory, a site of discipline, and economic development was guaranteed by an alliance between the bourgeoisie and the state socialists, relying on the Keynesian instruments of state interventionism and the management of circulation. However, the attempt to use the working class to further capitalist development fails to work not because the working class is inside or contained by capitalism, but rather because it can always be outside. It always threatens to assert its autonomy. Capital cannot do without labour, but labour can do without capital.

By 1974, the 'area of autonomy' was beginning to hold national meetings in Bologna and Florence, partly to discuss the relationship between the spontaneous mass movement, which was breaking out throughout northern Italy, and the traditional workers' organizations (the CPI, the unions). Many of Negri's arguments against the CPI strategy of 'historic compromise' in *Proletari e Stato* [Proletarians and the State] (1976) must be understood in this context. The CPI had elaborated a theory of capitalism that justified its participation in a political system that founded itself on the maintenance of capitalist development by preventing radical worker departures from the negotiated settlements which CPI unions made with the capitalist owners. This is the 'planning State' Negri targets, one that makes economic equilibrium a political law, so that autonomous wildcat strikes were considered illegal. The CPI theory relied heavily on Gramsci, especially his notion of 'civil society' as a way of justifying the separation of politics and economics, so that the party could partici-pate in parliamentary politics while doing nothing to change the basic structure of the economy. For Negri, there is no such thing as civil society, since all of society has become a disciplinary machine for enforcing the laws of capitalist economic development.

The focal concern of Negri's first major book on political issues – *Crisi dello Stato-piano* [*Crisis of the Planning State*] (1974) – is a critique of the collaborative arrangement between the unions and the planning state to assure labour peace. In this book, Negri argues that the law of value, by virtue of which labour time or power is converted into money, is a mechanism of political domination that merely appears to have an independent economic existence. Keynesian planning, which means that the government intervenes in the economy to regulate trade and money, is an extension of the law of value in that it seeks to regulate the potential autonomy of the working class; it is a political, not an economic, strategy. What Keynesian state planning seeks to contain is the potential for over-production in the economy, the potential that the productive force of labour can create more than capitalism can sell or use profitably. This potential represents the very real possibility within capitalism of communism, defined in the terms Marx used in the *Grundrisse* as an abundance of produced wealth that would satisfy all needs. That potential must be contained because over-production results in lower prices. This is why the law of value is an instrument of political control. It imposes the necessity of restraining production (through lower wages and unemployment) so that labour value can become money on the market in a way that guarantees capitalist wealth. Over-production, the making of too many commodities for the market, ruins that process, because prices fall, and with them, profit and wealth. The law of value, the rule that says the material wealth of goods can only be converted to monetary wealth if the amount of available goods is kept sufficiently low to maintain prices, prevents the real wealth of produced goods from expanding to satisfy all needs. Productive labour, conceived as the potential for over-production and for the realization of communism, is thus a political threat to capitalism because it attacks the law of value by threatening to make possible a world where needs would be satisfied independently of exchange value and money.

The political strategy that is appropriate to this economic reality is 'direct appropriation', the seizure of the wealth they themselves produce by the working class. This would be the basis of a communism in which the law of value would cease to reign; labour time (what Marx called the measure of the value of labour that ultimately is the source of surplus value and profit) would cease to be the measure of wealth; and exchange value (the transformation through sale on the market of goods containing labour time or value into money) would cease to be the measure of use value (the practical value of goods to fulfil needs independent of their exchangeability or monetary value). The attempt to control the potential of workers to over-produce is therefore crucial to capitalist political survival. The instrument of this attempt, according to Negri, increasingly assumes the form of direct corporate command. Consequently, the concept of the creative, productive, and inventive subject of labour is inseparable from the political task of overthrowing the law of value and the command structure that supports it.

In another piece from 1974 – 'Workers' Party Against Work' – Negri describes a major strategy of *Autonomia*: the refusal of work. Once again, he argues that the crisis of capitalism is caused by the composition of the working class. Capital created the mass worker in the 1930s in order to counter the falling rate of profit; a massified work force could produce more with the result that more goods could be sold. But the massification of the labour force also works against profit by giving rise to workers' tendency to over-produce, thus creating a glut of goods on the market. Because the response of the *padroni* is an increase in the direct exercise of factory command, the working class must discover a means of organization that meets the force of that command while yet respecting the power of its own potential for the production of wealth. Negri calls for what amounts to a non-party party form, an organization that would base itself in mass actions and in the idea of workers' power directly exercised. Such an organization would seek to empower workers' autonomy as 'the communist power of non-work'. Workers should refuse to work and thereby affirm their power over capital. In this direct exercise of counter-power, the party model has a certain function, but it is only as a relay in the circulation of continual wage objectives and factory guerrilla warfare (sabotage). Thus, political organization is needed, according to Negri, but only as an instrument of mass workers' power that does not require mediation in order to be effective. Rather than the party form providing the norm for the way workers should be organized, the form that workers' struggle takes should itself serve as a norm for the party.

Although he advocates the use of wage demands to attain larger political ends, Negri also at this time begins to argue that the struggles must expand to include the sphere of reproduction, the social sphere surrounding the factory that operates to reproduce labour power. He begins to speak of the broader proletariat, including houseworkers, the unemployed, the marginally employed, and so on. By creating a social factory, spreading its command throughout society, capital has also broadened the field of struggle and created more points where attacks can occur. In this realm, direct appropriation, of such things as public services, becomes an instrument of struggle very much appropriate to the composition of the class and to the ideal of communism as the potential for over-production of a sort that would satisfy all needs.

Given his critique of the party model, Negri's *La Fabbrica della strategia* [*The Factory of Strategy*] (1977), a critique of Lenin, seems a predictable next step. He argues that the minoritarian status of the industrial workers in Russia determined the form of political organization for Lenin as something external to the proletariat. In addition, the underdeveloped and highly dispersed conditions in the country made a developed and centralized organization necessary. But planning and massification have changed the composition of the working class, and new organizational forms are needed as a result, forms that address the new composition which is multisectoral and territorially mobile. Moreover, with the spread of factory control to all of society, the organization can no longer be centralized. For Lenin, all economic struggles were political, and political struggles were not always economic. But, now, Negri insists, economic struggle and political struggle are identified completely. Capital has conquered society, operating a real subsumption of labour, but in so doing it has created a social individual directly capable of communism.

It is possible, therefore, to read communism directly in the class itself rather than in an external political directive. Because the vanguard has today become a vanguard of the mass, the concept of organization has become internal to class composition. Acting autonomously, the working class itself becomes an obstacle to capitalist development. In addition, Negri argues, Lenin's concept of power as an absolute needs to be replaced by a concept of power as a relation of forces. Only in this way can one gauge the changing configurations of power between labour and capital. Rather than being a single instance

of power like the leninist party, autonomy consists of a plurality of
points of organization, a multiple mobilization of all legal and extra-
legal forms of struggle, the co-ordination of an entire 'molecular' web,
and the progressive accumulation of moments of encounter.

Lenin's greatest limitation, according to Negri, is that he could not
show that the struggle against the state is a struggle against work.
Control over economic development, the creation of wealth, as in
Lenin's state socialist organization of work, is not yet liberation from
the capitalist model of economic development (which presupposes the
tyranny of waged labour). The highly developed level of the productive forces today means that it is possible to move directly to
communism, skipping an intermediate socialist stage (state planning
which retains the capitalist relations of production) and extinguishing
the law of value once and for all. Today, socialist planning, rather than
being something positive as it was for Lenin, is the first object of
attack. Negri concludes that the politics of class must take their stand
in the autonomous particularity of the needs and interests of the
proletariat.

In his next book, *La Forma Stato* [*The State-Form*] (1977), a critique
of the 'political economy of the [Italian] constitution', Negri returns to
his earlier work on legal theory and gives it a political meaning. The
Italian constitution integrates labour into an ideal of economic
development sanctioned by a myth of democratic consensus, but this
ideal, Negri points out, is belied by the continuing necessity of labour
legislation. The constitutional ideal of a 'democracy founded on
labour' assumes there is no antagonism between labour and capital,
yet the ongoing necessity to produce law as a means of mediating the
difference between the two underscores the durability of the basic
antinomy and reveals the constitutional identity to be a myth. The
constitution implicitly acknowledges that labour is the general origin
of value and of social production, and since the constitution presents
itself as a general science of abstract principles, that is, as law, the fact
of the necessity of labour legislation cannot be dismissed as a merely
particular episode that does not touch the general principles or the
abstract form of the constitution. What it indicates – against the grain
of the corporatist mystification of the constitution's claim to social
integration – is the necessity of contradiction and the inevitability of
class conflict.

According to the constitution, anyone opposing economic development, defined as the development of capitalism, is criminalized. The
'socialist' obligation to work is made identical with such values as

democracy and equality. All of society thus becomes a medium of accumulation, a social factory. The working class is subordinated and integrated into a social organization whose sole purpose is the creation of wealth for capitalists. But as the concentration of capital promoted by the constitution leads to an expansion of workers' power through the increased massification of workers, a crisis of legality emerges. The constitution promotes an integration of classes, but capitalism produces struggle on ever higher levels. The basic antinomy that the constitution seemed to make disappear, merely reappears in new forms.

Negri also argues in this book against the leninist concept of law. Law, he contends, is not superstructural; there is a direct link between law and surplus value (the mechanism for extracting profit from the exploitation of labour). The relations of production are produced by law, and law therefore is a form of violent command integral to production. But at the moment when an identity of law and command seems to be most realized, the antagonism implicit in capitalist social relations expresses itself. Law is therefore both the identity of authority and the first line of crisis. In response to this, law can only become general domination, and consequently, in the transition to communism, the state of law can no longer be possible.

Negri also criticizes the Bolshevik (Pasukanis') idea that the transition can consist of the mere socialization of property, a replacement of the market with an ideal of social work and of social property. This is not enough, according to Negri; workers' struggles must move against the basis of property itself, the law of work-value which is the regulator of exploitation. Property is nothing more than a determinate concentration of capitalist command, of the enforcement of the law of value. Negri cites a passage from Marx to bolster his argument: 'The suppression of private property is thus realized only when it is conceived as the suppression of work. . . . An "organization of work" is therefore a contradiction'. For the Bolsheviks, law was saved by the myth of social work that supposedly exists outside of the process of valorization, the transformation of exploited work energy into surplus value and money. For Negri, law cannot be separated from exploitation in the transition to communism. The communist struggle against work and the state must also be against law as the specific authoritative form of the relation between the state and labour.

Against the coalition of capital and the state evident in the constitution, Negri proposes a strategy of self-valorization, whereby workers place their needs and interests first, and refuse to sacrifice for the sake of the general interest or consensus which the constitution seeks to legitimate. By affirming the independence of its interests by demand-ing higher factory as well as social wages, workers force capital to drop the show of democratic neutrality; it must become repressive to maintain itself. And the form that repression takes is public administration, new constitutional forms that operate through command to obtain labour peace. The state subsumes civil society (eliminating law, liberty, and equality), and this places the working class outside civil society entirely. The 'other' workers' movement responds by constructing in itself its own society (self-valorization).

Il dominio e il sabotaggio [*Domination and Sabotage*] (1978) is probably Negri's clearest exposition of the concept of autonomy. Autonomy as self-valorization consists of a separating of working class interests and needs from the prerequisites of capitalist development. It is a politics which brooks no compromise with the idea of collaborating in the exploitation of labour for the sake of a capitalist development that ultimately merely maintains its domination through such collabor-ations. The working class affirms its otherness, its difference, and its discontinuity with the capitalist project. It seeks to break the homoge-neity of interests that capitalism seeks to impose. Negri calls for struggles around the social wage; the struggle for the salaried wage must become more general and egalitarian. Although violence is a necessary component of these struggles, the goal is the total use of wealth in the service of collective freedom.

It is in this book that Negri comes to sound more and more like the French thinkers in the post-structuralist tradition who were writing at the same time (especially Deleuze, Derrida, Foucault, and Guattari). Whereas the orthodox dialectic, which provides the basis for Com-munist Party theory, operates in terms of homology, totality, and resolution, the philosophy of discontinuity emphasizes non-homologous otherness or heterogeneity, the fractured and incomplete nature of totality, and the impossibility of conclusive resolution. Negri argues that it is only by insisting on his own difference and otherness as well as on the difference and otherness of the class movement that there can be ruptures of the sort that would provide hope for renewal. The workers' movement is discontinuous because it constantly remakes its organizational forms, and by defining itself as other than or outside the totality of capitalist development, the movement operates a destructuration and sabotage of it. There can be no homology between the workers' movement and capitalist development, and consequently, the totality of capitalism must be seen as forced relationship, one ruptured from within by a destructuration exercised by the proletarian subject. Capitalism restructures itself by imposing conclusiveness, a finality or goal, on this internal rupture. The interruptions of strikes and wage demands can be countered by higher prices and the ideal of a continuous, though cyclical, capitalist development. But working class self-valorization is irreducibly discontinuous; it cannot be subsumed to the homologies of the capitalist logic of rational or historical progress. As autonomy, it refuses the goal of economic development. Negri: 'The rupture and recognition of the class' own productive force removes any possibility of a resolutive dialectic'. It is in the logic of separation and discontinuity with capital that workers' power resides.

Marx oltre Marx [Marx Beyond Marx] (1980) describes the relation between this concept of autonomy and the earlier concept of communism as a real possibility signalled by the potential for over-production in modern capitalism. Through a reading of Marx's *Grundrisse*, Negri argues that this model of communism is immediately given in inverted form within the categories of capitalism. For example, the characteristics of money (sociality, the representation of collective productivity, the measure and sign of patrimony) can be immediately reversed into communism. Class politics consists of carrying out this inversion and producing an immediate communism. Communism is the result of the activity of a constituting subject, one who makes the material world of goods, but this subject must liberate him/herself from the capitalist constraints of the law of value and of wage labour. Communism's future is not the telos at the end of capitalist development, as Italian Communist Party theorists claim, but rather it is a new subject formation constituting itself by affirming its autonomy from capital and thereby destroying capital. The communist refusal of work unleashes the multiplicity of free movement of this subject, its complete autonomy. The transition to communism is the material self-construction of an autonomous subject.

Negri continues this argument through a reading of Spinoza in *L'anomalia selvaggia, saggio su potere e potenza in Spinoza [The Wild Anomaly, A Study of Power and Potential in Spinoza]* (1981), the first book he wrote while in prison. Negri poses Spinoza's concept of potential against that of power, and argues that potential, the principle of the material constitution of being through human activity, resembles the principle of communism in the theory of autonomy. The concept acquires a political dimension through this reading, becoming identified with mass democracy and direct governance. The state is not to be founded on law, but instead on liberation, which is equatable with the principle of material constitution, the free expansion of human material productive potential.

Negri's theories have clearly placed him at odds with the major political forces of his time, most notably those on the left associated with leninism. In *Politica di classe [Class Politics]* (1980), he addresses these differences. Written at a time of great political repression against the extra-parliamentary left in Italy, the book calls for a greater level of political organization, though Negri as usual carefully distinguishes this from a leninist form, arguing that there must be an anchor in the composition of the class; the seizure of state power alone is not enough. Against the Red Brigades, Negri argues in favour of mass insubordination, resistance rather than tyrannicide. The political struggle must come first, and it must give priority to needs in the period of transition. There is a need for wealth and liberty in the proletariat that is not answered by the leninist alternatives.

Perhaps the greatest significance of Negri's work resides in the way it steals the principle ideals of liberalism – freedom, equality, democracy – for marxism by giving them a substance or materiality that liberalism, in its limitation to a purely formal commitment to such ideals, could not. Yet Negri also continues to operate within the liberal ideology of a decontextualized subjectivity; his theory of the realization of communism as self-expression remains beholden to a notion of self-identity that is metaphysical from the perspective of the post-structuralist critique of the subject. In that perspective, the subject is seen as an effect and as a site, as a product of non-subjective processes and as a locus of discourse where social and cultural codes are replicated in an appearance of expressive self-identity. But in the discourse of liberal metaphysics that Negri inhabits, the subject is thought to be prior to social representation, an essence subtractable without loss from its social context and its rhetorical instruments. It is an origin of expression in no way shaped by structures or codes.

Negri's absolutism of the expressive subject considered as a mass or collectivity is merely the liberal individual writ large. The subjective potential he ascribes to the proletariat, one that precedes (indeed exceeds) all social mediation, recalls the claims to interiority that grounds the very institutionality of property that Negri wants to eliminate. It is not shaped or given content by 'external' instruments or cultural representational forms. For this reason, he conceives of democratic communism as a simple direct expression of materiality as it is produced by human subjectivity. But do humans simply produce without any determination or formulation by their institutional context? Will that 'external' situation merely fall into place, find its remedy naturally, once communism as unlimited over-production is accomplished? Such issues cannot even be raised in the context of a political theory that rests on a metaphysics of subjective interiority and of essentialist materiality.

It is not as if the metaphysics of subjectivity inherent in Negri's work does not have an answer to some of these questions. The market as instrument of distribution, the argument would go, does not need to be dealt with as such, as an external instrument requiring reformulation, because it is nothing more than the expression of a capitalist subjectivity. Everything can be accounted for as a symptom of subjective power over another subject. The liberation of the subordinate subject will immediately remedy the oppression waged by such instruments as the law of value. But in locating the solution to this problem in a purely interiorist and essentialist model of subjectivity and materiality, Negri relegates to a position of accident or secondary externality what should, even according to the logic of his own argument, be a central concern – the form or rhetoric of social interaction. The very existence of the law of value, as an external instrument that exercises in a mediated way the power of capitalists over workers, testifies to the essential role such instruments play in determining the content of social existence. Otherwise, capitalist subjective power would exercise itself directly, without mediation. Because that law is essential to capitalist power, it cannot be considered merely secondary, merely an expressive form for subjects in no way shaped themselves by such instruments. As much as subjectivity, such instrumentalities pertain, by their very existence and necessity, to materiality.

Attending to the instrumental arena of social life, its practical, formal, and rhetorical dimension, means as well materializing one's own descriptions, seeing the rhetorical dimension of one's own logic as well as of the logic of power one describes. In his work on the Italian constitution, Negri points to ideological operations that should require a materialist or rhetorical description, but he remains himself within the vocabulary of liberal reason. For example, he accepts the ideological liberal description of the opposition between formal or abstract law and real or concrete labour. Such logical descriptions conceal the rhetorical or material mechanisms (the style of enactment, if you will) of subordination under the ruse of seemingly rational categorical distinctions (formal versus concrete). By accepting such descriptions, Negri accepts the terms of liberal ideology. It would have amounted to a more 'materialist' account if he had used a more rhetorical vocabulary of description, one that emphasized the anchoring of the constitution in language and that saw the formal/concrete distinction as a material exercise that is as much a matter of discursive shape or form as of logic or of social content. In the constitution, two metonymically connected parts of the system of social forms (labour, capital) are conflated to a metaphoric identity in which one substitutes for the other and incorporates it under its terms of action and understanding. Indeed, that incorporation and subordination is the social enactment of the subordination of rhetoric to logic and of popular mass democracy to republican authority in the constitutional culture of liberal capitalism.

Because the suppression of reflection on constitutional language and the concealment of the actual rhetoric of power is essential to liberal politics, a greater understanding of those forms, the instrumental and practical shapes social thought and social life assume, is indispensable to the reconstructive project which Negri theorizes. By allowing such issues to be demoted to problems that are secondary to the more essential task of subjective liberation, we run the risk of replicating the liberal repression of materiality. And without an understanding of the constitutive role of formal procedure and rhetorical instrumentality, we risk conceiving of social construction as a matter of pure content in relation to which the formal dimension of life assumes a merely expressive and secondary position. Choosing the right social content – democratic communism, say, conceived as the realization of a liberated subject and the fulfilment of material production – then becomes an excuse for ignoring once again the issues of form, shape, and procedure – the economic mechanisms for distributing goods, the legal forms for assuring freedom without exploitation, the everyday texture of life's arrangements and negotiations, and the political institutions for exercising democracy directly.

The content of social life is as much constituted by as expressed in those rhetorical forms, be they economic or cultural. For this reason, an issue such as the replacement of the instrument of money (which may be a metaphor of power but which is also an enabling metonymic connector) is not merely secondary in relation to the more 'material' issue of the realization of the freedom of the subject of labour. That freedom may itself depend on the construction of a system of distribution that makes such instruments as money available equally in a way that fully democratizes the economic system. Negri argues that money is simply a direct expression of capitalist domination exercised as the extraction of labour value from workers. But that is only the case in a context that gives money that meaning. In an altogether different context, the instrument acquires a different significance; it becomes merely a token of exchange, a means of voting on communal projects, or a way of crediting others' good work. This means that the very concept of value would lose its meaning and be replaced with a system of calculation in which the instrument is not capable of assuming value in itself, as with capitalist money.

In other words, the more ideal concerns of giving a more egalitarian and democratic content to social life hinge crucially on the choice of instruments or of forms, and forms that had one meaning in a capitalist context can be given new ones in a different context. The life of the subject will not improve simply by giving a new material content to social existence by declaring it an expression of subjective liberation; just the contrary, that new content will be dependent on the making of new forms (as much of exchange or distribution as of arranging work relations, for example), new practices and rhetorical procedures that will give both new shape and new meaning to social and subjective existence.

What we end with then is a position that fulfils materialism, in the sense of extending it into form, but that consequently also extinguishes it as an instance supposedly separable from the arrangements it assumes or is given in social existence. The radicality of the concept of form resides precisely in this removal of any possibility of a substance or a subject that is not situated within formal arrangements, distributions of elements in relation to each other, not as structures but as figures held together by forces playing off each other. Negri's importance resides in his reconceptualization of capitalism along these lines, giving it back the political meaning Marx assigned it. The so-called 'economic' system is a site where forces meet and interact, where the energies of workers (broadly defined as everyone in society who doesn't live off the ownership and accumulation of capital) collide with the constraining powers of capitalists. In this remarkably *political* understanding of economics, there is no room for a palliative of the Habermas variety that would suggest a possible socialism that preserves the labour process intact and that would deny a thoroughgoing democratization of every aspect of economic and social existence. The assumption of a materialist philosophic position implies a commitment to the immediacy of self-determination. Such a commitment remains captive to metaphysics, however, to the extent that it does not see forces as assuming forms that are the contingent figures in which substance and subject exist. And the foregrounding of that contingency (and indeterminacy) is the task of post-structuralism.[2]

3   The Politics of Deconstruction: Feminism

Post-structuralism names a broad field of work that ranges from psychoanalysis (Lacan, Deleuze and Guattari) to philosophy (Derrida, Irigaray, Lyotard), to literary criticism (Barthes, Cixous, Kristeva), to social and cultural theory (Foucault, Bourdieu, Baudrillard). While this work has on the whole shifted our paradigms of understanding from cognitivist analysis and totalizing dialectics toward more differentiated, materialized, and indeterminist modes of thought, as a whole it suffers from the absence of a practicable political orientation. Descriptions of ideal worlds or of subversive strategies of writing and living abound, but none of the theories either attempts the kind of social theory Habermas proposes or sketches models of political practice of the sort Negri provides. There is in post-structuralism an antipathy to systems and to the logocentric project of subsuming the world to the categories of reason that makes the avoidance of habermassian varieties of total theories understandable. But why is practical politics so alien to philosophies that seem so eminently political?

Part of the answer to that question can be located in the structuralist abolition of the subject. Althusser's 'process without a subject' was a process without politics, since radical politics, defined in Negri's terms, at least, as the revolt of subjective force against supposedly oppressive objective structures that limit its potential, is precisely the converse of the precipitating of subjects by codes or structures. The critique of ego-consciousness in structuralism and post-structuralism is a necessary part of the critique of liberal rationalism, with its exclusive emphasis on the individual mind as the centre and source of social action. But by emphasizing determining structures, discourses, and codes at the expense of the radical recoding and reinflection any person or group can give to those structures and codes, it can legitimate the privileging of higher forms of party and state reason over the needs, desires, and democratic aspirations of supposedly 'ideological' subjects.

It can also lead, as it does in Foucault, to a description of power that

seems to leave no space for the interaction of forces whose stabilization
is the origin of all power. The force in power is simply one part of a
larger dynamic arrangement, and it must be conceived as a reaction
and a response to countervailing movements of force that are as much
determining of the shape of society as that pacification of forces we call
power. At its most extreme, the critique of the subject becomes in
Lacan a fatalism that grants no importance to the reinflections an ego
can give to its determinants and that sees the instincts and the symbolic
order as exercising a power in relation to which a subject can only
adopt a position of resigned acceptance. The mid–1970s political
pessimism and passivity of the 'new philosophers' was a predictable
derivative of this perspective.

This is not true of post-structuralism as a whole, and such critics of
rationalism as Derrida and such materialist radicals as Deleuze and
Guattari have always pointed more optimistically to openings in the
walls of determination. In their work and in the French feminism of
Cixous, Irigaray, and others, one finds a post-subjective politics that is
not limited by models of over-determination. The breakdown of the
boundaries of the subject does not occur as a caving in but as an
exploding out. Yet Deleuze and Guattari's nomadic libertarianism
leaves the determination of the shapes of social institutions in the
hands of those who take the trouble to occupy them; as a prefigurative
politics, it leaves the present behind, and with it, present politics.
Similarly, while post-structuralist feminism offers an enabling model
for a revision of the system of determination, the movement runs the
risk of recategorizing the excluded as the ineffable, thereby reproducing the patriarchal privileging of the 'virtuous' woman. Setting oneself
apart leaves the inside of politics intact and troubles the integrity of
politics at best as a persistent othering that avoids capture. But the
process of capture is allowed to stand.

I will now consider the issue of the politics of deconstruction with
special attention to the issue of feminism. To what extent does
deconstruction follow the pattern of male philosophy when it
metaphorizes women into figures of indeterminacy? Is this merely a
repetition of the paradigm or an internal critique of its premises?
When Derrida argues that male western philosophy is available for
expropriative uses, to what extent is he repeating the game of
differentiating one-upmanship and the process of bonding that defines
the rhetoric of male philosophic practice and that is essential to the
maintenance of that tradition? By characterizing philosophy as open
and available to multiple, disseminatory uses, by making philosophy

'female', is he simply being quintessentially 'male' himself? I will begin by considering the use made of Derrida in the US. Then, I will offer a critique of his reading of the figure of a woman in Nietzsche.

The ascription of political values to philosophical methodologies is a risky endeavour. As much as meaning, such values are usually a function of use. Hegel saw the dialectic as promoting a monarchial republic, but Marx managed to use the method in favour of an ideal of radical political and economic democracy. Use is not without its particular genres and modes, its particular uses; it has its own shapes and forms, its own rhetoric. It is in the different modes in which philosophy is used that political values make themselves evident. The dialectic was conservative when it sanctified existing institutions, denied democracy, and foreclosed further knowledge. The radical use of the method takes different forms altogether. It promotes a sense that the social world is in movement, that previous conclusions are merely starting points, and that much remains to be not only known but also made. This radical use takes the cap off the dialectic, turning a triangle into a square with an open fourth wall.

Deconstruction appealed to liberals and radicals, while offending conservatives, in part because it provided a philosophical justification for the kind of radical use Marx made of the dialectic. As a result, what had been a matter of contingent practice acquired the generality of principle as well as a certain methodological permanence. While being a philosophy in its own right, deconstruction was also the philosophy of the radical use of philosophy. It explained just why methods like positivism that exempted themselves from critical reflection could not get away with it; the positivist method is itself a rhetoric that operates according to certain tropes and shaping procedures. It occludes its own social and historical positioning through a metaleptic reversal that places a social and rhetorical result – the method itself – in the place of a cause. For this reason, it can split into different uses; no ground holds it in place.

Derrida provided a philosophical description of why such uses were not only possible but unavoidable – and of why departures were not only likely but necessary. To a certain extent, Derrida closed the question of whether philosophy should be open-ended or closed (which is to say, critical and democratic or conservative and élitist) by providing a philosophical justification for the impossibility of closing. The radical position, he proved, could not help but prevail – simply by default. The closure conservatives sought simply was not possible.

No wonder they were so angry. Such anger has been expressed in the

US particularly in the form of consistently negative reviews of post-structuralism in the leading intellectual journal – *The New York Review of Books*. Writers like Denis Donoghue and John Searle, who are far indeed from being considered experts on the movement, are asked to present it to the larger public. The reviews are debatably accurate, and they are always condemnatory. I will consider more closely one review by Searle of Jonathan Culler's book *On Deconstruction*, since it suggests that while some of the trouble may have to do with a traditional American suspicion of things European and theoretical, it may also have to do with the difference between a more conservative and a more radical vision of philosophy and of language.

Searle's account of Derrida is largely based on Culler's account, so it may be inappropriate to accuse him of misrepresentation. To a certain extent, Culler's transformation of Derrida's philosophical and political concerns into almost exclusively literary concerns has to be given its due of credit. For example, when Searle, following Culler, defines deconstruction as a method for reversing oppositions like speech and writing, truth and fiction, he is being only partly accurate, since Derrida never discusses truth and fiction. Indeed, the discussion of opposites in his work is derivative in relation to the critique of logocentrism, the idea that truth consists of the adequation of language to being conceived as presence, of which those oppositions are a symptom. Truth in logocentric philosophy, from Plato on down, is conceived as what is subtracted from representation and empirical contingency, as what is proper to itself. Derrida argues that this concept of truth depends on a set of normative oppositions – inside/outside, ideal/non-ideal, transcendent/empirical, and so on. Because sound or speech seems closer to the mind, it is usually thought to be more 'true' than writing, an external, non-living, technique of representation that indicates non-presence (of the speaker or mind or idea). But this opposition is only important because truth is always prior to representation, and speech, as the sign of truth, is prior to writing, a form of representation.

Searle takes the speech/writing opposition as crucial when in fact it is ancillary. Derrida is not really interested in speech and writing as empirical events; he is interested in the philosophic values of which the opposition is a symptom. Searle begs the question when he says that Derrida does not offer empirical proof that writing is prior to speech; that is not the point. The point is that the logocentric model of truth as an immediacy of presence in the mind or as a trans-representational ideality requires that representation and mediation in general (as well as the specific practical, spatial, iterative, differential, graphic character of writing) be thought of as derived and secondary.

Derrida argues three things regarding this issue. The first is that the constitution of this sort of ideal truth depends on the expulsion of representation, mediation, and the sort of worldly contingency and indeterminacy associated with writing. But the prior term – truth as presence in the mind – is an effect of what writing represents – that is, representation, mediacy, difference, spatialization, and so on. The second argument is that the characteristics of writing that are denigrated – its repeatability in different contexts separate from the living presence of the speaker, for example – are in fact what allow speech in the mind to occur at all. Such speech requires signs, and no signs can exist without being in some way capable of being communicated or transferred out of their immediate context and into others. Moreover, all mental representation is 'like writing' in that it presupposes a space on which representation is deployed. The third argument is that if spatial representation can occur to presence (the speech of the mind, for example), then such representation is a structural possibility internal to such presence, and not a mere accident that befalls it from without. Representation is part of the system of truth; it cannot be declared outside in relation to a more pure (clear, precise, rigorous) inside of truth. The purpose of these arguments is not to privilege writing over speech; it is to question the sanctity of the values (the inside is better than the outside, presence better than representation, the ideal better than the contingent, the universal better than the historical, the natural better than the technical, and so on) that underlie the logocentric definition of truth.

Searle quotes a long passage to this effect in Derrida, but he ignores its evident implications. The major implication is that the seemingly simple determination of truth as what is present to the conscious mind or as something prior to contingency, representation, and difference is not innocent; it harbours value claims. The purpose of Derrida's work is to flush out those claims and to see if they withstand critical scrutiny. Usually, they do not. The outcome of this critique is not, however, to claim, as Searle contends, that there is no truth, no rationality, no logic, only a play of signifiers. It is to say that the condition of possibility of these things is something that the logocentric conception of them wants to declare irrelevant or secondary; indeed, Searle repeats the scenario by declaring the speech/writing question to be a marginal one that Derrida resurrects illegitimately.

One of the implications of Derrida's critique is that we should question seemingly self-evident notions of philosophic truth or philosophic value. Searle rightly points out that transcendental grounds of the husserlian variety are not necessary for science, logic, and rationality, but Derrida never makes that assumption. Derrida does say that every time truth, either as a foundation or as a goal of language analysis, is defined in a logocentric manner, it assumes certain predictable values – immediate presence is better than mediacy, identity is better than difference, ideality is better than practical, situational contingency, and so on.

Searle himself espouses these values when he says that 'first-rate' philosophers (himself included) are 'vastly superior' to Derrida because of the 'clarity, rigor, precision, theoretical comprehensiveness, and above all, intellectual content' of their writing. Clarity presupposes that visible presence, rather than the mediacy of presence and absence, is good; rigour and precision suggest that proper, limited determinations can be made that clear away the clutter of differential inter-relations and contextual differences; theoretical comprehensiveness assumes that a universal ideal closure, without remainder, should be established; and intellectual content valorizes the conscious mind's mastery over the contingent world of signifying form. Semantics lords it over syntax, as usual, and the fact that the condition of possibility of semantics is a syntax whose operations are asemic is forgotten. These are the very logocentric values that deconstruction questions. And it is not surprising, therefore, that Searle should have trouble with it.

When Derrida debated Searle, he pointed out that Searle was in many points in agreement with him and that occasionally Searle used Derrida's own arguments against Derrida without realizing it. It is interesting that one of Searle's arguments in his review against deconstruction is in part what deconstruction is all about: 'It is a condition of the adequacy of a precise theory of an indeterminate phenomenon that it should precisely characterize the phenomenon as indeterminate'. The difference is that Derrida would argue that our methods are embedded in language and therefore also subject to indeterminacy. Our theories are practical and contingent – part and parcel of the world they describe. Derrida would therefore question the possibility of 'adequacy', since that assumes we stand outside the world and describe it with an essentially non-worldly language (formalism remains the dream of analytic philosophy). He would also question the value of precision, since, given the nature of things, an imprecise language (one that evokes difference and contingency) might be more accurate, might be a better representation of the indeterminate phenomenon.

This is why Derrida's style of writing is so troublesome to Searle. Derrida assumes that the truth of the world is not determinable using logocentric presuppositions and methods. If the nature of being is differential and not determinable as a presence that can be precisely named by ideal theoretical categories, then the method that describes it accurately must itself be, to a certain extent, indeterminate, differential, contingent, practical, and so on. Everything is, as Searle quoting Wittgenstein and inadvertently and unknowingly echoing Derrida says, exactly the same. But it is also slightly different.

Searle's misrepresentation of Derrida is in part a confirmation of Derrida's claim that spirit (thought, ideas, ideal truth) depends on the letter (signifying systems, the history of word-concepts, the disseminatory potential of language to create meaning effects) and that the letter is never fully controllable by spirit. It can go astray, betraying unconscious values of the sort Derrida ascribes to logocentric philosophy. For example, Searle discounts Derrida's claim that logocentrism and phallocentrism have been one in western philosophy, but in the same section, Searle calls for a distinction between 'genuine knowledge and its counterfeits, and justified feelings of mastery from mere enthusiams generated by a lot of pretentious verbosity'. Now, Searle's negative terms are all terms that, throughout the western philosophic tradition, are ascribed to metaphor and to woman, two victims, if you will, of what Derrida calls phallogocentrism. Genuine knowledge is present as theory (visibility) to the mind, whereas metaphor is a 'mere' secondary representation or 'counterfeit'. Woman is given to 'enthusiasm', indeed hysteria, whereas men are rigorous, tough, and rational. Mill: 'A woman never runs wild after an abstraction'. Metaphoricity and metaphors of 'femininity' conjoin in Searle's value system, and he thus gives a good indication of what Derrida means by phallogocentrism.

Searle's 'presentation' of Derrida is itself more an act of rhetoric designed to generate negative 'counterfeit' effects than a representation of truth held firmly in his mind. The major misrepresentation is that Searle allows American Yale School deconstructive literary criticism to be confused with Derrida's work. There are large differences, and although Searle eventually brings out some, his opening gambit is to deliberately confuse the two. Thus, Culler's example of a nietzschean problem of causality (a pin and pain) is allowed to stand as an example of an undifferentiated 'deconstruction'. In fact, Derrida never deals with psychological examples of this sort. Searle also lets stand Culler's (not Derrida's) contention that 'truths are fictions whose fictionality has been forgotten'. This is in fact a quote from Nietzsche in which the words 'fiction' and 'fictionality' have been substituted for the orginal words 'metaphor' and 'metaphoricity'. Even Searle will acknowledge that metaphor and fiction are two different things. More marginally, Searle claims that Derrida only discusses Plato, Rousseau, and Husserl 'in any detail'. He neglects to mention Aristotle, Leibniz, Descartes, Condillac, Hegel, Marx, Nietzsche, Heidegger, Levinas, Austin, Searle, and several others.

More careful and extensive reading might have allowed Searle to live up more to his own philosophic ideal of precision. But the problem of misrepresentation of which this review is so fine an example is not idiosyncratic; it is inscribed in the very nature of communication and translation, especially across cultures. This problem suggests that knowledge, as Derrida contends, is a matter of practical work (careful reading, for example) and not a matter of spontaneous intuitive theoretical mastery in an ideal register.

The answer to the 'problem' of the structural possibility of missed effects or misrepresentation in communication is either to close it off (logocentrism) or to try to find out what happens when you leave it open (deconstruction). The traditional political critique of logocentric closure is that it requires a specious assumption of authority (bolstered by a sense of possessing Truth) on the part of an élite of true knowers. It is symptomatic, therefore, that Searle's review is full of metaphors of élitism (superior, first-rate, and so on). Derrida's work programme, I would contend, has more democratic, indeed democratic socialist, consequences. It suggests that we should stop trying to pin down what the world 'is' and instead begin building something new – new languages of knowledge, to start with. It is, ultimately, a *constructivist* philosophy.

The debate, therefore, I would suggest, has political as well as philosophical consequences. And although theories of knowledge and practical politics do not map onto each other, there are nonetheless practical implications resident in the form of philosophical theorizing. For example, one can imagine that if both Searle and Derrida were in charge of a planning commission charged with building a super highway through a poor working class neighbourhood, they would probably proceed in different ways. Searle would determine with precision, clarity, and rigour what would need to be done to accomplish the intention or meaning of the project. Costs would be

calculated exactly, expenditures regulated efficiently, the law exercised to move the inhabitants out of the way, and the goal of practically
realizing the theoretical project effectuated. I suspect Derrida would
dawdle a bit before beginning. He would ask what assumptions are
being made in formulating the project and what ends or interests
would be served by its realization. This in itself would introduce
enough indeterminacy, lack of rigour, and imprecision to cause
anxiety in the searlian camp of planners. Then, Derrida would
probably ask about the history and make-up of the community that is
about to be destroyed – still withholding any determination of truth in
the matter. He would ask if the people in the neighbourhood have
been consulted, and he would be likely to consult them, thus
introducing a radical difference of goals and interests into the unity of
the endeavour. He would do a study to weigh ecological and social
impacts. He would situate the project in the context of the city as a
whole, the nation, the history of urban planning under capitalism and
its assumptions, both theoretical and practical. He would construct, in
other words, a highly indeterminate network of contexts and differential relations around the seemingly simple project, whose truth could
just as easily be realized with clarity and rigour – but without raising
any questions at all.

Deconstruction is, I would therefore argue, not the masterpiece of
idiocy Searle paints it as being; it is an important critique of important
blindspots of philosophy, and it has its radical uses. Nevertheless, it
would be a mistake to become too uncritically starry eyed in its regard
without taking the obvious problem that if it has its radical uses, it also
has its conservative ones, into account. Indeed, as a method for
reading texts, deconstruction can be quite fallible, especially when
confronted with the necessity of performing political analyses. Its own
criteria of judgement are such that they limit its range of critique to
issues of identity, presence, and meaning. It is true that Derrida
incorporates the language of Marx's economic analysis (surplus value
and so on) into his method. And he has made his own political
allegiances quite clear. But the goals of deconstructive analysis – the
production of indeterminacy, the location of aporias, the demystifica-
tion of conceptual grounds – can be, and have proven to be, quite
troubling to writers and thinkers with radical political priorities. The
accessibility of deconstruction to their use seems by now beyond
dispute. But the fact remains that although radical critique must take
the side of indeterminacy when confronted with ideological models of
nature, or truth, or identity, such critique has a more difficult time

assuming indeterminacy or undecidability as allies in regard to the ⌡
formulation of affirmative positions. *Pace* Negri, Deleuze/Guattari,
and Irigaray, who do rely on models of discontinuity and difference to
ground a radical politics or an alternative philosophy, those struggling
for equality, democracy, and freedom often feel they require something more firm than an aporia under their feet as they carry on the
good fight.

I take Irigaray and Negri's position: indeterminacy, discontinuity,
and the critical questioning of philosophical hierarchies founded on
values of identity and presence favour equality. This does not mean,
however, that every deconstructive reading satisfies radical ends.
Deconstruction is consistent in regard to the proto-political values
implicit in western philosophy, but as a procedure of analysis, it does
not explicitly guarantee one political outcome over another. [Actually,
in revising, I have to take issue with myself here. It does, I think, imply
progressive, egalitarian, anti-hierarchical values. But this does not
mean that those values cannot be ignored in favour of, say, a tragic
pessimism, as in the work of Paul De Man.] As a result, problems can
arise when the method is confronted with actual political issues like
feminism. Indeed, by 'bracketing' or 'putting aside' political consequences, deconstruction can run the risk of becoming an aestheticism of
contradiction. And this can lead to the excusing of questionable
political positions on the grounds that the texts in which they occur are
undecidable or indeterminate. Derrida's 'La question du style', an
essay on Nietzsche's writings about women, is, I would contend, a case
in point.[3]

Derrida argues that Nietzsche 'is a little lost [in his own text]'; he
contradicts himself regarding women, sometimes portraying them
positively as an affirmative force akin to the dionysian, sometimes
condemning them as resembling the idealist or dogmatic philosopher
who believes in 'truth'. Ultimately, however, woman is a figure for the
non-truth of truth in general, and is therefore a positive force.
Nevertheless, in order to prove his contention, Derrida must quote
selectively, at times leaving out or only partially citing significant
passages, at times ignoring Nietzsche's irony, once generating a
mistranslation in accordance with his argument, once creating an
impression of causality by putting together two disparate citations,
and, throughout, overlooking Nietzsche's copious notebooks.

And while Derrida's argument is not without its virtues (he suggests
that there is no truth of sexual difference, which is to say, there is no
distinct identity of gender that can be the basis of a hierarchical

<u>empowermant of one over the other</u>), many feminists would rightly claim that such a laudable ideal does not help their cause much in the short run. It merely obliterates the identity all oppressed groups must claim as their own in the struggle to free themselves from their subordinate position. This ultimately is the difference between a deconstructive feminist like Irigaray, for whom the identities of reason are inherently phallocratic, and a political feminist like MacKinnon, for whom inequality is the primary term, one that imposes the necessity of an immediate reversal of the system of subordination.

The issue of reading or interpreting a text like Nietzsche's is therefore also a political problem. Derrida argues that Nietzsche's positions on woman are multiple and contradictory and that the figure of woman in the text is the name for that indeterminacy of meaning. Truth is a matter of dissimulation; it consists of metaphors that create identities out of differences of force and different experiences. Truth always hides this 'non-truth', this process of dissimulation that makes the concept of truth as identity possible. This is also the case with Nietzsche's text. Derrida claims that Nietzsche's multiple and contradictory positions on woman are evidence of an undecidability of meaning that eludes an interpretation (like Heidegger's) that would assign a single meaning or truth to the text. Nietzsche's own style is parodic, ironic, plural, and 'feminine' because, like the figure of woman in his text, it only feigns or simulates truth. But, like woman, whose identity passes into man's undecidably in the text, his style puts all notions of identity or of what is 'proper' in question. 'Style' is therefore in this essay a name for that process of semantically undecidable differentiation lying under all identities of being or thought that Derrida elsewhere calls 'writing'. Derrida concludes his essay by citing a line from Nietzsche's notebooks – 'I forgot my umbrella' – and by arguing that one can never really know what it means. It remains outside the horizon of meaning a hermeneuticist like Heidegger seeks to establish, an horizon that would fully saturate the meaning of a text. Style (inscription, rhetoric, metaphor, representation, and so on) is thus necessary for truth to have meaning, but style itself is unassimilable to truth.

Derrida acknowledges that Nietzsche attacks women in his writings. But he claims that woman also appears as a dionysian force in Nietzsche, someone who keeps the dogmatic idealist philosopher's desire for 'presence, . . . content, the thing itself, meaning, truth' at a distance. She is therefore an affirmative figure who undermines truth as identity through dissimulation and a plurality of styles (undecidability) that cannot be resolved into a single thesis or meaning. Consequently, Derrida claims, Nietzsche's propositions on woman cannot themselves be reduced to a single truth. Terms like truth, woman, and castration would have to be placed in decidable oppositions with other terms, and Nietzsche's parodic and heterogeneous style of writing precludes this.

What Derrida calls the 'graphic of the hymen' in the text always subtracts a margin from the control of the horizon of meaning, thus opening an infinite calculus of undecidability. What this means is that oppositions like truth/non-truth, presence/absence, semantics/syntax, woman/man, and so on are supplementary of each other. To determine one, it is necessary to call on the other, if only to establish a margin, a boundary of identity for the term being determined. But that addition or supplement is also a loss or subtraction, for it means that the identity of the term determined is never fully complete without its relation to its other. Its interiority or self-identity (what Derrida calls *propriété* or properness) is always also outside itself, somewhere in between the two, and this is why Derrida chooses the metaphor of the hymen to describe it. The identity of what is inside is guarded or kept intact, yet also breached and left open to an outside by the very thing that defines its boundary. What demarcates inside from outside in the determination of the identity of any oppositional concept like truth or presence also by that very token confuses the two. Syntax is always considered as something added onto a self-sufficient semantics, but without it, semantics would be lacking, would have no identity.

Something similar happens when a hermeneuticist tries to determine the identity of the meaning of a text like Nietzsche's. Something will always be needed to be added on, which is to say, something will always be subtracted from the horizon of meaning. It can never be fully saturated, if for no other reason than the very graphic (or figural, rhetorical, and metaphoric) element of the text itself remains meaningless, yet it is essential to meaning. But more importantly, an identity of meaning (of the figure of woman say) will always depend on relations to other uses of the figure in the text, and these can never all be fully taken into account in a single thesis. There are always differences, and consequently, a margin will always be subtracted; there can be no 'proper' identity of meaning. The very figurality or graphicality of the metaphor of woman can never be elevated to the ideal level of meaning, even though meaning depends on it.

One need not be a particularly astute observer to have noticed a rather large pool of hot water growing steadily under Derrida's feet. His choice of metaphors in this instance is not the most felicitous. Why 'hymen'? To understand his use of the term, it would probably help to recall that the essay in which it first appears ('La double séance') was written in the late 1960s. The modern feminist intellectual critique of male language or of the male appropriation of female metaphors had not yet come into being. Moreover, it was far from common back then for men to join the feminist cause in public philosophical forums. Claims of precociousness and of uniqueness (as a male philosopher launching the critique of phallogocentrism) might let Derrida off the hook for choosing womens' genitalia (and a sign of virginity at that) as the name for undecidability (shades of the '*ewige Weiblichkeit*', the eternal or ineffable female, also known as the inevitable housewife), but by now new standards have been fashioned, and the use of hymen in this way cannot easily escape critical judgement. Indeed, it is possible that the choice already reflects on Derrida's argument regarding Nietzsche.

For Nietzsche, according to Derrida, woman is a figure of the undecidability of sexual identity as well as of the necessary plurality or indeterminacy of style, which is to say, of representation or inscription in general. A nice idea, but is it true? Or to put it differently, is it an accurate description of Nietzsche's text? If not, is it still commendable as a nice, hermeneutic spin job that is meant to create certain political effects regardless of accuracy? Can we say that Derrida's text is therefore a good representation, a truer one, of what he is talking about for being somewhat faked?

Let's look at the inaccuracies first. Derrida claims that in *Ecce Homo* Nietzsche writes that he has a plural style 'because' he knows woman.[4] Check the text and you find that the notion of causality ('*puisque*', since or because) does not appear, and the two parts of the sentence come from different sections. At another point, Derrida cites only half a passage, leaving out a part that contradicts his contention that woman is the name for non-truth: 'When we love a woman, we easily conceive a hatred for nature on account of all the repulsive, natural functions to which every woman is subject . . . We refuse to pay any heed to physiology and decree secretly: "I want to hear nothing about the fact that a human being is something more than soul and form" . . . We ignore what is natural'.[5] Why would Derrida want to avoid citing this passage? Perhaps it is because Nietzsche consistently associates the capacity to tolerate physiology and nature and to reject spiritual ideas like 'soul' with his dionysian task of affirming all that is horrible in existence. It is true that woman is associated with that horror; but she is more associated with the attempt to cover it up than with its affirmation, and indeed, this is the role she occupies most often in Nietzsche's text.

In another passage which Derrida only partially cites, Nietzsche writes of woman's incapacity to accept or understand sexuality. Derrida leaves out the following: 'Women easily experience their husbands as a question mark concerning their honor and their children as an apology or atonement'.[6] This imposition of a moral meaning on the natural world is precisely what Nietzsche's dionysian task is directed against: 'Whoever is incapable of laying his will into things, lacking will and strength, at least lays some meaning into them . . . My struggle against the feeling of guilt and the projection of the concept of punishment into the physical and metaphysical world . . . To endure the idea of the recurrence, one needs freedom from morality'.[7] Which is to say, freedom from woman as the figure of christian moral idealism's imposition of a spiritual meaning on nature.

The figure of woman is undecidable in Nietzsche but only to the extent that she is both what the dionysian male philosopher must tolerate as well as an emblem of how idealist concepts of truth ('soul', and so on) have acted to dissimulate that horrifying reality. It is for this reason that she is usually associated with metaphors of bashfulness – '*Schäm*': 'One should have respect for the bashfulness with which nature has hidden behind riddles . . . Perhaps truth is a woman who has reasons for not letting us see her reasons? Perhaps her name is – to speak Greek – Baubo? [fn – Baubo is an obscene female demon, a personification of the female genitals]'.[8] Woman is a critical figure in that she names the gross materiality underlying the pretensions of christian idealist truth, but she also represents the hiding of that truth of materiality.

It seems unlikely, then, that she would represent the dionysian as an affirmative force, as Derrida claims, especially since, for Nietzsche, the dionysian is a pre-eminently male task, and it is always defined in contradiction to the christian idealism that woman most often represents in Nietzsche's text. That task entails looking directly at the horror of nature (female sexuality) and of avoiding the dissimulation of that horror by christian idealist concepts of truth as spirituality (what woman as non-truth always names in Nietzsche). One gets a sense of the masculist significance of the dionysian in the following equation of woman and truth that Derrida does cite: 'Supposing truth is a woman – what then? Are there not grounds for the suspicion that all philosophers, insofar as they were dogmatists, have been very inexpert about women?'[9] If the dogmatist is not sufficiently virile for the woman who is the figure of the truth of nature's horror, the dionysian philosopher will be. Indeed, the dionysian can be interpreted as little more than an attempt to compensate for the horror of castration that the female genitalia represent through a compensatory exaggeration of cognitive powers.

Consider the following passage deleted from Nietzsche's autobiography by his sister: 'The treatment that I have undergone on the part of my mother and sister up till now inspires me with an unspeakable horror . . . I don't know why, but Julius Caesar could have been my father – or Alexander, that love-bound Dionysus . . . At this moment, as I write this, the postal service is bringing me a head of Dionysus'.[10] The sense of horror at women and the accompanying emblem of castration are appropriate to a psychopathology that would seek compensation in such figures of paternal power as Caesar and Alexander. The compensation and the threat seem to coalesce in Dionysus, and indeed, the concept of the dionysian in Nietzsche also links self-empowerment and horror. Connotations of sexuality abound at those moments when Nietzsche equates woman with the horrible truth of nature: 'I treat previous philosophers as contemptible libertines hiding in the cloak of the woman "truth" '. And he speaks of himself in the same passage as being superior to 'disciples of "truth" ' in his 'severity towards oneself, in cleanliness and courage'.[11] The imposition of ascetic pain on oneself deflects the threat that woman poses by internalizing it. One hurts oneself rather than leaving oneself open to externally inflicted pain. It is significant as well that this entails cleanliness, and the avoidance of libertinism, contact with female sexuality. It should be clear by now that Nietzsche's attitudes toward sexuality are just a little bit weird, though understandable as a particular kind of masochistic psychopathology inspired by a horror of castration associated with woman's genitalia.

The dionysian task in fact is directed against woman; it cannot be described as feminine. And it is inaccurate for Derrida to claim that it is directed only against an idealist brand of feminism. Nietzsche does consistently associate feminism with lying and mendaciousness, the denial of nature, but he also identifies woman in general with christianity: 'Christian morality – the most malignant form of the will to lie, the real Circe of humanity . . . Consider . . . the great majority of . . . self-underestimates that believing women accept from their father-confessors, and believing christians quite generally from their church . . . How much "slave" is still residual in woman'.[12]

In one passage that Derrida cites, Nietzsche directly equates christianity and woman, but Derrida translates it somewhat eccentrically in order to create a sense that Nietzsche speaks positively of woman. The passage occurs in 'The History of an Error'. The error is the idea that there is a true world, as idealists believe, behind the world of appearance. Derrida shifts the meaning so that it seems to be about the very idea of truth as such, but this is not really the case. It has an altogether more limited and historical significance. In order to do this, to identify the platonic and christian idea of the true world with the concept of truth as 'presence', he translates the German passage 'Die wahre Welt, unerreichbar fur jetzt . . .'[13] ['The true world, inaccessible for the moment . . .'] as 'Le monde vrai, hors de portée dans le présent . . .', a translation that replaces an historical marker – 'für jetzt' – with a philosophic one – 'dans le présent' – that allows Derrida to speak of the 'non-presence of truth' when he interprets the line 'it becomes woman, it becomes christian'. To suggest that the true world's becoming woman is for it to become non-present unjustifiably eludes the political and historical implications of the equation of woman and christianity.

The feminine operation in Nietzsche, according to Derrida, consists of distance, dissimulation, and a plural style, but it seems more consistent to say that woman represents a christian dissimulation against which Nietzsche sees himself as struggling in his dionysian task and from which that task requires maintaining a certain distance. It is indeed true that, for Nietzsche, dissimulation is a positive value: 'My dionysian ideal . . . the force of all life that wills error; error as the precondition even of thought. Before there is "thought" there must have been "invention"; the construction of identical cases, of the appearance of sameness, is more primitive than the knowledge of sameness'.[14] But this untruth of all truth is precisely the knowledge that woman avoids when she posits christian ideals of atonement and guilt: 'In a world that is essentially false, truthfulness would be an antinatural tendency'.[15] The dionysian 'grand style' is therefore directed against the 'enthusiastic interpretations' to which women are prone: 'To translate man back into nature; to become master over the many vain and enthusiastic interpretations . . . that have so far been . . . painted over the eternal basic text of homo natura'.[16] And even more explicitly: 'The greatness of an artist cannot be measured by the "beautiful feelings" he arouses: leave that idea to females . . . [The grand style] disdains to please; . . . it commands . . . it wills . . . Does the concept of the grand style ultimately stand in contradiction to the soul in music – to the "woman" in our music?'[14]

This grand, plural style is the one Derrida claims is feminine in Nietzsche, but nothing in the text permits such an interpretation. What the text does suggest is that the grand style is the rhetorical equivalent

of the counter-castratory act of self-empowerment that is the dionysian. Rather than being feminine, it is designed to ward off the threat
of femininity. But as an act of male power, it must also find
confirmation in woman, and this is the curious ambivalence (though
not undecidability) of Nietzsche's attitude toward woman.

It is noteworthy, for example, that Nietzsche uses the same
metaphors – to redeem, *erlosen*, and riddle, *Räthsel* – to describe both
the act of redeeming woman by making her pregnant and the dionysian
act of redeeming existence through a grand affirmation of even its most
horrifying aspects: 'Has my answer been heard to the question how
one cures woman – "redeems" [*erlöst*] her? One gives her a child . . .
Everything in woman is a riddle [*Räthsel*] – everything in woman has a
solution: pregnancy . . . Nothing like this has ever been written, felt,
suffered: thus suffers a god, a Dionysus. The answer to such a
dithyramb of solar solitude in the light would be Ariadne, – Who
beside me knows what Ariadne is! – For all such riddles [*Räthseln*]
nobody so far had any solutions . . . Zarathustra once defines his task –
it is mine, too . . .: he says Yes to the point of justifying, redeeming
[*Erlosung*] even all of the past'.[18] The similarity of metaphors suggests
a similarity of content between a self-empowering act of sexual
prowess and the dionysian task of affirming the horror of existence, of
redeeming or solving its 'riddle'.

The similarity becomes even more striking if one pursues the
relationship between Dionysus and Ariadne. At one point, speaking
of his style, Nietzsche writes that it is necessary that there be 'ears –
that there are those capable and worthy of the same pathos'.[19] The
laws of style, he writes, must 'open the ears of those whose ears are
related to ours'.[20] Whenever Nietzsche writes of Ariadne, her ears are
a prominent feature of her description, and, of course, Ariadne is the
mythological figure capable of making her way through the labyrinth,
Nietzsche's favourite metaphor for his own style of writing. In 'Klage
der Ariadne', one of the *Dionysus Dithyrambs*, he writes: 'Be clever,
Ariadne! . . . You have small ears, you have my ears: stick a clever
word inside . . . I am your labyrinth'.[21] Bearing in mind that Nietzsche
always describes his dionysian task of revaluating all values in terms
that emphasize the active and powerful role of language ('Yes-saying,
Yes-doing'), it would seem that the power of language has a sexual
meaning for Nietzsche at a certain unconscious level. The female
genitals that the great male philosopher alone can tolerate become
curiously sublimated into a small ear pierced by powerful words.

Nietzsche's style would seem to be an incontrovertibly masculine operation that presupposes a debasement of woman. Even those moments where Nietzsche seems to be praising woman for being a creature of appearance, surfaces, and dissimulation can all be read as being consistent with the interpretation I have proposed. She is non-truth, but only as the non-truth of the 'garish finery . . . of moral word tinsels', 'the beautiful words: honesty, love of truth', 'the old mendacious pomp', 'the flattering colors and make-up', and 'the siren songs of the old metaphysical bird catchers' that Nietzsche hates so much.[22] All of these metaphors recall the way woman is usually described in male discourse as something artificial and superficial. In other words, her elevation belongs to the traditional dual male attitude toward woman that simultaneously elevates and debases her.

Derrida's reading of Nietzsche as a kind of muddled fuddy-duddy lost in his own text is indeed touching, but given the near psychotic quality of Nietzsche's ravings about women, the effort seems at best misguided. What is perhaps most curious is that Derrida ignores that dimension of Nietzsche's text that should be the basis for an argument in favour of the 'non-truth of truth', of the way ideas of truth cannot escape the representations, the rhetoric in which they are deployed. Nietzsche himself claims that his philosophical task of revaluation is dependent on a new style, an active use of language, and indeed, his psychopathology is most tangibly evident in his stylistic motifs. One could say that it is enacted as a particular rhetoric, a certain symptomatic disposition of discourse. Yet Derrida ignores this realm entirely. His reading computes conceptual meanings, but it does not attend to style itself, the very issue, supposedly, of his essay. Had he attended to rhetoric, the rhetoric Nietzsche claimed was the essential dimension of conceptuality, he would have found that the figure of Dionysus is a metaphoric substitution, that woman as truth is a sexual displacement, and that the grand style is a condensation of terror and compensation. These movements and processes are what shape the conceptuality of Nietzsche's text and transgress its boundaries into other texts, situating his own as a displacement or deflection, for example, of certain sanguinary and fantasmic postal deliveries.

Derrida's text fits into this broader one. 'Derrida' is as much a practice of rhetoric as the name for a conceptual content. And that rhetoric helps explain why he chooses to read Nietzsche's figure of woman as a name for the loss of presence, meaning, and truth in representation, a loss that should be tolerated with tragic laughter. Derrida uses the term 'more powerful', '*plus puissante*', three times in his essay to characterize the way this feminine loss of meaning escapes hermeneuts like Heidegger, who in other essays are described as '*trop faible*', too weak, or '*impuissant*', powerless (impotent?), to harness the graphic of the hymen. In this, Derrida's rhetoric resembles all too strikingly Nietzsche's own. What is at stake here, then, might have more to do with male sexuality than with female figurality. Or perhaps the point is that philosophy and sexuality are always somehow imbricated in each other, like philosophy and rhetoric?

To claim that, as a result of the arguments I have presented here for as well as against deconstruction, the politics of the philosophy are undecidable would be inaccurate. Deconstruction has much to offer, but it does not exist outside history. Derrida picks up certain strands of thought from his culture and his intellectual context that he processes and expands in ways that can be crucially useful in a radical project, but he also obviously replicates certain patterns that are symptomatic of the very world he wishes to critique. We can point that out, but I doubt any of us escapes the same trap. Indeed, look above at my remark that 'Derrida's text fits into this broader one'. My insight into that broader text that Derrida does not seem to acknowledge places me in a position of greater power. And even my acknowledgment of that carries a similar weight, unavoidably. And doesn't my use of 'unavoidably' seem to manage to excuse me by positing a necessary (and self-exculpating) structure at the root of all of this? The route of reflection always leads home. Derrida has drawn our attention to the fact that we can never step outside discourse, representation and rhetoric. It seems no less true that we can never step outside of our historical and social positioning, our codes of thought. What this suggests to me is that an important arena of work would be that boundary or margin where the conceptual and the anecdotal meet, where philosophy and sociology converge, offering us insights into our delusions and our victimage as well as our possibilities and potentials for overcoming them. It is, as Derrida puts it, a question of style.

In the next chapter, I will pursue further the question of how deconstruction and post-structuralism in general allow a bridge to be built between rationalism and materialism around the concept of form. Between the dictates of reason and the imperatives of material need and desire stand the eminently malleable and debatable issues of social and institutional form, of choice of mode of everyday existence, of style of personal and psychological formation, of cultural representation as a means of constituting reality, and so forth. What deconstruction adds to the political theory that can be constructed at the intersection of rationalism and materialism is a sense of how cultural representation and social form come together, not as a line of determination that sees the cultural as being shaped by a social world considered to be external to it, but as a process of fabrication that sees the powerful role cultural representation and rhetorical form play in constructing the substance of social life.

4   Post-Modern Politics

Post-modernism is to art what post-structuralism is to philosophy and social theory. The two came into being at about the same time, with post-modernism emerging in the late 1960s, as structuralism was moulting into post-structuralism. It is the name for a movement in advanced capitalist culture, particularly in the arts that emphasizes irony, pastiche, allegory, and the fake, readymade, and constructed character of art. Cynical regarding the progressivist dreams of modernism, which hoped to shape the cultural world in the image of technology, industry and science, post-modernism is resolutely ironic regarding the enabling myths of art, culture, society, and philosophy. In philosophy, it disposes of the master narratives of marxism and modernism alike, and in art, the emphasis shifts from expression or content to form or style. The metaphoric substitution of a meaning for signs gives way to the sheer contiguity, random and unpredictable, of forms.

One of the central objects of critique in post-modern philosophy, therefore, is the classical theory of representation, which held that meaning or truth preceded and determined the representations that communicated it. This theory is associated in post-modern philosophy with social normativity, so that the critique of representation comes to have a political value. The argument for the rhetorical power or material effectivity of representation is also an argument against classical patriarchal and capitalist ideologies that secured legitimacy by grounding social institutions in truths or ideas of substance held to be outside representation altogether.

The post-modern rejection of the traditional epistemological frameworks out of which such modern progressive movements as marxism emerged has provoked a negative reaction on the part of some marxists to the movement. Jameson, for example, in a classicist marxist gesture,[1] declares it to be the cultural expression of late capitalism. This judgement presupposes that culture can still be directly express-ive of economic phenomena, an example, in other words, of the theory of representation that is under critique in post-modernism. What post-modernism suggests is that late capitalism has the effect of creating cultural possibilities that become detached from the realm of economic necessity and with that from the logic of extra-discursive determina-tion by a pre-cultural substance. Those possibilities overturn the logic

If cultural signs do not represent an already given material substance, they can create new meanings, new institutions.

of representational expression and material overdetermination that restrains previous cultural forms and that shapes Jameson's argument.

What post-modernism as a movement has discovered is that what were thought to be effects in the classic theory of representation can be causes; representations can create the substance they supposedly reflect. This can be looked at in two ways – either as a movement toward artifice, informationalism, and a techno-culture of entirely simulated realities that supports capitalist ideology by further distancing the realm of raw, dirty production, or as a movement with progressive possibilities that signals the ability to reshape a supposedly immovable material universe that can no longer be thought of as external and determining in relation to culture. It has been subsumed to the realm of human invention and collective social creativity. In the cultural scene that high capitalism admittedly makes possible, therefore, the positive lineaments of a post-capitalist world can be glimpsed. Capitalism also digs its own grave on the cultural level.

To derive an analogy from Marx, just as capitalism at its furthest reaches is also the first indication of the possibility of communism, so also, one could say, capitalist culture at its furthest reaches (where culture or simulation subsumes reality entirely) becomes the instrument for fabricating a post-capitalist world. The crucial reversal in this equation is that of sign and thing, culture and the social, or the political, or the economic. It is this reversal that allows one to grant culture a power it could not possess when it still was accountable to a determining materiality. Rather than being expressive representations of a substance taken to be prior, cultural signs become instead active agents in themselves, creating and evoking new substances, new social forms, new ways of acting and thinking, new attitudes, reshuffling the cards of 'fate' and 'nature' and social 'reality'. It is on this margin that culture, seemingly entirely autonomous and detached, turns around and becomes a social and material force, a power of signification that discredits all claims to substantive grounds outside representation, and this discrediting applies equally to political institutions, moral norms, social practices, and economic 'realities'. Detached from the ontological, natural, and moral foundations that give political, social, and juridical institutions their meaning as representations of a prior referent or truth, the expressions of an inherent or already established moral or social order, cultural signs instead are revealed to be the instruments of the creation of new grounds, new meanings, and new institutions.

The political valence of post-modernism is therefore at least undecidable, rather than being decisively conservative. The reasons for condemning a cultural and social movement must come not from the fact that it was made possible by a certain stage of capitalism (so were universities and literary critics after all) but from an assessment both of its internal values and of its probable effects. Cultural movements are themselves semantically multiple, and they can have multiple uses. Parts of post-modernism may indeed fulfil the imperatives of late capitalism, may even express its values, but the same features of the movement can be interpreted as signalling the availability of a high enough level of social development to make possible the building of an alternative world (Marx's reading of automation, for example), and other parts of the movement can use the same post-modernist instruments for progressive ends or to further radical endeavours.

Indeed, post-modernism is in many respects the philosophy of such malleability or rhetoricity. It suggests that capitalist economic necessity can be transcended; play, with its logic of contingent connection, can replace work, which is shaped by the rhetoric of capitalist efficiency that subordinates needs and desires to the rules of symbolic and material accumulation. The post-modern questioning of the substance of social reality and of the determining power of material necessity is not only a troubling, and obviously frightening, philosophical possibility; it is also an important political opening that deprives those in social power of the grounds (material necessity, social reality) for imposing austerity, efficiency, and subordination on the large majority of people.

I will be primarily concerned with political, rather than aesthetic post-modernism. My argument will be that post-modernist insights need to be radicalized and pushed beyond the points achieved by such thinkers as Lyotard and Baudrillard. I will concentrate on the translations published in the Foreign Agents Series by Jim Fleming and Sylvere Lotringer at *Semiotext*.

Lyotard's *Driftworks*[2] consists of essays written for the most part in the early 1970s, and they bear traces of 1968 and of all that it represented in regard to a reconsideration of traditional left politics. Lyotard identifies political repression with reason and with the way semantic content or meaning implies the repression of the syntactic play of language. In this, he follows in the path of thinkers like Derrida and Kristeva, who also argued against the privilege of reason over rhetoric, abstract ideality over the materiality of language. Reason, Lyotard contends, is trapped because it requires language, yet its concepts are seemingly meta-rhetorical. It cannot be the ordering operation it claims to be so long as it is constitutively attached to language, whose materiality and productivity contain the potential for generating meaning effects that are quite disorderly and unreasonable. Consequently, Lyotard locates a radical political potential in aesthetic strategies of language, form, and figuration that undermine rational order and the order of meaning that sustain communicational efficiency and scientific operationalism (the translation of concepts into procedures).

This is in some respects a classic pre-formulation of post-modernist aesthetics. Lyotard extends these insights to the question of political organization. Like many other leftists of the time, Lyotard points out that political organizations merely reproduce the order of power against which they are directed. As the deconstruction of power discourse concerns not what is said but how it is said, the way discourse is laid out or deployed, so also the deconstruction of traditional politics means leaving aside large organizations and attending to the places and institutions of everyday social practice. Dealing with traditional political discourse in its here and now, its time and place, instead of in terms of its contents, reveals the repression in the system. In this programme, one finds an outline of the molecular politics of everyday life that characterized the new social movements of the 1970s and 1980s in western Europe.

Another way of stating Lyotard's point would be to say that those whose psychological training leaves them intolerant of the material, situational, and socio-historical character of language, of its open-ended semantic possibilities, and of the socially negotiated and contractual quality of meaning, are likely to be matched by those in political life who refuse to reflect on the politics of organization and who reject democratic forms as being anarchic. Both forms of rationalism are justifiably contested by Lyotard, but his alternative (like that of Irigaray in another register, which veers into religion) risks being a kind of mysticism that merely confirms the worst fears rationalists have regarding the irrationalist destiny of post-structuralism. For Lyotard, capitalism, the family, and personal identity form an alliance against the unconscious and desire. One must combat it by freeing up one's libidinal drives, decathecting from capital, and releasing oneself into the plurality of singularities Lyotard calls 'driftworks'. The trick is not to seek power over anything, but to dissolve oneself into libidinal 'workings'. This kind of zen marxism applies to discourse as well, since any consistent discourse ultimately will serve the ends of power. One must seek a level prior to discourse, abstraction, and logic.

All very well and good, but this critique fails to distinguish varieties of rationality or genres of use of reason, and it takes for granted that libidinal freefall will have a happy, rather than a tragic result. It operates with the unarticulated assumption that liberal reason is so embedded in western culture that release from its authoritarian aspects will give rise to a better world rather than to violence, brutality, and domination – all former stars of earlier rejections of liberal reason. This can be understood in two ways, either as a temper tantrum of release directed against a bad father that presupposes the over-arching presence of a good mother, or as a kind of advanced experiment in release from constraints that elsewhere in less developed contexts must be operational because violence is a real possibility. The latter option is the more generous, and it seems more in keeping with the opening Lyotard promotes to run with it.

In that frame, Lyotard's project, like Irigaray's, consists of moving to the other side of what reason requires – order, consistency, predictability, and so forth. Reason presupposes that the same rules must apply in the same way everywhere. On the other side of rationalism is the material reality of difference that requires that each situation elicit its own understanding, its own appropriate level of reason or feeling. From this perspective, living reasonably requires less consistency than flexibility, less the ability to remain the same in different situations, than the capacity to change and to assume distinct roles according to the requirements of each new context. A just society would as much require this skill, this ability to 'drift', as Lyotard puts it, as it would require the ability to participate in discussions of rational norms like 'let's not kill each other'. And those norms will always also be a matter of desire and feeling, as well as of material contexts and intersubjective structures. If libidinal release always presupposes an implicit norm of a reasonable world that will safeguard against violence, reason itself must always presuppose feeling and desire, those others with whom it seemingly has no commerce. For reasonable norms and rational laws ultimately come down to how people feel about each other, and the killing will not stop until the kind of libidinal release Lyotard proposes can occur without murder resulting. That is the stake (and the hope) of his version of post-modernism. It contrasts with a conservative reason that would seek order through restraint rather than through a material reconstruction, one that sees in the ability to express feelings without violence, the ability to drift, a positive therapy that builds rationality from below, as part of a social world that ultimately would replace external legal mediation with psychological, domestic, economic, and political modes that make ethical living without repression possible.

The French post-modern critique of reason can thus be said to have a certain reasonableness about it. In general the critique is directed at the kind of reason found in patriarchal capitalist culture, a principle of order that reduces the domains of indeterminacy, contingency, and democracy for reasons of efficiency, domination, and power. In the work of Jean Baudrillard, it begins to take a more mystical turn. In *Simulations* and *In the Shadow of the Silent Majorities*,[3] Baudrillard applies deconstructive insights to social phenomena, but his conclusions, rather than being affirmative, lapse into 'asemism', a celebration of meaninglessness and a despairing assessment of the uselessness of all political action.

In *Simulations*, Baudrillard takes ideas from Derrida and expands them into a social theory. Those ideas are:

(1) The referents of representational systems (especially of language) cannot be determined outside representational systems. At no point does a sign exchange itself for a referent or a meaning that is not itself in some way bound up with representation.

(2) Representation does not come after objectivity or meaning as something added on to it. The designation by the human mind of a domain of objectivity requires representation, and equally, the condition of ideality or meaning is representation.

(3) Because linguistic representation is made up of a system of difference whereby each substantive term is constituted through its interrelations with all other terms in the system, and because language is inseparable from its pragmatic context, the possibility of indeterminacy in the designation of objectivity and the communication of meaning can never be fully purged. Language units refer to each other, and it is this which allows them to function as referring to things or ideas. Thus, in reality, there is a circulation of signs rather than a one to one correspondence between signs and things.

Baudrillard gives these ideas a social, political, and historical spin in the following ways. Models, he argues, are now more determining of reality than they are representations of reality. Watergate, for example, consisted of a manipulation of representations on all sides. It was a simulacrum of scandal for regenerative ends. By falling for the lure by engaging in a moral critique of the events, the left ended up doing the work of the right. It took a simulacrum for something real and thereby lent it a credibility it didn't merit. More generally, Baudrillard asserts that stable positions of power or of discourse can no longer be determined; all is merely a vertigo of interpretation. The power of the media now means that the real no longer exists. Images or simulacra determine what 'is' as a constantly circulating play of representations. Order consists of reducing this play to a supposed reality. Even revolutionary discourse is guilty of this operation. Nuclear deterrence serves as an example in that it is a simulacrum that reduces all chance in society to a nuclear order, a balance of terror that amounts to a terror of balance. Because both capitalism and communism are forms of domination, the possible war is merely a feint that maintains power for both sides. Baudrillard concludes that all politics is a form of manipulation, even democratic forms, since they feign equality of participation.

In the second part of *Simulations*, Baudrillard periodizes modern history in terms of semiotics. The contemporary period is the age of simulacra, of endlessly circulating signifiers or representations that nowhere touch a reality. Production has given way to reproduction, and simulation is now determinant. For example, opinion polls predetermine results; the medium controls the message; and the image anticipates the real. In a deconstructive move, he claims that there is no real which is not 'always already' reproduced. The 'discontinuous indeterminism' of genetic codes now operates in society itself as the montage logic of the media, which allows no distinction any longer of true and false. The false image is as true as any supposed truth.

In the Shadow of the Silent Majorities is a populist libertarian polemic against the French socialist left. The silent majority or masses are privileged for rejecting all attempts to impose a meaning, a reason, or an order, even a socialist one, upon them. Baudrillard's populist neo-romanticism comes to the fore here. The masses reject all rational communication, but in their pre-articulateness, they are radical in a way that left intellectuals and revolutionaries cannot grasp; they block the economy in its attempt to administer a rational balance of behaviour and goals. They know there is no liberation and that the system can only be destroyed by pushing it into 'hyper-logic', an implosion that is centripetal, plural, anti-authoritarian, and non/representational. The silent majority, along with terrorism, carries out a rejection of all representational systems, of all traditional political meaning. They are therefore immune to revolutionary calls for expansion and liberation. (The translation leaves out an essay in the original French edition which carries the anti-left argument further in a critique of the French socialist government that originally appeared in the right-wing *Le Figaro*.)

Baudrillard probably represents the apotheosis of the post-1968 critique of the traditional left that gave rise to the slogan 'the end of politics'. Yet whereas that critique of statist socialism and leninist vanguardism led others to seek alternate social models in the 'area of autonomy', it leads Baudrillard to a sort of 'tactile mysticism' that mixes McLuhan with Castaneda. Nevertheless, there is an autonomous dimension to Baudrillard's work in that it posits a non-leninist political potential within the mass of people themselves.

More problematic from a political perspective is his contention that the advent of the Information Age in the advanced capitalist countries implies that reproduction has replaced production. Those computer chips are still produced by factory labour in Third World countries like Malaysia, the material basis of the First World's Information Age. And that labour is predominantly female, since women workers are more 'pliant' and less likely to unionize, Baudrillard's theory thus in some respects replicates the capitalist displacement of industrial work away from the white centre to the non-white periphery in that it obliterates the reality of peripheral labour in an analogous gesture of intellectual gentrification. By accepting the premises of capitalist modernization (which does indeed strive to replace a First World production economy with one based on tertiary or reproductive activities like information and entertainment, as it shifts industrial production to the Third World), Baudrillard's theory risks participating in the imposition of exploitative production on the non-white and the non-male.[4]

In addition, to claim that the Information Age has replaced production with simulation overlooks the fact that the information most corporations rely on has to do with such things as accounting, which is to say, with the tracking of efficiency based in wages paid and prices extracted, with in other words the very material world of production that informationalism supposedly displaces. This is not to claim that the world of economics stands outside representation. Women workers in Malaysia are lured to factories by the promise of money for cosmetics that allow them to refashion themselves according to prevailing advertising images of female beauty, and they are ideal workers because of the internalization of representations from the culture that induce in them social attitudes of obedience and conformity. Even the materiality of work itself is representational, since it consists of looking through microscopes at microchips all day long, a labour that ultimately results in semi-blindness, a deprivation of representational power. So it is true: capitalism is simulational, but the execution of an efficiency model (by the International Monetary Fund, for example, in the Third World) can be as murderous as a death squad, and informationalism only seems to change the language in which power speaks.

Baudrillard's despair over capitalist culture also overlooks contradictory impulses, tensions, and embedded resistant potentials. Much like Adorno, Baudrillard's reading of capitalist culture is excessively one-sided and pessimistic. Things that he reads negatively can be given a positive inflection. The power of simulation is also a power to produce models of alternative worlds; it can be turned against its capitalist use. But that turn requires a sense of the semantic plasticity, the polysemous character of social instruments. To envision an alternative use for simulation, one must see seemingly univalent social phenomena as being capable of giving rise to multiple semantic effects. The media, rather than being only a source of domination, must come into focus as sites of contestation, where meanings derived by audiences might be entirely at odds with the intention of domination.

Baudrillard's own description of the resistant quality of daily mass life opens up the possibility of alternative meanings to the dominant left reading of that phenomenon. It suggests that simply because left revolutionary intellectuals have failed to connect their fairly abstract concepts to the everyday material concerns of the people they supposedly address, it is not necessarily true that there is no counter-hegemonic power in the pre-conceptual needs and desires that seem to e the blind preoccupation of those people. Baudrillard is right to suggest that revolution is a matter of such needs and desires, not only right ideas, although the post-structuralist resistance to reason prevents him from working out the necessary mediation of those two sets of terms. Can revolution be blind to need-satisfaction alone without any reasonable, which is to say, principled and equitable, mechanism for distributing resources?

His theory of the power of mass resistance therefore threatens to lapse into a populist metaphysic that is the mirror image of his intellectual cynicism regarding culture. It is as if the theory of simulation carried embedded within it a hidden yearning for authenticity or genuineness that seems ultimately to be fulfilled by the silent majorities. Capitalist culture is bad because it has replaced the real with simulation, and what is real is to be found outside that culture amidst the undifferentiated *popolo*, in a sort of pre-verbal realm of non-reflexivity. The positing of such an outside is one of the characteristic tropes of romanticism. The gesture suggests the existence of an other that is genuine, a pre-simulational ground whose transcendental meaning resides precisely in that it is external to all syntactic figuring and semantic coding. Such is the silent majority, outside language altogether.

Had he wished to move more consistently within the categories that initiate his critique of capitalist culture, Baudrillard would have been obliged to describe the simulational character of even this supposedly extra-simulational reality, the extent to which its 'outsideness' or otherness is shaped by a representational power that expels such majorities into an undemocratic silence. The contouring of social positions is itself a rhetorical or simulational procedure, and it is necessary to describe the shape societies assume in rhetorical terms. Banished from a democratic determination of what their culture will be, the silent majorities of Baudrillard are the victims of a metaphoric substitution, a displacement that obliges them to relate in a part to whole or synechdochic way to a society whose shape should be wholly theirs to determine. As in psychology, the shapes given by rhetoric constitute social reality as a form of perversion, or to put it differently, as a formal skewing of what might be a more fulfilled existence into a shape that turns away from or misshapes that potential fulfilment. The life of the silent majorities is a rhetorical misshaping of certain other possible life shapes or forms. In this way, simulation can be located at the root of even those seemingly pre-simulational realities that Baudrillard places outside the culture of simulation as its other.

Similar problems are evident in Arthur Kroker and David Cook's *The Post-Modern Scene*, an important application of Baudrillard.[5] In his own sections of the book, Kroker convincingly threads together contemporary art and social theory, showing how infirm the boundary is between the aesthetic and the political. Yet, like Baudrillard, Kroker emphasizes domination effects in culture at the expense of other possibilities. Culture is not conceived as a terrain of struggle or difference; it contains no inherently progressive potentials, no radical lines of tension that outline alternative possibilities to the identity of power.

One of Kroker's major arguments is that Nietzsche represents the negative side of what Marx presented positively as his analysis of the capitalist commodity form. Yet one could, as indeed Negri does, read the description of the commodity in Marx as nothing but political force disguised as economic calculation. The commodity is merely a metaphor for command. Moreover, it is difficult to accept that the commodity form is now no longer a matter of production but instead entirely given over to semiosis when standing armies all over the world seem to indicate that although commodities depend increasingly on marketing signification, they are always also a matter of enforcement, the imposition of work, through the implicit threat of the infliction of bodily harm, on large, generally unseen and certainly unrepresented populations. And even though that threat is representational and pain is nothing more than a signal to the brain, what this suggests is that a recharacterization of reality (from substance to simulation, for example) does not affect the ethical modes of judgement applied to that reality. A painful simulation is just as bad as a painfully real thing.

Kroker, like Baudrillard, uses turns of phrase ('the disappearance of the real', 'the triumph of signifying culture') that suggest that culture has *become* increasingly simulational and that there might be or might have been at some point an outside to simulation. But one could argue that simulation always has been the case, from Plato and the sophists down to Reagan and prime time TV. All societies rely on ruses to maintain legitimacy, rituals to position subjects, and rhetoric to stabilize a communal representational world that assures the continuity of a shared phenomenal reality. Images have always sustained and produced power, and it is doubtful there has ever been a genuine or authentic sociality of the sort implied by Kroker's metaphors of artificiality and decline. As with Baudrillard, one could perhaps attribute to Kroker a nostalgia, a desire for a world prior to technology, cosmetics, mediascaping, and commodification, a world akin to that of religious faith, before the fall into doubt and rationality. (It should not be surprising, perhaps, that the book contains a positive meditation on Augustine.)

Baudrillard has been accused of sexism for his use of metaphors of seduction to describe simulated culture. Kroker seems less culpable, but there is nevertheless something troubling about the idea that culture has become 'cosmetic' (a metaphor with unfortunate gender presuppositions) in the age of the mediascape. Perhaps it is a similar gender unconsciousness that motivates him to read an Alan Parsons' song, 'Eye in the Sky', which is about male power over women played out through a power of surveillance, as a radical post-modern text about surveillance in general ('I ain't gonna take any more . . . The sun in your eyes/Made some of the lies worth believing/I am the eye in the sky/Looking at you/I can read your mind/I am the maker of rules/Dealing with fools/I can cheat you blind . . . Don't cry cause I ain't changin' my mind'). Bearing in mind that it is a male persona speaking to a woman, the song's gender-political inflection seems fairly clear.

Baudrillard and Kroker both practice the male intellectual genre of discourse (as I myself do here), a genre that permits us to describe world truths without marking the fact that we speak from a singular perspective that only pretends to generality. If post-modernism teaches anything, it would seem to be that reality is fractured and plural; it has different versions, and no version is complete. The white male position is a particularly privileged one, and there is nothing wrong, I suppose, with its having its day. But one must at least pose the question of the other, of the other's perspective and of the other reality it creates. Is the 'fun mood of America in ruins' really shared by those blacks who have been the primary victims of the Reagan era? Or would they describe the ruins slightly differently, as bodily pain or the denial of a sense of worth or the absence of pleasure? I make these remarks not in a spirit of moralistic highhandedness but rather in the hope of underscoring the limits we ought to place on our own discursive presumption. We white male intellectuals, that is.

It would seem from Baudrillard's work that there is no reconciliation possible between post-modernist political thinking and marxism. But that is to assume that marxism is as it has been traditionally constituted a philosophy of totality. Another book in the Foreign Agents Series, *Communists Like Us* [*Les nouveaux espaces de la liberté*], by Guattari and Negri, suggests that marxism need not be defined in those terms exclusively.[6] The tract brings together Guattari's molecular political and psychoanalytic concerns with Negri's more marxist macro-political outlook. Thus, they begin by redefining communism as comprising both molar struggles against exploitation and molecular struggles for singularity and liberation. The liberation of work and the generation of new modes of subjectivity are both necessary for the communist project. The political aim of the book is therefore also very much a reflection of the collaboration that produced it.

The year 1968, the authors argue, saw the end of traditional left politics and the relaunching of revolution. Because capital had spread productive command throughout society and the sphere of reproduction, to the extent of colonizing the unconscious, the new revolutionary movement combined for the first time the molecular and the molar, addressing issues of everyday life as well as the traditional class struggle. The women's movement was a token of this, as was the new importance given marginal sectors (the unemployed). State administered work as a model of socialism was rejected, and a new emphasis was given to the bodily character of liberation. Human ends and values of desire were now projected as what should orient production.

What they call Integrated World Capitalism, which includes both capitalism and socialism, was the determining force of the 1970s, superseding the nation state. The nuclear state is its central figure. The law of value ceased to function; intimidation spread throughout society; and hunger was used as a weapon to turn the Third World into the new reserve army of labour. Nevertheless, Negri and Guattari see new revolutionary subjects emerging in the underemployed sectors, in areas of management whose life is rendered precarious by crises, and in the various new social movements around feminism, ecology, and peace. They condemn terrorism, and argue that leninist and statist models of organization are incompatible with the new composition of revolutionary subjectivities. They call for a 'functional multicentrism' that would in a new organization establish a plurality of relations between a multiplicity of singularities or movements, a plurality geared toward collective objects that would be beyond bureaucratic control. The principle task is to reunify the traditional components of class struggle against exploitation with the new movements for liberation. One important element of the new strategy is 'work on oneself', as a singular collective, thus renewing the 'human roots' of communism.

They conclude with a list of tasks and diagrammatic propositions: the development, definition, and expression of the new productive subjectivities, dissident singularities, and new proletarian set-ups; struggle around welfare, rent, and the imposition of life-oriented time arrangements on work; redefinition of work independent of the 'capitalist and/or socialist' ways of organizing it; the necessity of addressing issues of workday legislation; a breaking with the state form; privileging the anti-nuclear and peace movements; and finally addressing the question of a new mode of non-leninist, non-anarchist organizing. The three propositions are that the North/South axis should replace the East/West one. The movement should promote alliances between the proletariats of North and South against East/West nuclear terror. Europe needs to be reinvented as a political terrain. Finally, they propose that peace must be seen as a primary condition for overturning the North/South power structure.

Communists Like Us is an important amalgam of political strains of thought and action that till now have seemed at least disparate if not altogether incommensurable. The term 'alliance' in their vocabulary is well-chosen for this reason, since it implies difference within unity, and

Negri and Guattari are wise to argue that there is no reason why different movements should have to be collapsible into each other in order to work together. The question of what the concrete form such alliances might take is, however, not engaged. At times, Negri and Guattari seem to be suggesting that the alliances are material and unconscious, rather than deliberate. For example, the Latin American proletariats are placed in material alliance with those of the First World when they provoke their national governments to threaten to refuse to repay debts. Even in this regard, the material connections are sometimes drawn, sometimes left to be guessed at. The logic of the necessary link between the anti-nuclear movement and the proletarian movement is made evident; nuclear terror is spread throughout society in a way that neutralizes class struggle. But the relations between the women's movement and the other movements in terms of the linkages between patriarchal sexual power, the hyperbolic aggressivity of the military institution, and the power drive of either the capitalist market or statist administration are not addressed. Without the establishment of such material linkages, the call for alliances can seem opportunistic or merely tactical. It would seem that truly effective alliances should be forged on the basis of an understanding of the necessary material connections between movements.

Nevertheless, the collaboration between Guattari and Negri indicates the possibility of certain catalytic combinations, of post-modern political collages that need not necessarily be beholden to material necessity or to historical determination for their validation and that still enrich, rather than deplete, the traditional 'metanarratives' like marxism. Even if the connections are contingent, their very making overrides any weakness that might result from leaving behind the old anchors. In this sense, post-modern politics would ultimately mean the evolution of a greater sense of leverage regarding what can be done, what can be created from the available political materials. A new political rhetoric emerges to the extent that metaphoric political forms, which stressed the subsumption of diverse subordinate movements to semantically more significant, higher-order ideals of organizational unity and identity, give way to metonymic forms that stress the greater variety of contingent connections, contiguous links that are not in the order of subordination but instead of co-ordination in an equal and diverse field of possibilities. Rather than discard the metanarratives (as much a male socialized gesture of exclusion and subordination as the metanarratives themselves), they are preserved, deepened, made more complex and differentiated. It amounts to adding detail and colour to a rough sketch, rather than destroying the sketch and claiming that only the detail is true.

The post-modernist and post-structuralist critique of representation thus has a political corollary. The belief that rhetoric is attached to reason as a secondary and dispensable appendage that has no productive power of its own creates a hierarchy that places semantic ideals over syntax or meaningful content over mere rhetoric or form. That theoretical hierarchy resembles the practical one in capitalist societies that places political ideals (freedom) over everyday materialities or that places economic fetishes (the free market) over the everyday forms of need and desire. On the left particularly, such semanticism (the assumption that social principles like communism are teleological ideals or contents rather than rhetorical procedures of democratic, material social constitution that are concerned with everyday forms of existence) allows the question of the rhetoric of everyday life – the forms it assumes – to be subordinated. It also places institutions like the patriarchal family and the workday in a secondary realm of social rhetoric that does not bear importantly on the more significant issues of the 'socialist' content of society. But that content is itself constituted and shaped by those 'secondary' forms.

A shift toward an understanding of how the procedures of political rhetoric constitute the ideational and institutional world they supposedly represented necessarily brings with it a shift toward an understanding of how the rhetorical procedures of everyday life, the shapes and forms of the workday, sexual relations, and so on, constitute the supposedly meta-rhetorical or extra-representational reality or content of social existence. What post-modernism suggests is that there is no content of society apart from the rhetoric of forms, procedures, modes, shapes, and genres that constitutes the embodiment in everyday life of that content.

The critique of representation can therefore be said to bear on left politics in crucial ways. The reversal of sign and thing also reverses certain polarities or hierarchies, the one that placed the form of the workday second in relation to the content of the state plan, or the one that placed the form of gender relations second in relation to a more primary non-sexual concern (one usually associated with male socialized forms of reason) like efficient organization. This is a politics that addresses the formal dimensions of social life as much as its materiality. Its orientation is horizontal and egalitarian rather than vertical and hierarchic. It privileges lateral connections between different political dimensions and refuses to subordinate one to the other. The authority that traditional political representational systems sanctify melts into an entirely democratic and levelling movement. Subsumption ceases to be the principle of political life, and conjugation takes its place. Aware of its own status as a rhetoric, such a politics seeks to posit new worlds through representation, to develop models of alternative forms of social existence. Rather than being beholden to a spurious ideal of extra-discursive substance or pre-representational truth, it works to create new forms, and in so doing to give rise to new substances, new meanings, new realities.

What one gains from this insight in the conclusion that social power and social politics are forms, malleable shapes, particular dispositions of mouldable elements, configurations given over constitutively to reformulation. From a post-modern perspective, politics comes into focus as a radically contingent arena of imagination, strategy, and creative manoeuvre around stakes that are at once material and representational. For the purpose of power is to secure the accumulation of the goods of desire, the commodities that are as much factors of material need as of psychological cathexis. If they are things, they are also signs. In Mystic, Connecticut, where I am writing this, the signs of power are large lawns, high trees enclosing hermetic estates, beautiful large buildings – space, quiet, beauty, exclusion. These significant things are all quite material, linked to desire both as the fulfilment of psychological images and as felt pleasures. And they are linked to the normalized brutality of wage labour elsewhere in the world, the source of the power to buy estates.

But materiality can no longer be taken as the term for necessity or for what is outside simulation and contingency, or for what is true in an extra-rhetorical sense. A rhetorical (that is, a post-structuralist or post-modern) theory of social politics sees materiality as inseparable from the shapes given it by social construction. To embrace politics in a post-modern sense is to place a stake on contingency, on the insight that power, no matter how grounded in 'reality', how seemingly bound to 'material' necessity, is up for grabs, movable and therefore removable. This is why the anti-political strain of post-modern theory does not take its insights far enough, far enough to see that society is not a reality that can become simulational, but an arrangement of rhetorical forms and materialized tropes that has never been anything but simulational. And it is precisely at that point, with that insight, that a post-modern politics can be said to begin.

5 Neo-Political Art After Post-Modernism

Jean Baudrillard's commodity radicalism has influenced the anglophone art world and even generated a sub-school of 'Neo-Geo' art. Ever cynical regarding the fallen consumer culture of the middle class and ever romantic regarding its own capacities to negate that culture, art in the modern age is an appropriate landing site for a nostalgic theory of simulation, one that sees everywhere an increase of degradation that can only be matched by an inflation of lethargic dismissiveness. Baudrillard is in some respects the perfectly modern post-modern aesthete, the purely detached figure of pure detachment, Pater as a semio-fetishist. He synthesizes a grandiloquent inflation of discourse with a marketable discourse value that is in keeping with the tremendous increase in sheer money worth of modern art itself, which has become a magnet for capital fleeing less enduring forms of value. The theory of commodities becomes through the production of books like *Cool Memories* that aestheticize the most fragmentary droppings of the world-travelling tourist-cum-theorist a commodification of theory. Life itself is a version of romantic art, an object of detached, cynical contemplation, one more item in the repertoire – post-modernism as the art of neo-colonial pillage.

But Baudrillard is not the only possible derivative of post-structuralism and post-modernism for art. Indeed, other more radical and engaged alternatives, ones that take the deconstruction of social identity as a point of departure, are to be found in neo-political Anglo-American art. I will concentrate on the work of one neo-political artist – Fiona Burns – arguing that it points toward revolutionary uses of post-modern insights into the fluidity and conventionality of the boundaries that secure the identities of power.

Specifically at issue in Burns' work are the boundaries that separate museum art form public life and that separate aesthetic values from economic and political ones. Seeking not so much to use art to criticize a society that is taken to be extra-artistic, her work investigates the very artistic quality of social existence itself, and it seeks to insinuate an artistic consciousness into political and economic life. Taking her cue from Derrida's contention that there is no outside to the text, she contends that what art should be about is extending the domain of art, both as a remaking of such social scenarios as domestic power according to principles of artistic harmony and as the erosion of structures of economic domination whose continuance depends on being sheltered from the negativity, as well as the positive values of art.

Burns' work ranges from pure negative art to pure popular entertainment, from museum work to Hollywood films and even television commercials. Her performance and exposition pieces in association with the Institute for Contemporary Art in Boston attempt to redefine the boundaries separating the museum from its surroundings, as well as the work of art from its social context and its audiences. Her popular work is less resolutely reflexive and radical; it presents itself as entertainment and exploits the traditional figures of the Hollywood genres. The point of both the high and the popular work is to find ways of <u>forcing art into life,</u> and consequently, the crucial boundary she investigates is the one between '<u>doing art' and living.</u> Social existence itself, defined as a practiced set of conventions and formulae, is what is at stake in her work. In her 'lived pieces' especially Burns seeks to draw attention to the figurality of everyday experience and activity, the way it, like art, is shaped according to line, composition, colour, mood, figure, and frame. At its furthest reaches, Burns' art extends into the workplace and the living room, attempting to suggest new configurations for social organization and interpersonal interaction that would be normed by artistic rather than economic rationalist values.

In Burns' museum work, the idea of museum art itself is at issue. Her exhibit at the Documenta show in 1987 entitled 'The Essentials of Civilization' consisted of a room fitted out with a transparent plastic sewage system that was in fact the functioning sewage system for the museum itself. In the centre of the room stood an object shrouded in black veils. Behind the veil, she could then see an imitation of Moses' tablets on which were inscribed the essentials of civilization: 'First create a situation in which someone else does the work for you, a servant or slave, or someone you hire and who could not live without being hired. Second, put together an army to make certain that those you subjugate and hire don't steal your house and goods. Third, hire artists to portray all of this in a good light and to build monuments to your glory. Fourth, build camps in which your army puts those who find you disagreeable. Fifth, draw a picture of yourself and name it god. Sixth, call what you have accomplished civilization'. Beneath the tablets was a large plastic sewage container, the endpoint of the plastic pipes, in which spectators' excrement floated.

∴ Post-Modern process of art dissolving into everyday life has returned forward for it allows art to escape its compartmentalization —as a safeguarding value 'above' the world of politics?

In such pieces, Burns is still working within the format of museum art, but she does so ironically, drawing attention to the markers that define museic propriety and identity even as she inches over them, daring the spectator to follow. Art itself is placed under critique, but at this point, in 1987, Burns was still operating within what she would later call 'the artistic attitude', the 'position verging on contempt toward the spectator that gives lessons from the museum wall or from the center of the exhibition floor'. That attitude itself becomes an object of critical revision in her subsequent work.

Implicit in Burns' agenda at this stage is what would become elaborated more clearly later as a critique of the very possibility of an institutionally autonomous art. Indeed, one could say that her Documenta exhibit was meant to make art so scandalous and repugnant that it could no longer be contained within a museum. By early 1988, as her disillusion with the possibilities of working within museum formats became more marked, Burns would write in her essay 'The End of Art': 'It is as if the camp guards had built a play house where anything was possible, and they called it art, and got all the creative young people to go play in it while they went about the business of brutalization'. She argues not only that museums are so many elegant prisons but also that the very idea of art as a category separable from economics or law or politics is highly questionable, one certainly that she and her generation of artistic radicals should be about undermining. The world of power is structured emblematically and aesthetically, she contends, 'but part of that particular figural construction of the world entails caging art, which, like a veal calf, becomes as a result more tender and less threatening'.

Given this, it should not be surprising that Burns concludes 'The End of Art' by calling for just that – the end of art as a figure within the larger figurational process of capitalist culture that structures creative play and the imagination into discrete realms that neutralize its negative as well as its incitive powers. 'Art belongs in the world, not in the museum', she writes. 'Its power to deconstruct the boundaries that separate things that should not be separated must first be applied to its own status as something separated from social life. We must abandon the genre of art, stop taking the institutional framework of art for granted, with all that it implies in regard to the segregation of imagination from daily life, of pleasure from work, and of a managing subject from a managed and exploited object (be it nature or women or workers) that is one of the major legacies of the invention of capitalism. That segregation is internalized even in radical art as the

(fm Duchamp to Kosov)
[Craig Owen]

(What is right about Burgo/moca)

decision to place an art object before a spectator in a setting (the museum) that draws attention to and reinforces the objectival status of the work of art and the passive position of the spectator.' Her answer to this problem is the strategy of making art public. 'We must speak beyond the museum, be more than "artists". That category belongs to a world we can no longer inhabit.' Burns' 'strategy of debasement' directed at the highness of even radical post-modern art aims at destroying the 'entire apparatus of art conceived as an artifact of a segregated cultural system that reserves access to things like art to an educated élite'.

Two of Burns' undertakings in 1988 in association with the ICA consisted of the placing of art works in public spaces and the distribution of works on a mass scale. The work 'You Too Can Have Power' was set up in the spring of 1988 in the square in front of the Boston Public Library. Designed to draw attention to the way social and commercial life is constructed as theatrical roles and dramatic relations between people, it was also a participatory piece. Intended not so much to speak a meaning at the spectator as to engage the spectator in some action that would lead to a change in consciousness, it tried to draw attention to the way importance, power, or centrality is distributed in society.

It consisted of different rooms, set out as a maze. People going through the work had to pair up, and Burns, who supervised the project daily, usually tried to pair men and women or people of different generations and races. In each of the rooms, the participants were given costumes and scripts and roles to follow, some of which were predictable – the boss and the secretary, the philandering husband and the betrayed wife – and some of which were new or liminal – two cows approaching the slaughterhouse and discussing how much they missed their pasture. The incentive for participation was the fact that the routines were taped, and each participant was given a copy of the video at the end. They also filled out a questionnaire before and after, so that one could gauge how successful the work was in raising certain issues in people's minds. Burns found that they had slightly different perceptions regarding such things as the way power is distributed between people after the 'show', and this was especially true of the many young people who were taken to the exhibit on school field trips.

A related show in the autumn of the same year was called 'You Too Can Be An Artist'. Designed around Benjamin's influential essay, 'The Work of Art in the Age of Mechanical Reproduction', it took

Benjamin's point one step further and suggested that not only the aura of the work of art must be deconstructed but also the figure of the artist herself. In the 'catalogue' for the event put together by Elizabeth Sussman and David Joselit of the ICA, Burns writes that post-modern art, for all its radicalism of content and style, still seeks aura, that sense of being unique and elevated that Benjamin attributes to classic art, before the 'fall' into mechanical reproduction made public access a mass phenomenon. 'When I go to a Cindy Sherman show', Burns writes, 'I still feel that I'm supposed to be looking at art. Not surprisingly, I'm in a museum when this happens'. By art in this sense, Burns means not just the thing hanging on the wall but also the system underlying the object, 'the way we produce things to be looked at in what are fittingly called "shows", the set of assumptions that go into that relation of object and looker, art and public'.

The only way around this system she conjectures is to deconstruct the ideal of the artist as someone who expresses a meaning, even if it be a radically deconstructive meaning. What she calls the 'presumption of art' places people who are rendered passive by a social system of domination in yet another passive position. She finds this presumption at work even in brechtian art that attempts to promote critical reflection in the viewer. 'Only when we finally break down the division between artist and spectator will we leave what remains of aura behind', she writes. 'Only when art ceases to be art and becomes part of the fabric of life will it be liberated from the forms of capitalist passivity in which it still exists.'

It is this interest that lies behind the 'You Too Can Be An Artist' show. Curated by Tim Norris of Arts International, the show was conducted at the Boston Trade Center and lasted two weeks. Digital Computer was enlisted as a supporter (Burns' family owns the company), and it donated the supercomputer that was the centrepiece of the exhibit. Its immense screen was set up in the lobby of the building, and there people were encouraged to work at a keyboard, producing works of computer art that they were free to take and to copy for others. Participants were aided by several dozen art students from the Boston schools, who were enlisted into the project. The works produced were printed on high quality paper and constituted 'works of art' in their own right.

While these experiments in artistic extension beyond the bounds of the museum attracted a great deal of attention, they do not, Burns claims, live up to her ideal that the lived world itself should become infected with a contagion of refiguration that would imaginatively realign the existing shape of things. This 'post-auratic' ideal entails crossing the boundary not only between artist and public but also between art and economics or politics or sociology.

Her most successful experiment at such a crossing was the so-called Arts Block in the impoverished Roxbury area of Boston, a predomi- nantly black section filled with dilapidated houses and public apart- ments. Burns had inherited a row of old redbrick buildings with her family fortune, and she did them over as a public space fitted out with gymnasia, cafeteria, child care facilities, artist studios, computer design rooms, screening rooms, film processing facilities, and so on. It quickly became a neighbourhood commune where local people received free training in artistic production, where children could be left off while their mothers worked and could be given early training in creative skills, and where the artistic energies of the young people of the community could be developed and encouraged. The Arts Block also became a quite successful crafts shop where well-designed household goods and furniture were manufactured and sold. By the end of its first year of operation (1988), it was a self-sustaining economic enterprise, although the beautiful design objects that were originally made for the sake of adding imagination to the homes of the people of the neighbourhood quickly became fetish objects for upscale buyers from across the river in Cambridge, the home of throngs of white upscale professionals. Nevertheless, the Block survives with its indigenous links intact, and these are probably most evident in the music produced in the Block studios and performed in its concert halls, music composed and performed by local black artists.

It was as a result of the Arts Block that people became aware of Burns' great wealth, which apparently originated in a small gold mine her father discovered near her home town in Ireland. The fact that private wealth enables her sometimes grandiose artistic experiments is troubling to some of her supporters and admirers, but Burns argues that using capitalism against itself is an appropriate strategy. Few people knew when this issue was first raised of the extent of her immersion in that particular strategy – the fact, for example, that she had already acquired the Orion production company and was already producing several films – but in early 1989, several 'pieces' were unveiled that confirmed her move away from museum art entirely and into the realm of the popular or as she puts it the 'lived'.

The first, 'Radio Free America', carried out in conjunction with Japanese performance artist Tetsuo Kogawa, consisted of the initia- tion of a new radio station in the Boston area that carries out the same function as 'Radio Free Europe'. It broadcasts 'true' news about America ('Your prices rose again today, America, which means that you got poorer and the wealthy people who sit at the top of the heap got that much richer'), while also broadcasting both popular rock as well as experimental programmes that mix theatre and poetry with modern music. As in Burns' other public works, the new radio station has an interactive component that democratizes the listening process. Regular call-in shows permit people to express their resentments or to communicate with each other or to tell their life stories.

At the same time that Radio Free America began broadcasting, Burns' 'lived pieces' began to attract attention. They extrapolated from her experiments in public art and tried to further undermine the boundary between art and social life. Burns suggests that she wanted in making them to draw attention to the aesthetic character of reality. 'The very world we inhabit is a work of art, something made from papier mâché words, sculpted images, well painted canvases of experience. All of our thoughts are figures', she writes. 'All of our actions by dramatic design'.

This might stand as a kind of epigraph for this genre of 'work', if indeed it can be called that at all. The most controversial consisted of hiring several dozen actors who were found actual jobs in local companies where they worked side by side with real workers and lived out supposedly real lives, going home to families at the end of each day and returning to work the following morning. They were, however, acting parts, and their parts were all designed to 'humanize' the particular corner of the economic or social system in which they found themselves. With nothing really to lose, they spoke out against even small abuses of power in their office spaces and questioned the habits of efficiency and hierarchy that prevail in the work world. Charged with demonstrating a charitable and equalizing attitude toward others at every turn, they attempted to introduce a new rhetoric of human action into the everyday. The experiment went on for several weeks, but it had to be called off when one of the actors was arrested for fraud. She had taken her role so far as to begin disbursing the funds of the bank where she worked to poor people on the street.

A related 'economic piece' operated on the same margin between art and the work world. In 1987 Burns bought a factory in the nearby area of Dorchester, an extremely poor part of Boston. The factory was entirely refurbished, not simply as a production unit but also as an artistic site. The interior was turned into a beautiful and comfortable place in which to work; the walls were covered with attractive designs and lively paintings; and the work stations were designed in such a way as to maximize the pleasure of the endeavour. The workers were not hired but instead given the factory as a worker-owned, self-managed unit, and the workforce was deliberately chosen to be composed of equal numbers of men and women, as well as whites, blacks, Asians, and Hispanics. Burns calls the piece 'Economy by Design', and at its opening her catalogue described it as a piece of 'economic art' in that it brings artistic principles to bear on an area of life usually considered immune to those kinds of ideals. Its purpose, she writes, is 'to show that there is no world of necessity, that the economy is no different than art, a particular design that can be changed'. The factory still operates successfully, though some claim it is subsidized by profits from Digital and is therefore not really the successful post-capitalist experiment Burns claims it to be.

Burns' work in popular culture under the auspices of Orion has lost her a good number of her earlier acclaimants. They argue that she has sacrificed her commitment to art as a viable radical political endeavour. Gone now are all signs of artistic negativity, and the 'jargon of popularity', as one critic put it, has taken over. In an interview Burns dissents and argues that the popular is the arena where artists must work if they are to be effective at accomplishing what they claim to be doing by working within the public format.

Through Orion, Burns has set about making films, television shows and commercials. Her commercials are exact replicas of some of the most famous ads on American TV, but they advance slightly different messages – 'Listen to the heartbeat of America', for example, an ad for cars full of warm images of the western landscape that carries a nationalistic message in the original, is done over as a message about the American nuclear arsenal ticking away in missile silos hidden beneath the prairies, 'the heartbeat of America – nuclear destruction, genocide, no more prairies, no more America, no more life', as the voiceover puts it.

Not all of the work through the new Orion cable television network can be attributed to Burns, but much of it has her mark (some would say her ego) on it nonetheless. Numerous young writers have apparently been commissioned to write the new television shows, a number of which play of traditional formats and a number of which seek to establish new terrain for television viewing. Among the more traditional shows is 'Sammy and Jane', which concerns a working class family undergoing the stresses, tragi-comedically presented, of women working and job instability. 'Boygirl', on the other hand, is somewhat

more adventurous. Devised by Burns herself, the show concerns a
bisexual black high school student who must force her/his parents and
friends to come to terms with his/her difference. The same can be said
of 'Mrs President', another Burns creation, which features a black
punk angel named Felix Culpa, who oversees life in a somewhat askew
White House. Perhaps the most interesting feature of the new network
from a political perspective is its attempt at radical popular democracy.
All issues before the government are presented as referenda for public
voting by telephone call-in. According to Burns, popular culture has
reached a point where it now supplies the means for the opening up of
government to mass participation, and this is one of the points she
hopes to make through Orion.

Only one of Burns' films at Orion – *Vamps* – has actually appeared.
Its moderate success at the box office was an encouragement to some
performance oriented film-makers who thought Burns' popular
experiments would certainly fail. But the film also became a focus of
debate regarding the kinds of representations of women that women
should make. The film – the story of three female vampires in
Manhattan trying to outwit witch-hunters who are on their trail – is
indeed entertaining, and it has its moments of black tragedy as well as
strong resonances with the experience of the Holocaust. The 'vamps'
are sympathetically portrayed as emblems of the weak, the deviant,
the minoritarian, the oppressed, and the hunted. Positing vampirism
as a disease akin to AIDS, the film plays to a number of contemporary
motifs of oppression and deviancy, and the quite traditional nemeses –
a couple of ex-Nazis whose passion for killing vampires is equated with
the desire to exterminate all deviants – are ready stereotypes of
oppression in all its forms. Yet the film also associates women's power
with sexuality, and it is this aspect of the film that has drawn the most
fire, with some contending that it merely caters to popular prejudices
and risks reaffirming a subordinate 'bodily' position for women.

Burns insists the film emphasizes a resistant female power that
refuses male domination. As an alternative, it does not offer an ascetic
sisterhood, but rather a spectrum of positive sexual possibilities. One
of the vampires is lesbian, while another has a deep and abiding love
relationship with a doctor who brings her blood so she won't be
tempted to prey on people. Neither does Burns allow sexuality to be
portrayed entirely as a field of power. There are several erotic scenes
that are made aberrant by the suspense motif of the female vampire's
bite, which serves as a metaphor for a power the women choose to hold
in reserve – most of the time. Moreover, Burns neutralizes the

negative stereotype of the female vampire to the extent that they do not kill, and they only extract blood from men they take as lovers.

'The point', Burns insists in an interview with Peter Biskind in *Graphication*, 'is that the horror motif needs to be inhabited and refigured. The fear-of-women that has characterized it throughout its history needs to be recoded, given a new inflection that takes away some of its bite, if you will. We must pacify it, and one way to do that is to invert its dominant figures, give woman a positive power that is not so much horrifying as defensive, a defense against a horrifying violence that is emblematized in the conservative male characters, the two Nazi witch-hunters.' Burns responds to the claim that she panders in the film to the ideological form of Hollywood narrative with its orientation toward spectatorial pleasure by criticizing the asceticism of that critical position, its assumption that what entertains must be ideological, that pleasure is necessarily delusion or domination, that consumption is the one true object of a marxist cultural critique.

'I take issue with the idea that the culture of consumption is a form of capitalist domination', she writes in 'Response to My Critics', in her book of essays *Cinders from a Human Bonfire*. She traces the origin of this 'asceto-marxism' to the intersection of phenomenology and marxism in Europe in the early twentieth century, in the work of Lukacs particularly, where, for the first time, the critique of production is replaced by a critique of consumption. For Burns, it is appropriate that this idea should be perfectly coequal with the duration of stalinism, the imposition of socialist duty and the annulment of personal pleasure for the sake of the state-party-collective. But with the end of stalinism should also come the end of the critique of consumption, she argues. That critique was a means of deflecting energy away from the critique of productive relations and of the preservation of capitalist work domination under the rubric of state socialism in the Soviet Union. 'For orthodox marxists', she argues in a provocative note, 'being fast and artificial can seem inherently bad; but it isn't. That capacity, not some naturalist wallowing in the slumber of a neo-natal and maternal authentic community, is what will ultimately get us out from under power and into a world of equality.'

It is doubtful that an artist like Burns could continue the line of work she has established for herself without eventually confronting the necessity of how the ideals she espouses and the artistic practices she engages in are applied to or lived out in her own life. Would it too be 'art'? The account of her struggle with these issues is contained in the pieces collected in *Cinders from a Human Bonfire*, the work of

criticism and fiction she published in 1988. There she describes her
attempts to work out personal relations that combine the 'deeply
restorative powers' of identity with the 'necessary dangers' of boundary crossing. In her stories (or her autobiographical accounts?),
characters like Sylvia maintain stable relations with single lovers, but
also move freely around the world, working in Africa one year, Italy
another, New York city the next. 'There are new subject possibilities
emerging', Burns writes, 'new ways of forming ourselves that are both
matters of identity and multiplicity'. A polyvalent sexuality is essential
to this new psychology, but more so for Burns is the capacity to assume
different identities, to actually be different people. In 'Masquerade',
she describes a character who dresses up in different guises, taking on
different roles, moving from context to context and assuming the
attitudes required by the situation. 'This is the one truth', Burns
writes. 'That we have to be capable of being more than one thing'. If it
seems Burns is describing a level of experimentation available to only a
limited few, she is at least aware of this problem. She confronts it in her
essay 'Torture': 'At the fringe of what capitalism makes possible, we
can begin to glimpse the shore toward which we have been striving.
And if guilt is the price we pay for being able to work that far out, then
we must assume it and live it, for guilt, as much as hope, is a spur to
further reflection and, perhaps, even further action'.

Burns' most recent efforts have been in video, where she has sought
to give voice to those without any representation in mainstream
culture. She has particularly sought out women from rural areas or
from working class environments. The result – 'Other Voices' – is a
video done in partial collaboration with French anthropologist Anike
Allumette that allows women from around the world to speak about
their everyday concerns as well as to give voice to their grievances
about politics and economics in general. Meant as well as a critique of
male rationalist social theories, it works by juxtaposing the theories
and the lived realities of women's lives. Perhaps the most interesting
segment concerns an Indian woman in Peru. Set in the small mountain
home she inhabits with two children (her husband, we gather, was
killed indiscriminately in an army sweep of the area), the film focuses
on the woman's worn hands, as well as on the deep lines in her brown
face. After reading some quotations from the work of German theorist
Jurgen Habermas, the film-maker and the anthropologist ask the
woman to give her theory of society.

'What is theory?' Almatoomi asks.

'It's a general description of things, that tells you what's wrong and what needs to be done to set them right', Allumette responds bravely.

'Stop the soldiers from killing us', Almatoomi responds, turning her head to spit out the black liquid from her chewing tobacco.

'Right, but you see, a theory is more than that', Allumette says. 'It requires that you justify that assertion, using good rational reasons; otherwise, what you say won't be accepted as valid.'

Almatoomi shakes her head.

'Stop the soldiers. And give me back a husband to share my bed with at night. It gets cold up here, and I'm getting too old for the young men of the village. Change them too while you're at it. Make them love older women.'

Allumette nods and continues. 'Right, Almatoomi, I see your point. But a rational justification requires that we state our case using valid ideas so that our interlocutor will accept them as rational. Don't you see?'

'I see that your countries are rich, and mine is poor. I see the big men in big cars behind the soldiers. I see you doing nothing about it. Is that . . . what was the word you used, valid?'

'Almatoomi, come now. Try to follow the argument. How can you envision a just society that would end those problems if you don't learn to provide reasons for your propositions.'

Almatoomi pauses and looks at the camera. She turns her head and spits again. Then, she wipes her mouth and speaks.

'I see the sky coming to the earth as in the old legend. I see the corn in the field coming alive. The sky and the corn are warriors, and they are women warriors. They cover the soldiers in their blanket of air and make them sleep, their weapons falling from their hands. And the corn feeds us then, and gives us back all that was ever taken away.'

She pauses, and turns to spit once again. Then, she looks at the camera and says, 'Pass the yams'.

In Burns' work, then, we see one possible alternative to the passivity and cynicism that Baudrillard brings to post-modern art. On the other side of reason is not madness, but a return to politics, and in the post-modern insight into the semic character of social reality is not an invitation to capitulate, but rather a spur to engagement. This renewal of artistic politics nevertheless draws on the deconstructive arguments as well as the ironic posture of post-modernism. Posing art against something extra-artistic called 'society' is not, according to practitioners like Burns, the answer. 'We are in the works ourselves', she suggests. 'But that doesn't deprive us of power. It gives us the power to be ourselves staging points for acts of social refiguration. Here and now. What should we do?' If this neo-political art seems to take us back to versions of political engagement of an earlier era, it does so in part with a wink and a nod, as well as with a tutored sense of post-political experience. 'As much as what party should we join', Burns suggests, 'we should ask when does the party begin? After the darkness at noon, there shall be a light at midnight.'

6 Rhetoric and Ideology

Theoretical investigations into the nature and function of ideology have been dominated for the past two decades by the work of Louis Althusser, indeed by one essay by the French marxist philosopher – 'Ideology and Ideological State Apparatuses'.[1] It is not my purpose here to rehearse the numerous critiques of Althusser's position. I will concentrate instead on offering an alternative way of understanding the practical rhetorical operations of ideology (understood as those modes of experience that promote allegiance to systems of domination) and the political implications of the rhetoric of ideology as it operates in Hollywood film.

According to the althusserian theory of ideology, one of its primary operations is to dissolve social conflicts and political contradictions into representations that enact imaginary resolutions to those contradictions. What the althusserian theory ignores is the fact that, as a result, even the most speciously resolved pieces of popular cultural entertainment contain social conflicts and antimonies embedded within them. For example, in converting problematic public issues into purifying private stories, films invert, displace, and condense those issues, turning what is negative and contradictory into something positive and gratifying. But, consequently, films that seem most absolved of social antimony or of political significance are often the most political in the sense that they most strain to place such central features of society as inequality and domination offstage. If a pastoral painting were made of a ghetto, it would be assigned a political value by what it strives to avoid, regardless of its strainedly apolitical intent.

Given the dual character of ideological cultural artifacts (resolution and embedded antimony at once), a reading of such artifacts that sees them simply as unproblematic exercises in domination or hegemony would be one-sided. The althusserian theory of ideology holds that domination is the primary focus of cultural analysis, but one could argue that ideology is a secondary term, a response to other factors that may be more worthy of analysis. Those factors are what calls ideology forth as a response, and as things that *must* be silenced, they are sites of positive political possibilities.

Using this conceptual matrix, one could conceive of ideology as being itself made necessary by the tensions that are inherent in an inegalitarian society and by the potentials for upheaval that are

111

resident in any social system that exploits a majority of its members for its survival. Such societies contain irresolvable aporias at their centre because they rest on irrational principles of distribution. They are characterized by persistently repetitive dilemmas arising from the force exercised by the oppressed against the system of domination. Such dilemmas and those forces are contained and kept at bay by ideology. Ideology in this perspective is less the determinant of public consciousness, as in the althusserian framework, than a defensive operation, a response to factors that, were they not pacified, would tear the society apart from inside. Ideology is thus an exercise in power, but it is also a response to the power of forces that, if they were not channelled in ways conducive to hegemony, would push the society toward an altogether different distributive arrangement, one antithetical to those currently in power.

Thus, one can say that structures of power tend toward equalization by virtue of their own internal tensions, and ideology is simply an attempt to prevent this from occurring. It is less a positive vector of domination, therefore, than a negative attempt to prevent the internal erosion of domination from occurring. Its being defined by an 'anti-ideology', another world altogether that it prevents from coming into existence, a world that would turn the existing one inside out. And that other world can be deciphered, like a photo negative, within ideology.

Structures of inequality tend inevitably toward equality both because of the material movement of need and desire and because of the rhetoric of analogy that prevails in social consciousness. The accumulation of wealth or power in the hands of a minority breeds desires for imitation in the deprived majority. The stability of the differential is constantly threatened from within and must repeatedly be adjusted. What in economic mystification is called inflation (the upward spiral of prices and wages) is merely the name for this constant structural adjustment. A similar inflation of power, either as right-wing authoritarianism in underdeveloped contexts or as republican executive élitism in industrial situations, occurs in response to democratic threats to the differential of political inequality. Such adjustments, however, merely replicate on a higher level the situation of stabilized instability, augmenting the desire for a share of the stakes even as they raise the ante of exclusion. The tendency to erode inequality grows with each attempt to pacify it.

By calling that tendency a desire to emulate, I wish to underscore both its material dimension as a literal hunger and its rhetorical dimension as a figure of analogy guiding consciousness. For what is

— Thatcher's cults of self, & acquisition is a double-edged sword.

sought is imitation, an acquisition of the same for oneself. Thus it is that the wealthy and the powerful, simply by being what they are and by trying to preserve their condition, give rise to a tendency in others that works against their interests. Inequality, if you will, breeds equality.

Ideology can thus be read as a symptom of the very thing ideology acts to conjure away – the potential for a radical inversion of structural inequality. By attempting to pacify, channel, and displace the forces that would generate such an inversion were they not neutralized, ideology testifies to the power of the very thing it denies. Inequality and oppression create an irreducible structural tension that makes ideology necessary as a response but that remains immune to the therapeutic operation of ideology. Therefore, ideological cultural artifacts can serve as barometers of the potentials for radical change in a society. By reacting against those structural tensions and those potentially disruptive forces in a way that renders them invisible, ideology must also simultaneously put them on display – just as excessively washed hands indicate offstage guilt or as an abundance of white blood cells testify to disease.

For these reasons, I would argue that cultural ideology requires a double reading. On the one hand, it discloses the way desire and fear are channelled to assure hegemony. On the other hand, it provides a measure of those forces that threaten power. Even conservative artifacts, therefore, can yield socially critical insights, for what they designate in a sort of inverse negative is the presence of forces that make conservative reactions necessary. A literal reading of conservative anti-feminist films of the modern period, for example, might suggest that feminism was weak or even defeated. But conservative films can also be read as metaphors, attempts to deflect or turn away from the feminist challenge to traditional institutions. The deflected historical or social referent of such metaphorics is more often than not something that threatens the world that conservative politics defend. In other words, even though they are ideological, the conservative films are as much a testament to the power of feminism as overt feministic polemics.

Ideological films particularly are thus two quite contradictory things at once. They are ideology as a positive project (the affirmation of a technocratic vision of society in *The Towering Inferno* or of a slightly liberalized patriarchy in *Kramer vs Kramer*), yet they are also negations and denials of other social possibilities (popular democracy or a positive feminist project, to follow through on the examples).

They are thus marked in some way by what they deny, deflect, or displace. The absent presence of what is deflected or displaced casts its shadow over ideology, depriving it of the self-evident authority of simple affirmation. The monologue of power invariably turns out to be a dialogue.

The critique of the althusserian theory of ideology is furthered by recent developments in non-leninist marxist political theory and in object relations psychoanalysis. The althusserian theory is classically leninist, and it also owes much to the neo-freudian psychoanalysis of Lacan. Althusser's theory is leninist in that it defines ideology as a feature of individual subjectivity. To be ideological is to be 'interpellated' as a subject; given an identity by ideological social apparatuses like the family. A sense of self-identity is thus portrayed negatively as a symptom of an anti-communitarian bourgeois capitalist ethos. This concept of individual subjectivity carries with it unfortunate political implications, implications that have come under severe critical scrutiny in the post-1968 era. It pertains to a leninist discursive matrix that situates the individual as of lesser importance than the social group and that, implicitly, situates the party as the locus of political power, the ultimate mediator of individual wills. Under leninism, socialism is defined as the sublation of the individual into the large whole. Totality, unity, and identity are privileged over difference, autonomy, and multiplicity. Recent marxist theory, especially the autonomy theory developed by Negri and others in Italy in the 1970s, takes issue with this political-philosophical equation.

The autonomist approach argues that capitalism can only be overcome when the oppressed come to place their own needs, their own desires for value and self-worth, over the profit requirements of the economic system.[2] Self-valorization, turning the dominating impulses of capitalism to one's own use for the sake of creating counterforces to capitalism, not self-denial, should be the motor of a marxist politics, in economics as in culture. This strategy of counter-power is simultaneously an ideal of a post-capitalist society without state domination – a self-managed and fully democratic arrangement. Marx envisioned communism as giving rise to the possibility of full self-development within a co-operative context, but the leninist tradition down through Althusser reversed that description; self-annulment was equated with the socialist ideal, and austerity was imposed on workers denied democratic access to the determination of their own lives. Residues of that politics carry over in the conservatism of the structuralist theory of ideology. The autonomous marxism of the 1970s and 1980s revives precisely those texts, especially the *Grundrisse*, that were declared non-canonical by Althusser, and in this perspective, capitalism is condemned not because it creates subjects, but because it prevents a fully developed subjectivity from coming into existence.

Just as more enabling, non-leninist marxist models are available, so also more politically promising psychoanalytic models than the lacanian one Althusser employs are to be found, especially in the very object relations psychology that Lacan spent so much of his life disparaging. Absent in the freudian-lacanian tradition is any sense of the way social differences, determinants, and contexts play a role in producing psychopathology. In Lacan particularly, patriarchal paternalism is assumed to be natural and normative, rather than being seen as one contingent formulation of social life that might be replaced by a less pathological one. Object relations theory underscores the role of representation in constructing the subject; it emphasizes both the continuity between culture and psychology, and the malleable character of the psyche. Seen as a construct made from internalized representations of others, the self becomes more amenable to change and to progressive reconstruction. More so than in lacanian approach, which emphasizes drives that are outside determination by social relations and that consequently cannot be socially reconstructed, this approach suggests that all dimensions of the psyche, even those that are unconscious and instinctual, are historical and social, that is, changeable.[3]

A theory of ideology derived from this psychoanalytic approach would attend more to the malleable needs, desires, and fears operative on the pre-reflexive level of popular culture, rather than to the overdetermination of social life by unchanging drives. And it would attend more to the representations that shape those needs and desires in ways conducive to the maintenance of power. Those needs, fear, and desires are inseparable from representations because to fear or desire something is to bear a relation to a mental representation of what is feared or desired. The prevailing cultural representations, if internalized, shape those feelings into ideological attitudes, modes of thought and behaviour conducive to the reproduction of domination. But those feelings are not themselves ideological; they can be remade through alternative representations.[4]

This reformulation of the theory of ideology would notice the counter-ideological possibilities resident within the representational system of culture. Cultural representation designates a materiality of need and desire which cannot be fully shaped to suit the prerequisites of domination. There is a necessary misalignment between the idealizing representation ideology imposes and the material need or desire the representation addresses, and progressive political possibilities reside in this aporia. If ideology consists of the shaping of potentially counter-hegemonic needs and desires in ways conducive to the maintenance of domination, then that undecidable difference of force is likely to be enacted as a difference of rhetorical modes.

Rhetorical figures of representation and dramatic enactment range from pathos to hubris, metonymy to metaphor, irony to hyperbole, invective to elegy, and so on. None of these figures aligns with an inherent political meaning, and they all have a variety of political uses. However, conservatives favour modes that stabilize inequality and hierarchy, while progressives, from liberals to radicals, favour modes that destabilize power and promote equality. Conservative uses of rhetoric posit grounds of nature underneath merely contingent social arrangements, while progressives use the figure of nature to suggest liberation from the constraints of rigidified social orders. While both sides make use of the same figures, they do so for different ends, and they use them in different ways.

I will suggest that the conservative use of rhetoric can be described as being aligned with the vertical pole of linguistics, which is usually associated with metaphor, substitution, and the paradigmatic register (sets of terms that, though different each from the other, serve an identical function or fit into the same slot in a sentence), while the progressive use of rhetoric can be described as more in line with the horizontal axis, which is associated with metonymy, displacement, and the syntagmatic register (which concerns the serial order of terms in relation to each other in sentences). This is not to say that only conservatives use metaphors, or that metaphors are conservative in some inherent sense. It is to say that conservatives favour vertical social arrangements, whereby those with wealth and power rightfully rule, while progressives favour a horizontal levelling of such arrangements, both politically and economically. And that difference gets configured rhetorically as the difference between the metaphoric axis and the metonymic.

I will suggest that this rhetorical difference is understandable given the values at stake. But I would also argue that this particular understanding is not the only possible one. In other words, one could just as easily argue that certain kinds of progressivism, especially religious and non-materialist transcendental or idealist varieties, such as liberation theology, are metaphoric in character. Moreover, the metonymic, materialist pole is privileged as a critical lever against ideologies that configure themselves metaphorically, but one can imagine a post-revolutionary society in which equality would be achieved as one in which the metaphoric axis would assume new uses and meanings that would be quite different from the ones they assume in a conservative society. One thing that I associate with what I will call the metonymic register is a pliability of meaning that undermines the conservative attempt to make meaning a matter of identities, and this means that even the model I am using here can be given other meanings.[5]

The rhetorical pole that most readily lends itself to conservative ends is the vertical one associated with such tropes as allegory, symbol, and metaphor. All three consist of an evident or literal meaning and a hidden meaning. The hidden or unstated meaning is frequently something abstract or ideal, of a higher order than the empirical vehicle of that meaning (ealge = ideal of freedom, for example). It elicits a sense of awe and produces a sense of mystery both of which can be congruent with the political attitudes of devotion and obedience that conservatism favours. I will use the term metaphor to name this pole of rhetoric and to name tropes that operate in this way, and I will be particularly concerned with how they sustain conservative values.

Metaphor is a static structure that implies a world of identities outside history that are not subject to change. They exist simultaneously in an order akin to that of nature. The American eagle means freedom, and this static identity is not displaceable, nor is it available for negotiation or debate. The eagle is an immediate and total emblem of the higher ideal of freedom, not a partial sign connected in a mediated way to some other material thing (as 'big wigs', say, stand metonymically or contiguously for those with power because wigs were part of the aristocratic paraphernalia of government). Metaphor is associated with tradition and authority; it works through codes, a process of deduction, and a method of analogical thinking that makes identities out of different things. In order to know what a metaphor like eagle means, you have to be familiar with a traditional way of understanding it, a code that determines its significance in advance; you yourself cannot choose its meaning; rather, the meaning is deduced from an already established paradigm. The eagle is 'like' or analogous to the idea freedom, to the individual, to free marketing, or to any number of alternative meanings within the paradigm set.

Metaphor is context-independent and universalistic in orientation; that is, a metaphor like eagle does not depend on its real, concrete situation. The idea or meaning of freedom is a universal one that transcends the specificities of social place or historical time. Metaphor implies an autonomous ego who is free, like the meaning metaphor bears, from determination by his contexts and independent of constraining links to others. The style of metaphor is paradigmatic (implying order), hypotactic (entailing a subordination of terms), and disjunctive (operating as either/or propositions). A metaphor like eagle is one thing or another but not both; its meaning is decisive rather than being a matter of decision. Moreover, that meaning subordinates the actual material image to its higher-order, ideal semantic significance. In understanding metaphor, the actual material figure disappears entirely and becomes unimportant except as a sign of the ideal. That sense of meaning implies that the world is composed of predictable and consistent equations between signs and ideas. Figures of idealization (symbol, allegory, metaphor) thus work to promote thought patterns (obedience, awe, allegiance, order, and such like) that conservative social institutions require.

Consider a film like *The Deerhunter* which many people, myself included, thought to be highly conservative. Michael Vronsky (Robert DeNiro) is a metaphor for a new leader, one who heals wounds done to the community. He rises above his context and seems to acquire a meaning that transcends the material world. He is often associated with high mountains and with a shamanic knowledge that seems almost spiritual. Other characters in the film are subordinated to his higher power. As metaphor establishes an authoritative meaning that cannot be disputed, only learned, Michael assumes an authority in the film that seems endowed. Like a metaphoric meaning in a figure, that power is inherent in him, not given by his context or relations. It derives from a code that is already established. Moreover, Michael is elevated above others, just as meaning is elevated above its material figure in metaphor. He is idealized, and his most transcendental moments are rendered in a representational form that seems almost to stress its own artificiality, its own transcendence of ordinary material realism. If metaphor names the vertical axis of representation, it is associated in this film with the establishing of a vertical social ideal. Michael becomes the metaphor for a leader who exercises power from a position of inherent superiority.

But anyone familiar with the way the film was received in 1979 also knows that it appealed to a populist spirit; many workers in steel towns apparently liked it because it represented their world accurately. In addition to presenting an ideology of authoritarian redemption, it also described the everyday reality of material life that prompted the need for such an image of redemption in the late 1970s, when economic recessions, high inflation, and rampant unemployment (especially in the steel industry, the setting of the film) were gutting workplaces. In addition to providing an ideological cure in metaphoric form, the film also put on display the originating wound. Thus, the film contains (and is contained by) another rhetoric that anchors it back into the material context against which its idealizing metaphoric rhetoric strains. The name for that horizontal pole of rhetoric is metonymy.

Metonymy consists of associative links between contiguous terms that are in some way connected and on the same level. Instead of eagle substituting for the idea freedom as in metaphor, eagle as metonymy is linked contiguously or horizontally with empty mountain nests, with other scarce species of wild bird, with actual damage done the environment by capitalist industrialization sanctioned by the ideal of freedom, and so on. Metonymy represents a materiality that ultimately contradicts and undermines the idealizing tendency of metaphor. Michael Vronsky, rather than being a superior leader, appears metonymically as a victim of class oppression, a working class man tied to his material context who attempts to transcend it through compensatory activities like hunting deer. Metaphor leaves materiality and social context behind, but in metonymy those realities come to the fore, and no transcendent idealization can escape them.

If metaphors have ideal meanings that are different from their empirical vehicles (freedom in relation to eagle), metonymic signs are connected to other empirical signs; no ideal or hidden meaning elevates the metonymic rhetoric to a higher order of semantic significance. If metaphor establishes a deductive order of meaning that is fixed, metonymy creates connections that are potentially infinite and that never leave the ground for the ether of ideality. In contrast to the traditionalist orientation of metaphor, metonymy is future-oriented, dynamic, and indeterminate. Contiguous relations and connections are unpredictable, necessarily multiple, and impossible to limit to an order of subordination or analogical equivalence. A metonym is connected by part to something else (wing indicating bird, or empty nest indicating endangered environment) that can always in turn be connected to another part of the actual material world in some significant way. The meaning of these signs can never be fully saturated or determined, and no one of them transcends the others, placing them in a subordinate position.

Metonymy is therefore empirical and particular, rather than ideal —

and universal. The codes that sustain metaphor are depleted as metonymic connections generate contingent meanings that are beholden to no code or paradigm. Metonymic meanings are context-dependent and combinatory, paratactic (or co-ordinative) and conjunctive (operating as both/and propositions). A metonym links two things together, rather than decisively separating them into a superior meaning and a subordinate concrete figure. A metonym can only be understood as part of a context to which it is connected, as eagle refers to nest, to environment, and so on. No code determines its meaning; rather, the sign 'eagle' can be connected to other things in any number of ways. Its very figurality, it represents a more democratic or radical kind of 'freedom', than the hypostatized natural ideal of metaphor, which, as a cognitive entity or idea, seems the property of a single mind. Rather than designating an authority of meaning that must be recognized and obeyed or a superior individuality elevated above others (the person privileged with access to higher meaning), metonymy implies that meaning is social and constructed, a matter of what the existing material relations create as possible meanings or of what people wish to posit as conventional meanings between themselves.

One can see why a metonymic representational form might avail itself more readily of democratic, egalitarian, and anti-authoritarian social principles and values. Indeed, one way of distinguishing a quasi-radical film-maker like Robert Altman from conservatives like Francis Coppola, the director of *The Godfather*, or Michael Cimino, the director of *The Deerhunter*, is to say that while Coppola or Cimino are predominantly metaphoric in their representational approaches, Altman's rhetorical mode is predominantly metonymic. No individual male hero stands out above the others; all Altman's characters operate through contiguous relations or connections which maintain them on the same general level. The political values implicit in his style are democratic and anti-conservative, questioning of authority rather than sanctifying it. If metaphor is associated with the authority of tradition, metonymy is associated with the open-endedness of a democratic orientation toward self-reconstruction. Metaphor is also linked to the authority of leaders as well as to individualism, while metonymy implies collectivity and co-operation. In the latter, I see a more socialist and democratic representational principle.

These terms can be used to describe the ways films construct representations of the social world. My contention is that while metaphor is perhaps the most powerful ideological representational form, metonymy is the principle of the inevitable undermining of all metaphoric (that is, authoritarian, inegalitarian, and hierarchical) cultural representations and social arrangements. I have argued that ideology prevents alternative worlds from coming into being, as much as it stabilizes the present conservative reality. I suggested as well that the inherent tendency of social arrangements is deconstructive; that is, they tend toward equalization, a running-down of hierarchies and inequalities. I will describe this process in rhetorical terms as a move from metaphor to metonymy. And I will suggest that there is a relationship between what happens on the level of the representational strategies used to construct the social world and on the level of the actual world itself.

Social power depends on commonly held representations, and the form of those representations has a morphology similar to the structure of power. Metaphor as ideology seeks to erect vertical ways of understanding the world that legitimate vertical social structures, to establish proper boundaries of identity and meaning that limit perception to concepts that reproduce an appropriate sense of what social reality is and should be, and to route understanding toward idealizations that deny the way the material inequalities of the social system are structurally derived. Metaphor establishes an authority of meaning as well as a sense of proper thought and behaviour, and it is linked to the maintenance of social order and the authority of conservative ideals. All the political principles of liberalism and conservatism come down to metaphors that determine the political meanings or values of society in this way.

Metonymy cuts against the grain of these ideological operations in that it produces a lateral movement away from vertical stablizations, in that it undermines the propriety of meaning that prevents alternate understandings from emerging, and in that it represents the insistence of the literal and the irreducibility of the material vehicle of all metaphor, even the most idealizing. The concept of metonymy is ideology-critical because it suggests that contiguous relations, multiple and indeterminate deviations from authoritative metaphors, cannot be reduced or transcended. And it indicates the material determinants that are couched within the pretence to metaphoric ideality and identity. The ideal meaning 'freedom' in a pro-capitalist sense cannot prevent eagle from generating associations that overrun and undermine the metaphoric meaning of capitalist entrepreneurship. Either eagle can mean threatened species, or freedom can become something else – the freedom to overthrow capitalist freedom, for example.

Nothing is impervious to recoding; nothing immune to such indeterminacy and indecidability. And this is so, I would argue, not for contingent reasons of interpretation, but because the structures of representation are themselves characterized by a levelling tendency, a metonymic running-down of metaphoric hierarchies, a diffusion of authoritative meanings in irrecuperably plural and democratic directions. I will relate this levelling metonymic tendency to political potentials and forces within the existing system of social power which I see as moving toward alternate, more democratic and socialist social arrangements. Whenever I use the word 'socialist', I will primarily mean this equalization (of power, rewards, and so forth) that is implied by metonymic representational dynamics.

Metaphor, the trope whereby an image substitutes for an idea (Michael Vronsky for the ideals of patriotism, for example), seems more fundamental than a trope like metonymy that works by lateral or contiguous association (Michael as metonym for actual felt resentment over the loss in Vietnam). But all metaphors can be read as metonyms; the ideals they promote can be interpreted as linked contiguously to actual, material desires, interests, and needs. Metaphoric ideals are merely translations of materiality into a semblance of transcendent universality. The ideals of deer-hunting patriotism thus can be read as metonyms of feelings of loss which those ideals compensate.

Moreover, ideological social metaphors depend on a process of metonymic displacement (the contiguous relations generated by lateral connections of reference) that constructs yet simultaneously undermines their propriety and authority. Displacement is necessary to the construction of metaphor because it permits a meaning to be shifted onto a figure or image that otherwise would not generate that meaning. Without the mechanism that allows the ideal meaning 'freedom' to be attached to the image of the eagle and thereby to inegalitarian and very unfree social arrangements, ideological metaphors would not be possible. An idealization that overlooks empirical reality and a displacement that attaches to that reality meanings it does not justify are necessary for metaphor-as-ideology to function.

Yet the very thing that allows such ideological meanings to come into being prevents them from becoming stable and absolute. The very process of displacement that makes metaphor possible, by allowing transcendent ideals to be attached to fallen social realities, implies that further displacements of meaning are inevitable; displacement continues uncontrolled and uncontrollable, generating references and opening significations that counter and necessarily undermine the metaphoric meaning. Conservative meaning schemes require that 'freedom', for example, refer only to a certain kind of freedom – the freedom of capitalist entrepreneurs. The displacement of that meaning onto other social institutions – popular control of the economy, for example – uses the same rhetorical principle that establishes the ideological metaphor to generate meanings antithetical to it.

Another way of describing this is to say that metaphor erects a vertical meaning structure whereby an abstract ideal meaning stands in for a non-ideal material or literal reality, but a lateral movement of reference that links this ideal to contextual or contiguous references undermines this vertical structure. The metaphoric meaning is generally given out to be absolute and unequivocal, a semantic identity whose truth is guaranteed by its ideality, its transcendence of mere material life. But metonymy indicates an inevitable horizontal or lateral movement away from such vertical hierarchies, both representationally and socially.

The exaltation of the character traits of the male hero in Coppola's *The Godfather* is an example of the erection of such a vertical ideal. Don Corleone is a metaphoric demi-god, a natural ruler according to the ideology of the metaphor, but lateral metonymic connections fan out from him, anchoring him in a debased material reality of ethnic social life, patriarchal family structures, neighbourhood provincialism, and so forth. Those connections point to alternate meanings from the conservative ones intended by the figure. These connections are lateral and horizontal because they do not move upward from materiality to an ideal; they remain on the same level of reference connecting material signifiers rather than moving away from them to a higher order meaning. The film's metaphoric ideals can thus be read as metonyms of a certain sexually inegalitarian, quasi-tribal family form, or as material symptoms of the male psychopathology generated by such a form. And from a certain leftist perspective, the metaphor of the mafia family means the demise of traditional communities in the face of the onslaught of market capitalism. Both of these meanings tend to undermine the sanctifying idealization of the male leadership principle and of conservative family authority promoted by the film's metaphors.

What is placed at the top of a vertical social hierarchy is supposedly there because it is unique, proper, uncommon. Metaphor as a trope suggests a unique and special meaning appropriate to such a social institution. The Don is uniquely capable of exercising patriarchal authority; Luke Skywalker is uniquely endowed to defeat the Empire; Michael Vronsky is uniquely empowered to salvage Vietnam. A sense of individual uniqueness and power is usually accompanied by a strong feeling of one's own ideality or superiority, and it is fitting therefore that metaphoric or idealizing rhetorical forms execute this ideology. To be supremely charged with leadership of society is to feel that one's own mind is above the world, capable of managing it from above. One's own meanings are authoritative; they take precedence over democratic negotiation and difference. Metaphoric forms suggest such a self-identity or propriety of meaning. The Don as metaphor suggests an ideal of uncontestable patriarchal authority; Luke as metaphor is the embodiment of a 'natural' and indisputable élitist republicanism; and Michael metaphorizes an ideal of community leadership.

Thus, one function of ideological metaphors is to establish proper boundaries of meaning, by positing a universal and transcendental truth that defines and protects the sense of subjective uniqueness. 'Freedom' comes to mean the universal value of unconstrained will, and the metaphor posits a boundary around that meaning that attempts to prevent it from coming to mean general social liberation, for example. Its 'proper' interpretation is this meaning alone, and no other. Such propriety is a correlate of self-identity and social power. And just as that identity and power are predicated on the exclusion of the other (to be unique is to be un-common, not like others), this meaning must also be exclusive and fully decidable.

I have suggested that metonymic displacements imply that meaning can never attain such a decisive and determinate identity. Meaning can only be determined as a metonym for a specific, non-universal material social context. What this means is that a highly improper plurality of meanings is unavoidable, since social contexts entail a plurality of points of view. The other cannot be reduced or eliminated. *Rambo* acknowledges ('means') the power and reality of the Vietnamese, even as it strives to eliminate them. It is a token of the reality of defeat, even as it enacts victory. This duality of meaning inhabits all the proper meanings of ideological metaphors. As ideology, they are reaction formations, attempts to conjure away literal realities or to unify material differences which leave their mark or trace on the ideological meaning, undermining it by inflecting it away from its self-identity.

All ideological metaphors, even as they posit ideals of social harmony or unity, necessarily point to the reality of disharmony. That material metonymic connections cannot be erased and sublated into the male ego-gratifying ideal of *The Godfather* is an indicator of the irreducible instability of the social power which these ideals sanctify. Cultural representations would not be troubled in this way if the social system were not itself a site of difference, contention, and disharmony. At its root, the figure of Rambo is indicative of a radical difference between social groups, an exercise of force against one by another. Thus, *Rambo* can either mean successful militarism or the pathos of oppression, or both at once. Ronald Reagan can cite the film as justification for war, and a worker can, according to Dan Georgakis, praise it as a 'revolt against the system'. The undecidability of meaning is symptomatic of the duality of the social life the film metaphorizes.

If metonymy is the trope that reveals the commonality of the supposedly proper and the undecidability of the supposedly self-identical, it also signals the materiality of the metaphoric ideal, the literality of the figural. The idealizing metaphor is inseparable from the literal, material vehicle that communicates it. If the Don is tied to materiality by lateral or horizontal metonymic connections, he is also literally tied to the material world by his very image on the screen. A metaphoric ideal of patriarchal leadership, he is also someone protected by the womb-like darkness of his inner sanctum, a literal child at one point overseen by an image of a large woman that suggests her neo-maternal power as something fearful to be deflected and dominated. The literality of these images, their material connection to a world of male socialization, undermines the ideality of the metaphor. The purpose of metaphor as ideology is to idealize certain aspects of social reality, but the material vehicle of metaphor cannot be reduced out, made to disappear into the idealization; it remains, suggesting a materiality that resists incorporation into the ideological vision. What the Godfather metaphor presents as the ideal of male freedom or the beneficent nature of patriarchy it must also show literally to be a neurotic structure intolerant of psychological boundary fluidity and of sexual ambiguity. Male family fascism is a literal representational style that belies the pretence of male self-idealization.

Thus, ideological metaphors are undecidable to the extent that they propose a successful transcendence of material reality, but they can only do so by putting on display their own anchoring in that materiality. They are presented as universals or as ideals (*Beverly Hills Cop* as an ideal of race harmony, *Terms of Endearment* as a universal truth of family life, *Deerhunter* as a universal meaning of natural male leadership), but they are in reality idealizations of one aspect of material life (professional black incorporation, conservative family socialization, right-wing working class pathology); that is, they are in fact metonyms, tropes of material connection to a specific part of reality, not to a transcendental universal. These symptomatic material connections drag down the ideal proposed by the metaphors to its common ingredients. The sense of the propriety or truth of the ideals is thus inadvertently made questionable by the very instrument of its communication.

If ideological metaphors sustain social power, what is the consequence for social politics of the inevitable undermining of such metaphors by metonymic processes? The purpose of ideological cultural representations is to bring about compliance with a system of material inequality, in which power and rewards are unequally distributed. The small tribe of white men that rules the United States resorts to overt police force and incarceration to control the predominantly non-white underclass, but the predominantly white working and middle classes require less overt means of cultural control because they are steeped in the ideology of individualist 'freedom' that also justifies the economic power of the ruling class. This sort of system requires that metaphoric satisfactions be provided as compensations for the inevitable frustration of need and desire that structural inequality requires. But the trouble with metaphors is that, because they are ideal rather than real, they leave material needs intact and unsatisfied. It should not be surprising then that metaphors inevitably contain metonymies that indicate desires and needs that exceed the ideal solutions offered by the metaphors of ideology. By analyzing back from metaphor to its material referents, its psychological roots, one finds desires and needs at work that generally are for a more egalitarian world. Ideological metaphors are thus always 'critical' to the extent that they invariably contain metonyms that indicate real desires, felt needs for transcending the constraints of life in capitalist America.

The white family in *E.T.*, for example, presents a universal ideal of reconstituted family harmony in the end. The initial absence of a father is compensated by the acquisition of an ideal father. But the literality of the film's images generate material connections that permit the 'universal' white male ideal to be read as a metonym, a specific reference to a small, upper middle class suburban segment of the population. Those images link that world to the excluded 'other' world of the black urban underclass, whose poverty is a structural precondition of white wealth. Moreover, the dream of the perfect family requires a material vehicle or image that undermines that ideal. The family is in fact broken, and although the metaphoric representation cures this lack, the literal image points to a reality of declining patriarchal family life, a reality that generates needs, fears, and desires that nostalgia for patriarchy cannot alleviate.

The necessary non-alignment of figural meaning and literal image in ideological metaphors thus implies the irreducibility of material realities, realities of structural inequality and of need, desire, and fear that exceed idealizing metaphoric solutions simply because they are material. Similarly, by analyzing forward toward the alternate meanings that metonymic displacements make possible, one also comes upon transmutative desires. Meaning is always an issue of desire, of what one wishes or wants things to mean or to be. Metaphoric idealizations are the most evident example of desire operating to transcend material reality, to make it out to be what it is not. 'America' was triumphant only on the level of metaphor in the Reagan era precisely because in reality (*pace* diminutive Grenada) it was nowhere triumphant. The metaphoric ideal of the reconstituted family in *E.T.* indicates real needs for security in a time of economic hardship; it was a metonymic displacement of public sphere conservative tribalism into a compensatory liberal vision of private sphere therapy. Metonymic displacements of meaning away from metaphoric idealizations are also examples of desire operating to transform the world, turning Rambo into an example of revolt, for instance.

I would argue that these metonymic forces at work undermining ideological metaphors are the bearers of a 'progressive' potential in that they indicate desires (for community, security, and self-worth) that exceed the acceptable boundaries established by ideology for maintaining inequality. Such forces would tend society necessarily toward equalization if they were to be realized. The generation of alternate meanings that fan out horizontally or laterally away from a vertical idealization like Michael Vronsky, either anchoring it back into a material reality of need and desire which it seeks to transcend or skewing its intent to produce counter-ideological meanings, indicates an irreducible levelling tendency on the material plane of signification, and this unavoidable levelling and indeterminacy on the level of cultural representation points to similar levelling tendencies in the social world. People's needs and desires tend toward material satisfaction, and a broadscale satisfaction of the needs designated by the representational processes I have described would necessarily lead to a levelling of unequal social hierarchies. If I suggest that metonymy is the dimension of cultural representation that points to this social potential and possiblity, it is because if meaning is a function of desire, then the metonymic dissemination of meaning is indicative of a proliferation of needs and desires beyond the proper limits established by metaphoric ideals in American culture. If films mean more than they intend, it is because the desires they address are also for more than is provided. If a certain literality or materiality is both necessary for metaphor to exist at all and ultimately subversive of the idealizing operation of metaphor, so also the material desires and needs addressed by ideological metaphors both permit the metaphors to be successful and threaten them with a necessary excess that can never be retrieved by cultural ideals, simply because their material tendency is toward a very non-ideal satisfaction. If, instead of being offered ideals of 'freedom', Americans were offered an actual power of choice regarding the satisfaction of material needs, they would choose a redistribution of rewards that would threaten the unequal hierarchies and vertical social arrangements which those cultural ideals sanctify.

It is for this reason that meaning, as much as people, must be policed. Meaning is a matter of what people desire; what something means is shaped by their needs, desires, and fears. Hollywood offers meanings that orient thought and feeling and action toward vertical-individualist as opposed to horizontal-communitarian social structures. If film and the cultural apparatus of which it is a part did not accomplish this task, the levelling force of desire would erode the existing inegalitarian structures. Metonymy, therefore, is something more than a mere representational style. It points to the erosion of social structures as much as of representational ones.

For example, the social representation that establishes male parental authority as the model for conservative political policy is a metaphor that operates as an analogy between two vertical structures, the patriarchal family and the republican polity. But that metaphor is constantly threatened with erosion by a lateral force of reference, a process of literal material connection that works against the vertical ideal. This metonymic movement appears when such new institutions as serial monogamy, single parenting, lesbian parenting, and so forth are spawned by the original patriarchal model, resorting to its conventions without fully honouring them. The original makes possible deviations or simulations that underscore the conventionality of the original and thereby displace its authority by revealing that it is merely itself a construct, one possibility in a series of possible social configurations. Similarly, the patriarchal family makes possible contiguous relations between oppressed wives, initially, then liberated independent women. Each term generates new relations of contiguity and connection, against the proper order imposed by the metaphoric substitution of an ideal (the perfect wife) for a debased reality (domestic slavery). All instances of social power and propriety are subject to this eventuality. All social metaphors are subject to the generation of metonymic associations that undermine them. It is from within the system of social power itself, then, that the principle of deconstruction and reconstruction emerges.

I will briefly consider a major film of the contemporary period, using this method of analysis. *Star Wars* (1978) performs an essentially metaphoric rhetorical operation by substituting an heroic individualist (Luke Skywalker) for an entire people. Luke is special precisely because he is common, that is, someone with whom everyone can identify. This undecidable structure of political representation – both individualist and collectivist at once – must be occluded if the republican form of government (the substitution – metaphorically and vertically – of an élite of superior male individualists for an entire people) is to appear legitimate. A different representational form might have posited a narrative that entailed co-ordination between a large number of equally competent people, none of whom was privileged as an elect individual. Thus, a potentially more democratic principle of permutation, by which no singular term would have governed the generation of new combinations, is displaced in favour of a principle of commutation, whereby each finds its value in being replaced by or identified with a central term that governs the field of possibilities and in effect closes off further combinations or permutations. Luke takes everyone else's place; this is his meaning as an ideological metaphor. This rhetoric thus privileges a unique individual who is also a leader-authority figure in social terms. The rhetoric resembles that of the American Right in the late 1970s and early 1980s, the period when the 'Star Wars' series appeared, which argued for 'free' individualism and political élitism or republicanism simultaneously.

But the ideological metaphor of *Star Wars* is undermined from within. Metaphor, as an idealizing trope, often promotes, as I have noted, a sense of hidden, ideal meaning, a sense of a higher reality behind the material vehicle of the figure. Luke's uniqueness is founded on his sense of his participation in a higher ideal reality (the 'Force'). Yet the film's metaphor displays its literal origins in metonymic or material connections that undermine the idealizing pretensions of the film's ideology. For example, Luke's home is a small farm where he is raised as an orphan by relatives. In the final battle with the Death Star,

Luke saves the day by resorting to rural skills learned down on the farm. The ideological purpose of this metaphoric equation of superiority with rurality is to promote the conservative values of self-reliance and 'natural' male individualism against the values of the liberal bureaucratic federal government, the urban bogeyman of the Right in the late 1970s, when *Star Wars* was made, which is represented in the film by the 'Empire'.

But the metaphoric equation displays a metonymic connection underlying the paradigmatic identity of ideals (rurality/male superiority) that the film seems to establish. That connection shows the conservative ideal of the great male individualist leader to be nothing less than a displaced farmer, or the displacement of the undereducated, pre-civil values of rural conservatism into a political and social programme. It thus displays the hick origins of populist authoritarianism and conservative republicanism, from Hitler's Bavaria to Reagan's Dixon, Illinois. The reading of the metaphor as a metonymic displacement reveals that the great male individualist is in fact a rather humble member of a larger communal chain, the occupant of a determinate and limited material position in society. This indeed may in part account for the hyperbolic inflation of the male in the film's metaphor; it is a reaction to the material reality from which it arises and which it deflects.

In addition, a noteworthy trait of Luke's rural family is the absence of a father and the presence of a fairly patriarchal substitute, an uncle. The (self-)inflation of the male is also inspired by a desire for a caring and ideal father who compensates for the uncaring, authoritarian structure of the conservative patriarchal family. The inflation is both a compensation for the sense of lack the uncaring and powerful father promotes as well as an internalization of the image of power the father represents. Such structural lacks can never be filled, and this literal truth is signalled by the fact that the actual father is (supposedly) already dead in the film when the narrative begins and is replaced by a substitute. In each of the three *Star Wars* films, a new parental substitute is found, until the actual father reappears, only to die again. A metonymic displacement, in other words, precludes closing off the seriality of need and desire, sealing the aporia caused by the double bind of conservative patriarchalism (the double need to flee the authoritarian father and to identify with him). The conservative family model operates around a powerful father, and this promotes in male children a sense of lack regarding such power. The absent father is sought both as a model of self-development and as a public political instance of social authority, yet he is sought precisely in order to throw him off, to reject the paternalism of the state in favour of a radical model of rebellious individualism. Once again, the literal origins of a public metaphor are on display in the film. The cultural metaphor of heroic male individualism is nothing more than a temporary and necessarily unsuccessful plug for the sewer hole of oedipal trauma created in males by conservative family tribalism, the social structure whereby bullish males exercise unquestioned authority over their family and (by metaphoric displacement) over the lives of everyone else in society.

In this way, the metonyms harboured within ideological metaphors can be flushed out to deconstruct the ideology of a film. But that deconstruction has positive implications; it is not merely an exercise in negative hermeneutics. For what it suggests is that material adversity predictably creates psychological needs that, in a patriarchal, individualist, and inegalitarian society, will be satisfied culturally through idealizing metaphoric representations like *Star Wars*. In other words, the metaphoric transcendence of material adversity (and *Star Wars* appeared at a crucial moment in US social history, a period of great economic hardship for many and of a tremendous decline in public confidence in liberal governance) is itself an indictment of such adversity as well as an advertisement for needs that cut against the requirements of the social structures that create adversity. For this reason, such needs are bearers of progressive potentials.

In addition, a film like *Star Wars*, despite the objective meaning I have assigned it as a structure of signification and as a symptomatic artifact of social history, is open to multiple interpretations that resist its stabilizing, over-coded idealization and promote a more lateral, metonymnic, and democratic sense of its possible meanings. Although the film metaphorizes conservative values, it also points to wishes to overthrow unjust power, to escape from constraints, and to attain self- worth, feelings that are not themselves necessarily 'conservative'. Indeed, some of my radical friends read the film (quite legitimately) as an allegory of the revolutionary struggle against injustice or as a democratic struggle against monarchy. And an audience survey I performed turned up numerous examples of people who read the film as an example of liberal or even radical values.[6] The film, in other words, can be used in any number of ways, and this pragmatic and contextual dissemination of its meaning beyond the boundaries the film itself (in my reading) seeks to establish is also a token of the impossibility of ever fully or in an absolute way institutionalizing the sorts of semantic authority and political hierarchy the film advertises.

To conclude, my theoretical differences with the althusserian approach to cultural ideology come down to a difference of politics. Rather than dismiss Hollywood film by assigning it a determinate meaning as ideology, I read it in what I hope is a more politically enabling manner. My method of analysis suggests it is possible to seek out what in contemporary culture points toward the realization of an alternate social arrangement, using the indices of unanswerable fears and unallayable desires. If cinematic ideology is as much a reflex as an exercise in domination, a response to things that it seeks to neutralize but that are fundamentally beyond its control, then the study of ideology in American cinematic culture is necessarily the study of its inverse, that against which it operates – the potentially explosive tensions of inequality, the antinomies of an unjustifiable social regime, the hopes and fears of the oppressed, and the desires for self-worth and identity that run counter to the stabilization of the extraction of wealth in a patriarchal, white-dominated, capitalist society.

This reading method is deconstructive to the extent that it conceives of ideology as an undecidable phenomenon, a marker of instability as much as of the stabilization of inequality. Indeed, the very thing that permits althusserian film critics to condemn Hollywood film – its persistent and repetitive use of ideological themes and forms – is itself an indicator of needs and desires whose repetitive recalcitrance indicates the inability of the current social system to meet them. White patriarchal capitalism, by virtue of its fundamental laws of operation (greed, competition, survivalism, the denial of charity and empathy, the atomization of communities, the idealization of efficiency, and such like), could never satisfy the broad desires for security, self-worth, welfare, equality, and community that are evident in film culture. Although these needs and desires are frequently channeled in conservative directions in contemporary American cinematic culture, the theoretical paradigm I have sketched suggests that they contain progressive possibilities that can be given different political inflections.

This itself constitutes a deconstructive strategy, an attempt to refrain from either assigning a political essence or meaning to such popular aspirations or accepting the substitute political formations into which those aspirations are translated in the contemporary conjuncture as defining their only possible meaning. The indeterminacy of meaning applies as well to social phenomena. And the populist reaction to government taxation in the US in the late 1970s becomes in the mid-1980s a reaction to excessive government spending on defence. My contention is that the needs and desires that seem most recalcitrant are ones which often are for things that only a socialist social arrangement could provide. And by that I mean the principle of equality as it would operate socially, culturally, politically, psychologically and economically.

I would conclude, therefore, by arguing that deconstructive analysis provides a model for locating forces in the existing system of ideology and domination that point toward an alternate social system, one in which a deconstructive levelling of economic inequality and social hierarchy would be realized, not as the execution of an ideal, but rather as the carrying out of material potentials, potentials that strain now against the boundaries and limits which ideology imposes.

A deconstructive reconsideration of the althusserian theory of ideology does not so much disable politics as make possible a politics quite different from that implied by the althusserian position. If that theory suggested that the masses were duped and needed leninist guidance or avant-guard tutoring in the cultural upper class' reflexivity, the deconstructive rewriting of the theory points toward an insoluble problem at the heart of ideology. The persistence of that irreducible antimony suggests that the more ideology is needed the more it fails, and it points toward forces at work at that fault line where material desire and cultural representation intersect and determine each other, forces that push the world that ideology sustains toward the edge of collapse and that hold the potential of giving rise to a different world altogether. It is for this reason that I would argue in conclusion that the major political consequence of this reconsideration of the theory of ideology is a recognition of the importance and necessity of working within the terrain of popular representation, since it is there that the needs and desires that are the bearers of those progressive potentials are most accessible to reinflection.

7 The Rhetoric of Liberalism

I have argued that the substance of social reality is figural or constructed, an effect of an arrangement of instituted tropes – the narrative of progress or 'growth' that transforms economic power structures into temporal figures of movement, the structuring of democracy as a displacement from popular participation to representational élitism, the metaphor of individual freedom that effaces interrelational social realities, the metonymic shaping of happiness on the mass level into fragmentary fetishes or part objects like drugs or sports, the patterning of sexuality as a doubly negated dynamic of repression and violent effusion, and so on. The substance of the social is constituted as these shaping procedures, these arrangements that create an effect or appearance of a pre-rhetorical reality that is 'represented' by existing institutions. What is interesting about such social-rhetorical structures is the tension they contain between the stabilization of the existing format and the forces that push against that stabilization, pushing it beyond its boundaries. In this chapter, I will consider how such tensions are played out in the social theory of liberalism.[1]

Few social theories so actively demonstrate the power of rhetoric in the construction of social reality as liberalism. Yet few social theories so strive to refute rhetoric's claims. Liberalism presented itself originally (in the late seventeenth century) as a rational social system; it placed itself in direct contradiction to the irrational exercise of force that characterized feudal social relations. Yet this rationality was formal and ideal, universal and transcendental, rather than democratic and material, or substantial and egalitarian. It privileged logic over rhetoric, and it guaranteed rights only in a formal or abstract sense, not in a realized material one.

Because liberalism as a social doctrine, for all its claims to universality, was wedded to a quite specific social form – capitalism – whose inequalities required justification, liberalism quickly found itself faced with a number of logical problems. Most notably, it could proclaim the ideal of abstract individual freedom but only in a way that promoted substantive inequality. Because liberal abstractions never could live as embodied materialities, the ideals of liberalism seemed

134

invariably at odds with their practical outcomes. Moreover, in order for the ideals to be universal, rational, and logical, they had also to transcend rhetoric, the mere exercise of force or the shoddy shaping of ideas according to prescribed forms in language. Liberalism was about right ideas, not practical discursive manoeuvres.

But, of course, the more it strove to transcend its practical side, the more evident it became that liberalism had to be a fairly sophisticated exercise of rhetoric, a very practical system of subordination and displacement, of condensation and substitution, if it was to justify capitalism. And this rhetoric was more than merely a matter of language; it also constituted the formal procedures for arranging and constructing liberal life forms. Rational politics would consist of representational delegation rather than direct democracy. Economics would consist of mediated and displaced ownership and control rather than direct distribution or equal allocation. Social arrangements would revolve around the idealization or hyperbolization of male individual freedom defined as unrestrained material acquisitiveness, the condensation of economic and political power into one, the displacement of majoritarian concerns into the margins, and the subordination of the interests of women, non-whites, and workers to those of a commercial class of men. Certain formal liberties would substitute for a fully realized or universal material freedom.

The forms of liberal social discourse were inegalitarian and radically unfree, except in the most formal and abstract sense of the terms freedom and equality. Consequently, it became evident early on that liberalism was an ideological social form, one that substituted certain idealized claims for certain real perceptions and that offered limited possibilities for more general potentials. The claim that all were free would substitute metaphorically for the reality that all were unequal, while the restrained freedom of opportunity in the market would substitute for the general freedom of owning what one needed outright. But the price of such metaphoricity was a disjunction between the rational ideal and the irrational actuality, the promised utopia and the limited reality, a disjunction that produced a constant unbalance and slippage within the system while leaving open the possibility that the ideals might be taken seriously, the pretence to universality applied practically. The real metonymic displacement of majoritarian interests in favour of a metaphoric idealization of individual freedom might be held up for inspection, compared to the metaphoric hyperbole, and found wanting. This in fact is what transpired.

As in the structure of metaphor, which establishes a comparative equivalence between two different terms, so in liberal theory, civil society and nature were seen at the outset of liberalism as being interchangeable: 'All the great laws of society are laws of nature'.[2] In liberalism's great early texts, from Locke to Rousseau, civil society is compared by analogy to both nature and to the science of natural laws: 'Freedom of Men under Government is . . . common to everyone of that society . . . As Freedom of Nature is to be under no other restraint but the Law of Nature . . . Just as nature has set bounds to the stature of a well-formed man . . ., so, in what concerns the best constitution of the state, there are limits . . . Administration becomes more difficult over great distances, just as a weight becomes heavier at the end of a long lever . . . The state if it is to have strength must give itself a solid foundation . . . for all peoples generate a kind of centrifugal force . . . like the vortices of Descartes'.[3]

Why nature? Nature connotes freedom from restraint, as well as order and harmony between parts subsumed under a whole. It suggests, in other words, the dual quality of liberal capitalism as a regime at once of freedom and of restraint. Capitalists would be free from royal domination, and workers would be kept in control. Property would be safeguarded by police charged with keeping society as close as possible to the harmonious whole that was nature. Thus, the analogy or metaphor served an ideological function by legitimating entrepreneurial individualism and justifying the political and juridical forms (sovereignty, contract) that maintained a frame of order around the anarchy of the capitalist market.

Liberalism acquired the logical or rational form it pretended to possess from the outset only once a number of initial analogies were accepted. The initial analogies were, first, that civil laws, like natural ones, prescribe that everyone in society is free and equal, and second, that civil society functions according to the scientific laws of nature; that is, civil society is an orderly and rational machine. From the first analogy derives the doctrine of individual rights. Everyone, as a free, self-possesed individual, has the same right to speech, property, and so on. From the second analogy is derived the doctrine of political sovereignty. The state as a whole must be maintained as an integral, orderly harmony of parts.[4]

One purpose of the analogy with nature was to make individual freedom a metaphoric or purely formal principle that regulates society from outside its everyday material operations. Freedom and equality would not be substantively guaranteed or constructed in liberal society, and so the probability would always exist that there would be people who possessed merely formal equality, but who would be substantively unequal. Within the form of the initial analogy with nature, therefore, lay a possibility of tension. This possibility was answered by the second analogy. If the first gave freedom to everyone but only in a metaphoric or formal sense, the second analogy – that society was a harmonious whole that operated according to the scientific laws of the machine of nature – provided a rationale for exercising force against those who were inspired by this tension to seek to rectify substantive inequality.

Liberal theory spoke otherwise of course. Compromises would be worked out between individual freedom and the order of the whole (Mill, *On Liberty*), or a theory would be advanced that claimed that the free natural exercise of individual self-interest would result in social harmony (Smith, *The Wealth of Nations*). Or it would be claimed that the institution of political sovereignty would mediate between the ideal of a natural right of equality and the actual fact of social inequality by recourse either to a concept of a contractual exchange of rights for security (Hobbes, *Leviathan*) or to the concept of a scientific ratio or proportion in civil society between its parts (Rousseau, *The Social Contract*). In any event, the two analogies operated together to secure freedom for capitalists on the one hand, while assuring that the radical potential for a materialized, rather than a purely formal, equality implied by the analogy with nature would be kept within bounds.

In addition to being a figure of analogy with civil society, nature also acted in liberal theory as the other it must vigilantly keep at bay. Nature defined as the civil war of all against all, as the prevalence of force over law, and as the absence of any guarantee of property right was the name for what must be left behind and kept permanently outside liberal civil society if it is to exist at all. In this imagery, nature came to name that tension within civil society that arises from inequality. The threat to property from within civil society constituted, according to liberalism, the possibility of a return to nature, to a world based on force rather than reason.

The dual meaning of nature thus pointed to the necessary duality at the heart of liberal society. Nature was something unconstrained and threatening (especially to legally sanctioned and protected property), but nature was also the principle of order and legality that justified constraint, the exercise of law to protect property. The boundaries of the autonomous male ego (the only legal property owner when liberalism was invented) were secured by a maternal principle of order (nature), one that established safe boundaries around a threatened self and an unstable self-possession, but the maternal (by which I mean all that materiality of women, work, slavery, witchcraft, and so on, that was excluded from the boundaried identity of rational propriety, the mark of male individualist, abstract freedom) also was that which most powerfully bore the possibility of overwhelming and engulfing property and the self-identity upon which it was built.

It is then fitting that a male-socialized principle of purely objective, anti-affective, and decontextualizing reason should be the instrument for keeping that threat at bay. Early liberalism and early capitalism constitute a history of battle between fathers and mothers, and the mothers lose (if by 'mothers' we mean those who, by virtue of being chained to the materiality of labour, could not rise to reason's heights of abstraction).[5] Liberal theory presented this operation as being purely logical, but it could just as easily be characterized as purely rhetorical. The logic is that the ideal of individual freedom (unrestrained male egoism) which originates in the analogy with free nature is rational both because it confirms scientifically deduced natural law and because it is the mode of operation of the individual mind, the repository of reason, as it engages the world objectively. To decide freely or naturally is to be rational. And such free self-possession translates logically into the right to decide freely how to dispose of one's self and of one's property. As Hobbes put it: 'Where there is no own . . . there is no commonwealth, there is no propriety'.[6] The ideal of a pure logic and of a purely scientific rationality are crucially allied with these social ideals. But the linkages between these ideals (nature, freedom, individual will, property) are merely contingent and figural, moving from metaphor (the analogy between nature and society) to metonymy (the continuous links between the individual and a social institution or piece of materiality like property). Liberal reason rests on rhetorical processes that contradict its premise of natural or non-rhetorical foundation. Nature suggests a non-rhetorical ground of self-evident meaning, but the very analogy that allies nature with liberal civility insinuates rhetoric into that apparent ground of self-evidence.

Moreover, the founding of liberalism on the metaphor of nature presupposes a process of displacement that makes metaphor possible as an analogical displacement from one thing to another (nature to civil society).[7] Civil society is a displacement from nature to civility or law, and that entails transferring rights from the people to the sovereign: 'Where-ever therefore any number of Men are so united into one

Society, as to quit every one of his Executive Power of the Law of Nature, and to resign it to the publick, there and there only is a Political, or Civil Society . . . And this puts Men out of a State of Nature into that of a Commonwealth, by setting up a Judge on Earth, with Authority to determine all Contro-versies'.[8] But the authority that liberal metaphors strive to establish by making society analogous to 'natural law' is strikingly contradicted by the very movement of displacement that allows those metaphors to come into being.

The structure of displacement that makes metaphor possible assumes that meaning is not inherent and that it can be transferred from one thing to another, like political rights during the entry into civil society. But if this is the case, then nothing is natural in the sense that liberalism pretends; nothing possesses a power over itself, over its own meaning, that is as compelling as a law of nature, which supposedly stands on its own, outside human mediation. Because of displacement, no meaning can be as self-sufficient as natural meaning must have been for liberalism to come into being in the way that it claims it did, as a simple mirror held up to nature. For liberal theorists, nature is something entirely outside displacement that is inherent to itself, fully self-sufficient, and independent. Yet displacement implies that a certain alterity, a possibility of being other than oneself, of passing outside one's own boundaries of meaning or being in an act of metaphoric transfer, makes possible the very ground of nature that anchors these assumptions. Nature must be inherently displaceable if it is to give rise to a displacement of natural law into liberal civility, and if the supposedly inherent meaning of nature can be transferable to the supposedly post-natural institutions of liberalism. The very thing that seems to grant a compelling power to liberal social forms (the analogy to natural laws) thus threatens to subtract as much as it adds to liberalism. For liberalism to lay claim to the self-identity and independence of nature, it must resort to a principle of displacement that disables such self-identity or properness.

The problem bears especially on that centrepiece of liberal theory – the individual right to property ('every one his Executive Power of the Law of Nature'). There can never be an inalienable or non-displaceable right to property because displacement, which grounds the liberal theory of individual property right, simultaneously destabil-izes the very idea of individual self-sufficiency. The need to establish rights claims in a manner that suggests their inalienability testifies to the possibility of the removal of that right. A right is only declared inalienable because it is eminently alienable. The assertion of right is therefore always a defensive confirmation of the possibility of what right (as a claim akin to nature) seeks to deny. In other words, property must be affirmed as a socially guaranteed 'natural' right precisely to the degree that it is unnatural and contingent.

The displaceability of property is at once affirmed and denied by the right to property. The right to own property implies that some other might own it or might deprive one of it. The self-identity of property ownership is consequently divided; what is 'proper' is so only in so much as it is not 'common'. Indeed, Locke defines property as something 'subtracted' from the commons. Property right, therefore, is not something inherent to itself or proper to a person; it is the denial of the possible commonality of property, of its potential displaceability. And the threat of displacement would not exist, would not need to be defended against, if it were not already present within the institution of property as the very process that constitutes it as a metaphorically 'natural' right.

The defensive character of the liberal discourse of nature is evident in the implied threat that is fended off in the assertion of property right. Because the very claim to property right implies the existence of a group without property who threaten to expropriate it, in liberal society property ownership can only be universal as a formal right, an abstract idea, not a substantive reality. But this is precisely the characteristic of pre-liberal nature, the war of all against all, that liberal civility supposedly supersedes. The necessity of a legal right to property in liberalism that has the effect of excluding people from property ownership (liberalism would still be rational and logical even if only one person owned all the property) indicates that certain people can only relate to property as an unexercised formal right. The legal protection of property is necessarily also the legal deprivation of property, since no legal mechanism guarantees equal distribution or a minimum of ownership, and any legal protection of some property means that ownership is never sufficiently universal to waylay the possibility of expropriation by some other. The very existence of a 'right' to property means that a social situation exists in which the contingencies of property ownership must be protected against those without property. Liberal law itself, therefore, the sign of a universality akin to natural law and of a civility transcending mere nature, points out the natural, that is, particularistic and antagonistic, character of liberal civil society, its true nature, one might say, as a civil war. The very necessity of law to guarantee property indicates that property itself is not universal, and this casts property right as a non-general particularity that exercises a force at once of privation and deprivation against those without property. Property right is a sign of nature within liberal civil society, a mark of the uncivility of liberal civil society.

A progressive possibility resides in this deconstructive antimony. The scientific principle of rational universality is coercive when applied to a non-universalist or disproportionate reality; nevertheless, the principle implies the changes needed to make that reality proportionate. To satisfy the principle of rational universality that was the real stake in the liberal metaphor of nature, liberal society would need to guarantee a universal equality or uniformity of ownership. And that, of course, would mean the disappearance of property as liberalism conceives of it – as a particularistic exercise of exclusion. Universality implies non-properness or non-particularity; what is universal cuts across the boundaries of individual identity. Property as something own, subtracted from and protected against the common, could not exist in a society of universal principles, principles that necessarily imply equality of distribution. Liberalism thus provides the instruments of its own dissolution, and liberal civil society, while betraying its own lack of civility, points the way toward a more civil social arrangement.

The proleptic quality of liberalism is nowhere more evident than in the principle of displacement implied in its founding metaphors. Displacement is a condition of possibility of liberalism that is simultaneously a condition of its impossibility as a system that remains intact within the outlines or boundaries it establishes for itself. The instability displacement produces at the origin of liberalism also operates to push it relentlessly beyond its outlines. Liberalism assumes an initial transfer or displacement of meaning, from nature to civil society (either as the giving up of natural rights to enter a commonwealth or as the analogy with natural law that provides a model for the laws of that commonwealth), but nothing prevents the process of displacement from continuing to move. Indeed, the instability within liberal rights discourse that it implies continues to operate, so that the history of liberal social theory becomes a narrative of attempts to shore up the openings that the displacement inherent in liberal institutions inevitably produces. If the landed gentry and the urban merchants can have rights transferred to them from the monarch and the aristocrats, why can't women, slaves, and workers have rights transferred to them from the merchants and the gentry? If government can be initially a matter of transfer or displacement, why should it not be a matter of infinite displacement? Liberal thinkers will strive to answer these questions in ways that contain their radical implications and that neutralize the effects of displacement. But the limits they impose will simply be the markers of an uncontrollable over-run, closed doors whose overly precipitous closing testifies to an anxiety over a very real opening.

Consider, for example, Montesquieu's *The Spirit of Laws*.[9] Montesquieu would like there to be only three kinds of government, and each one has its particular form of corruption. Yet the corruption of republical democracy is not so much an external accident or evil, as an indicator of the possibility within liberal civil society of the dissemination of power beyond the bounds set by liberalism toward a fourth form of government: 'The principle of democracy is corrupted not only when the spirit of equality is extinct, but likewise when they fall into a spirit of extreme equality, and when each citizen would fain be upon a level with those whom he has chosen to command him. Then the people, incapable of bearing the very power they have delegated, want to manage everything themselves . . . This license will soon become general . . . Wives, children slaves will shake off all subjection. No longer will there be any such thing as manners, order, or virtue'. Montesquieu provides an accurate description of what would occur if the founding principles of liberalism were allowed to become indefinitely displaceable, if the displacement that founds them were not curtailed by law, custom, or force. Equality, rather than being a right to be restrained and limited by law ('In the state of nature, all men are born equal, but they cannot continue in this equality. Society makes them lose it, and they recover it only by the protection of laws' [p. 111]), would become an unrestrainable force, a right to be claimed by all. Like Hobbes and Locke before him, Montesquieu recognizes the danger of displacement. Rights transferred to a sovereign can be transferred back; rights transferred from nature to propertied males can be assumed by 'wives, children, slaves'.

Fittingly, one of the first liberal theorists to use the principle of the transferability of rights beyond the bounds set by the classic liberal theorists was a feminist – Mary Wollstonecraft. In *A Vindication of the Rights of Woman*, she writes: 'Let woman share the rights, and she will emulate the virtues of man'.[10] Patriarchal hegemony is not merely a secondary characteristic of liberalism, however; in its first theoretical formulations, liberal doctrine is essentially male. Property right depends on the ability to know who owns what and who inherits what. The transferability of property is controlled by the name of the father passed to the son. Patriarchy is thus crucial to the preservation of property, the very basis of liberal civil society. The patronymic is the sign of the male essence of liberalism. But like other markers of propriety, control, or restraint in liberalism, it testifies to a danger of unlimited displacement, even as it defends against it. Property must be transferred, that is, preserved, if liberal civil society is to survive, but what assures survival also carries the possibility of annulment. The patronymic restrains but simultaneously indicates the reality of the possible uncontrollable transfer of property.

Wollstonecraft's promotion of the transferability of rights from men to women therefore concerns more than the mere broadening of civic freedoms. It touches the heart of liberalism's commitment to property right and to the political economic power of property-owning males. John Stuart Mill provides liberalism's answer to this challenge by acknowledging women's rights in principle while calling for their non-exercise in practice. Woman is 'entitled to choose her pursuits . . . entitled to exert the share of influence on all human concerns which belongs to an individual opinion, whether she attempted actual participation in them or not'.[11] The argument follows the outlines of liberalism's justification of property. Property is an abstract, formal right, and as such it is universal. But it can never be universal as a concrete and substantive reality. The form of the universal principle is itself a way of protecting against the effects of the real non-universality of property because it situates right on the level of formal abstraction. Similarly, women are accorded rights in principle, but in practice, Mill argues, their first duties are in the home. In these liberal arguments, a tautology of power is at work. For as the abstract and theoretical (or meta-practical) right to property suggests, the attitude of abstract principle that bestows yet withdraws rights from women is, according to Mill, due to a form of thinking – abstraction – with which men, more than women, are endowed.

Along with feminism, the other movement that promotes a displacement of rights beyond the bounds established by the founding fathers of liberalism is socialism. Rights are first demanded for the poor, then for workers and other dispossessed people. Paine makes social welfare a right: 'This support [for the poor and the elderly] . . . is not of the nature of a charity, but of a right'.[12] Marx would eventually turn Locke's principle of property right (that it is determined by labour) against liberalism and expand the idea of democracy to include not only political but also economic institutions. Like the liberal response to feminism, the response to socialism tends to follow rationalist lines that place logic over rhetoric, abstract or formal theory over concrete or substantive practice. The material claims of rhetorical analogy (if you own, so should we) are denied by the ideal calculi of mathematical efficiency. The formal equilibrium of the market, predicated on the rational choices of individuals, is rational, according to liberal theorists, while state or social planning is irrational and inefficient. And where the calculus fails, the formal universalist rationality of state power expressed in law will assure harmony. Logic ceases to be descriptive and becomes prescriptive.

Yet these negative moves testify to something against which they are reacting. That threat is the possibility that the force of displacement inherent in liberalism from the outset might give rise to a different social arrangement, one predicated not on a logic of identity (society = nature, capitalist social relations = scientific laws), but on the very rhetoric of displacement that lies behind or under (which metaphor is appropriate?) that logic. Generally, that threat is expressed in theories that emphasize the material and rhetorical dimensions that liberal universals and the liberal calculus of efficiency are designed to overlook or suppress. That materiality or rhetoricity necessarily appears irrational from the point of view of liberal logic, with its emphasis on self-evident principles of truth that are akin to natural or scientific laws and that transcend rhetoric. In the marxist tradition, the materialist perspective emphasizes the concrete inequalities of liberal civil society that its ideals of freedom and harmony either conceal or justify ideologically. In the nietzschean tradition of cognitive criticism, the perpsective is more rhetorical, emphasizing the processes of analogy, contrast, differentiation, condensation, and substitution that give rise to the apparently logical or rational categories of liberal theory (the individual as the original social agent, the state as the representation of the whole, the market as the objective ordering of preferences, and so on). Both point toward the possibility of a social form that would be predicated on the displaceability of the fundamental social categories of liberalism – the individual, rights, the market, property, and political sovereignty – and on the recognition of the material rhetoricity of all of these categories.

The rhetorical critique of liberalism is as essential as the materialist one. It points out the materiality of liberal theory, its necessary imbrication in concrete word forms that shape the image of the world liberal thinking projects and in fact constructs. If liberalism has been founded on a repression of materiality in favour of abstract rational ideals (thus emphasizing formal equality of access to property rather than substantive equality of ownership), it has no less been founded on a repression of rhetoric, of the concrete forms or styles of language in which its ideas are represented and constituted. If an emphasis on materiality undermines liberal pretensions, so also does an emphasis on rhetoric, for it draws out the mechanics of construction that go into the making of liberal concepts that only seem to be detached from the concrete historical world.

As the shift to a materialist understanding of liberal society brings with it a deconstruction of the self-evidence of the founding institutions of liberalism (property and sovereignty), so also a rhetorical understanding of liberal theory brings with it a deconstruction of the self-evidence of the justifications for those institutions. As liberalism cannot acknowledge the material reality of labour, the fact that all its ideals of property and freedom depend on the neo-feudal oppression of a majority for the enrichment of a minority, so also it cannot acknowledge the materiality of rhetoric, the fact that all its legitimating theories depend on linguistic forms (analogy, for example) that cannot be acknowledged without disqualifying the theories.

Liberalism does not choose to repress rhetoric; it cannot afford to acknowledge it and still preserve its institutions. For rhetoric not only implies the necessity of acknowledging materiality in a way that liberal thinkers must not do, it also entails a displaceability of inherent meanings that liberal theory cannot sacrifice – the inherent meaning of the individual as locus of free economic will unaccountable to communal concerns, of the institution of property as an object assignable to a single subject, of rights claims specific to individuals or groups that are not shaped by social structure, and so on. Logic must be chosen over rhetoric in legitimating liberalism because logic is the rhetorical mode appropriate to a universalist rationality of the sort that permitted liberals to overthrow feudal particularism. But logic also follows rules of necessity that limit its implications, and it permits liberal ideology to remain purely formal while withstanding the implications of the contingencies of substance.

In rhetoric, on the other hand, substantive concerns prevail over merely formal ones. A rhetorical plea is usually for some specific item of justice or is against some concrete injustice. A trope is a particular image, not a general idea, or a form rather than a content. But equally, rhetoric is governed by no rule of necessity; its implications cannot be limited by a principle of causal accountability. Its possible connections are random and open, its principle of operation the imagination. Nothing has an inherent meaning that is not subject to displacement or substitution by another or condensation with yet another. The openness of permutations and combinations is what matters, not the need to adhere to forms of procedure whose rules are established, as in logic, or to honour an already existing world immune to imaginative reformulation, the computation of whose existing, self-reinforcing rules is the charge of reason.

Like the emphasis on materiality in marxism, then, the emphasis on rhetoric in the cognitive deconstruction critique of liberalism leads to the unfolding within liberalism of a principle of democratic movement that pushes against the boundaries of liberalism. This means, more concretely, that things deemed external from the perspective of liberal identity become part of social debate. Background assumptions, contexts, and structures become foregrounded in the consideration of putatively individual concerns. Logical rational calculi, which tend to ignore history, are supplemented by narratives that lend context to social decisions. One can no longer calculate the efficency of wages and prices without telling the story of the structure of class power that make such seemingly rational calculations into exercises of force against subordinated groups. One can no longer try to settle the issue of the hiring of blacks and women instead of white males for scarce jobs without addressing the contextual structures that make jobs scarce as an integral part of the identity of the issue of rights. Like materiality, which anchors formal logic in concrete concerns, rhetoric expands the range of what liberalism's logic of identity must limit as the proper boundaries of such issues. That expansion is not merely discursive or theoretical; it implies that the issues themselves, the substance, is changed by choosing the route of a different rhetoric, one that, for example, takes context, the contiguous connections between things, into account. If logic drew boundaries around things that gave them an identity akin to that bestowed by nature, which was supposedly inherent to itself, rhetoric works to overrun those bound-aries, mak-ing connections that disallow rigorously defined or deter-mined identities.

The obvious rhetorical analogy to make would be that the logic of identity resembles the logic of capitalist individualism with its bound-aried notions of right and property, while rhetoric with its emphasis on the displaceability of identity in relations, connections, and contexts from which it cannot be subtracted is more like the logic of socialism. The truth may lie in between, since rational universals, at least when held responsible to materiality and rhetoric, are essential to the socialist project. Simply because liberal theorists misused them and refused to permit them to be materialized does not mean they are illegitimate.

I will conclude with an example from the liberal tradition that exemplifies what I have just described. Darwin describes a world of necessary contextual relations and responsibilities where one party's right is mediated by collective needs and where the doctrine of logical identity is supplemented by practical systemic relations and connections, yet he analogizes from liberal theory to natural science and thus displaces the evidence of these rhetorical connections and relations in nature with an interpretive grid that declares decisively in favour of liberal rationalist principles of individuality and identity. This is evident in his metaphors of competition, rank, entitlement, individuality, profit, subordination, and so on, as well as in his own account of how he arrived at his conclusions: 'This is the doctrine of Malthus, applied to the whole animal and vegetable kingdoms'.[13]

Darwin describes natural life as a liberal-capitalist economy where the strong competitors survive. In this way, rank and order are assured; a kind of smithian harmony results from the general pursuit of self-interest: 'All those exquisite adaptations of one part of the organization to another part . . . follow from the struggle for life' (pp. 75–6). Darwin chooses to emphasize competition between individuals, but at a number of points in the text his description indicates a certain undecidability between individual competition and structural or systematic inter-relations. What he describes could just as easily be interpreted structurally, relationally, contextually, or differentially as an eco-system where the different parts necessarily relate to, depend on, and support each other. Yet he consistently chooses the liberal interpretive grip, describing possibly systemic processes in liberal individualist terms: 'Thus I can understand how a flower and a bee might slowly become, either simultaneously or one after the other, modified and adapted to each other in the most perfect manner, by the continued preservation of all the individuals which presented slight deviations of structure mutually favourable to each other . . . Battle within battle must be continually recurring with varying success; and yet in the long-run the forces are so nicely balanced, that the face of nature remains for long periods of time uniform, though assuredly the merest trifle would give the victory to one organic being over another' (pp. 104, 85).

The most telling example of his decisive interpretation of something which his own observations seem to indicate is undecidable is the metaphor of the tree that closes the chapter on natural selection: 'As buds give rise by growth to fresh buds, and these, if vigorous, branch out and overtop on all sides many a feebler branch, so by generation I believe it has been with the great Tree of Life, which fills with its dead and broken branches the crust of the earth, and covers the surface with its ever-branching and beautiful ramifications' (p. 137). Darwin privileges those fresh buds, which, through good fortune and positioning, happen to thrive. By focusing on these stronger and more 'competitive' individuals, he downplays the fact that a tree is an aggregational and relational system in which parts lend each other support. The 'feebler branch' in the liberal interpretative scheme seems subordinate, but from a more relational or contextual point of view, the fresh buds can be said to depend on it. Its deprivation is their gain.

The example of Darwin is symptomatic of liberal thinking in general in that it describes the principle of displacement, yet it chooses to declare in favour of a logic of individual identity and a logic of rational universality that permits it to overlook both the communitarian dimensions of nature and the representational or projective power of its own rhetoric. For if Darwin had attempted to integrate the materiality of his own discourse and the constraints of his own frame of reference to his analysis, he would have been obliged to acknowledge the power of a rhetoric of connection at odds with the logic of identity that dominates his conclusions. And he would have been obliged to admit one significant exception to the so-called general rule he was adumbrating – his own species, which allows weak-budded scholars like himself to survive, despite the little they contribute to the logic of survival.

8 The Law of the Subject

Post-structuralism is sometimes described as a critique of the humanist subject, the 'man' created by the Renaissance in a post-feudal, republican mercantile era and nurtured to the full extent of his powers in the era of capitalist liberalism. According to liberal humanism, the self comes into being independently of the social grounds in which it is located. In this conception, the way the self's categories and word schemes are given to it by the culture is secondary to its psychological and political essence, an ideational and moral capacity that grounds man's freedom of thought and action. The languages, taxonomies, and images of the mind are derivative features of a more primordial subjective substance. They are appended to free thought and action, but they in no way are constitutive of that rationality and freedom.

The post-structuralist argument is that the subject is constituted through the intermediary of social and cultural discourses. The subject, rather than being the originator of the social institutions and the languages in which it moves, is seen instead as the product or effect of those institutions and languages. The theory thus offers a 'post-liberal' account of the self. The concepts of the freudian, the nietzschean, and the marxian unconscious are important to this reformulation. According to the freudian account (transposed into structuralism by Lacan), the ego is only a marginal and derivative (and generally neurotic) feature of the mind. Unconscious forces, mostly libidinal and instinctual, drive the mind as much as the seemingly self-directing activities of rational consciousness. Much of what happens in human life is a symptom or effect of unconscious processes. Lacan makes the freudian account structuralist by linking it to language. The subject emerges as an apparently independent being by entering the symbolic order, that realm of social rules, rhetorical forms, and language structures that gives shape to all of our actions. Consequently, the subject who thinks of itself as independent or free is operating within the realm of imaginary ego identity, a false consciousness structurally alienated from its unconscious essence. According to the nietzschean account (which is featured most prominently in the work of Foucault and Derrida), the unconscious does not have to do so much with libido as with language and rhetoric. Our thinking is shaped by operations of language that create appearances of identity in the world and in the self. The very idea that there is an 'I' that speaks, for

149

example, is a delusion created by discourse. Behind that 'I' stand a
multiplicity of rhetorical processes and discourse formations, as a well
of desires and forces. According to the marxian account (represented
in post-structuralism by the work of Althusser and Bourdieu), the self
is the effect of class structures. All of our seemingly independent
feelings and actions are shaped by our social positions. What we are
capable of being is not a matter of freedom; it is rather a range
determined by the axioms of our placement in the distribution of social
power. The idea of the subject is simply an ideological construct
designed to obfuscate the structural differentiations and reproductive
processes of a class society. When we act most freely and most
unreflectingly or spontaneously, we act most ideologically because we
merely reaffirm the marks of distinction that situate us as class specific
and determined subjects.

The post-structuralist critique of the subject has a dual impact on
liberal legal theory. It removes certain grounds – the concept of the
individual most notably – that lie at the root both of the conservation of
inequality and of the struggle against it, but it also provides the terms
for an alternative legal order. More particularly, the critique of the
subject has a negative effect on the philosophical basis of rights while
at the same time providing a means of overcoming the limitations of
liberal rights theory.

Rights in liberal legal theory are borne by subjects that are self-
identical. Rights assert the existence of boundaries around self-
identity that cannot be crossed either by the state or by others. Yet
rights theory is paradoxical in liberalism. While the doctrine has the
clear ideological function of sanctifying the private accumulation of
social wealth, it also provides instruments of struggle for those who
suffer the negative consequences of liberal capitalism – claims against
the state for welfare, demands for the empowerment of workers as the
right to unionize, actions against corporations for negligent harm,
assertions of the right to equal treatment, and so on. While those
actions cannot constitute a different institutional reality from the
existing one because they derive their logic from the institutions
against which they contend, they nevertheless are levers that imply a
radical alternative to liberalism within liberalism. There is no right to
establish a socialist economy in the United States, for example,
because the doctrine of rights is welded to the claims of property
ownership and to an individualist model of the social good, but the
doctrine of rights nonetheless implies the possibility of the assignment
of powers to workers that point toward socialism. Consequently, there

are clear limits on how far rights can be expanded within the institutional context that supplies rights claims with legitimacy; but this does not mean that the doctrine of rights does not harbour a certain deconstructive potential. While it operates within clear structural constraints, it also gives rise to possibilities that exceed those limitations in ways that offer openings toward an alternative structuration of society.[1]

The concept of the subject in liberal social theory, the basis of all rights claims, is inseparable from the institution of property. The right to property in liberal capitalism grew historically in conjunction with the right to personhood. Encroachments on speech and thought were enjoined as much as encroachments on property by the initial formulations of the liberal doctrine of rights, and it is difficult to separate the two either theoretically or historically.[2] The two belong to the same discursive system in that each exists differentially in relation to the other, and each provides the other with legitimation by supplying it with the metaphor that grounds its authority.

The metaphor of property ownership defines the right of personhood and therefore all other rights, while the metaphor of personhood provides a ground for the concept of property. Property defines personhood in that the rights not to be harmed, or to obtain certain provisions, or to act independently without constraint are all constructed around the image of self-ownerhsip. One owns one's self, and no one else shall determine how one disposes of one's self. No one shall, as it were, transgress the boundaries on one's subjective property. By catachresis, the substitution of the name of one thing for another (leg for table support, for example), rights come into being as the claim to ownership of one's thoughts and one's actions, and out of these claims emerge the legal doctrines that protect civil liberties, guarantee one against negligent harm, assure the keeping of contractual promises, and so on.[3]

And the catachresis is reversible; property as a legal concept is constructed upon the metaphor of the person or subject. To own something is to lay claim to it as part of one's self-identity. Ownership presupposes an owner, and there can be no ownership without a subject who owns. Property is sacred because it is an extension of the self. What preserves property through time and changes in space is the self-identity of the person (and this is particularly clear in corporate ownership where the fiction of a person must be transferred onto the corporation in order for it to function as an owner).[4] But this putative self-identity itself rests on the metaphor of property.

At the root of liberal theory, according to post-structuralism, therefore, is not a reality whose truth needs to be tested or disproven, but instead a rather metaphoric analogy that does not provide access to any extra-rhetorical ground of validation. Such metaphors are not the 'cause' of capitalism, of course, but they are a very important part of the socio-cultural movement initiated in the Renaissance that enabled the development of capitalism. Commercial trade was essential to the rediscovery of lost Greek and Roman texts and to their translation, and those texts (centrally, the codes of Justinian, which gave post-medieval Europe the Stoic idea of an equality of personal freedom) helped produce the humanist and liberal social theories that supply the arguments for and the justifications of individualist capitalism, with its emphasis on secular or 'humane' as opposed to sacred authority. Behind the liberal doctrines of the right to trade freely or to own privately or to determine political institutions lies the humanist invention of the subject conceived as a boundaried whole, hermetically sealed and appropriative, and protected from state authority as well as from encroachments from other freely operating subjects. That invention operated as certain figures or tropes, as a deployment of a certain discourse designed to secure desired powers and privileges against the entrenched authority of feudal investiture.

Liberal capitalism is in the best sense of the term an aesthetic invention operating under the guise of social rationality. Its constitutive mechanism is little different from the one that constructs literary meaning. It should not be surprising then that Kant, the great liberal theorist of abstract property right (that is, the capacity to own in the absence of the empirical object, through a concept or contemplatively, as it were), should designate abstract ownership as a capacity of Reason (*Verstand*), which is also the mental apparatus charged with the highest attainments of aesthetic contemplation. Indeed, *The Critique of Pure Ownership* could easily have been the title of Kant's unwritten fourth critique.[5] All of this is not to say that the regime of liberal property right is either frivolous or beautiful. (It is frivolous, if by that we mean without a necessary ground or reason.) Liberal legality purports to replace force with objective rules that function independently of subjective will and are rationally derived. But each of its fundamental principles – personhood and property – must sacrifice its claim to objective rationality at the very point where it gains credence for itself through a metaphoric comparison with the other term or principle. Each one's claim depends on a metaphoric relationship to the other term. But the claim to rationality must assume that the other term is not metaphoric. The term to which property, for example, is compared must be a ground of truth, not another metaphor. Each metaphoric relation (person is like property; property is a part of person) requires a non-metaphoric term of comparison, but the other term can only appear to be non-metaphoric by comparing itself with the first term. The legitimacy of the liberal concept of a private, non-social, and 'free' subjectivity presupposes a 'reality' of property ownership that in its turn can only legitimate itself by claiming that private subjectivity is a substance outside rhetoric.

The primary contribution of post-structuralism to a critique of the liberal doctrine of subjectivity and rights is the idea that the self is not, as liberalism would have it, a 'proper' interiority sealed off from an exteriority of social and cultural discourse. It is instead constituted as a complex of differential boundary relations where the internal subjective world and the external social world are tied together in a way that precludes a clean demarcation of the two. Along those differential boundaries, things thought to be external to the self are shown to in fact be internalized components of self-identity (relations to others, cultural representations, institutional conventions, symbolic orders, social codes, and so forth). Implied in this reconceptualization is an expansion of the subject into social relations and cultural representations that can no longer be thought to be merely contingent and external features of personal life. And with this reconceptualization comes as well a necessary refiguration of the right of property.

The post-structuralist concept of subjectivity has a psychological, an economic, and a political dimension. It assumes that a person is always at least two people, in the sense that one internalizes relations to others as one grows and that one's mature life is determined by replications and projections of those internalized intersubjective relations. The concept of internalized relations in subject formation also includes the idea that representations, taken from the culture, operate to establish self boundaries. The capacity to represent the world, which is founded on the ability to represent caretakers in their absence, places the world at an objective distance, thereby establishing a boundary of subjectivity. What is taken to be secondary in relation to a more primary and therefore authoritative subjective foundation for social action is in fact a primary constituent of that interiority. There is no such thing as a 'proper' or self-identical individual in the liberal sense; the person is always in relation, always to some degree other within itself.

The post-structuralist concept also points to the necessary interconnectedness of economic participants, even under the ideological regime of individual freedom, and the unavoidable interdependence of political agents in any social arrangement. The deconstruction of the individualist model of subjectivity has the political value of proving that there can be no concept of non-relational action within civil society. Political life especially consists of a pooling of political resources, a collecting together to attain certain ends. Even so supposedly subjective an act as voting has value only in numbers. And government by individualist premises, against the will of the social collective, is even to liberalism a contradiction. Similarly, there can be no properly self-identical pursuit and accumulation of property that is not also differential and boundary fluid. The very concept of market exchange, the centrepiece of liberal economics, assumes that one gets from others more than one gives. To own, therefore, is to be constitutively other, to contain others and what they have to offer within oneself. Self-identity defined as the right to ownership is always the extraction of the other, the appropriation of alterity to the self.

This is especially true of supposedly private property, which is in fact nothing more than the bringing together of many small pieces of other people's property into one piece of one's own. Private property is always heterotopic and differential in that it is a collecting together, an agglomeration, of what others own or used to own. Thus, so-called 'free' ownership under the liberal regime is in fact already social or communal. If a public trust were to pool communal resources in the same way, the same end would be achieved of creating economic power sufficient to carry out large, meta-individual projects. And indeed, this is what liberal economics accomplishes, but it does so for individuals. It permits the transindividual to be realized, but it places power over it in non-communal hands. Thus, as with psychology and politics, liberal economics is two contradictory things at once – the institutionalization of individualism and the prefiguration within those institutions of larger, more relational, communal possibilities.

Something similar occurs when one considers the liberal doctrine of rationality that comes into being with the concept of the 'free' subject and that legitimates liberal political and economic institutions.

Liberal social life and liberal legal rationality are constitutively intertwined. The self-identical liberal subject, the capitalist pursuing his interest and holding his property regardless of social effects and relational origins, is mirrored by the self-identical and independent authority of the liberal ideal of truth or by the authoritative and substitutive power of the republican representative, the legislative sovereign who originates law in positivist thinking. That truth and that political sovereignty is in each case an authoritative instance that is not differential or relational, not solicited or called forth by a substantive situation or material context radically at odds with its identitarian form, and not determined by rhetoric or the discursive-conceptual stage on which it is enacted. It is truth and sovereignty precisely to the extent that its interiority is shielded from all of these things.

If concept of differential boundary relations replaces the individual as the primary category of social life in the transcendence of liberalism, the workings of rhetoric and figuration replace the liberal concept of a self-evident truth or an authoritative sovereignty that transcends discursive determination, material context, and social history. Rhetoric names the textures of relation that make external situations and contexts internal to the truth of law. What this means is that a liberal legal rule such as all people stand equally before the law and are entitled to equal protection should be understood not as the property of a free subject or as a self-evident truth or as an expression of a sovereign authority of law. Rather, it is one element in a discursive field that includes social institutions. It would not need to be true if certain institutions and practices did not exist, making it necessary or calling it forth as a guarantee against them. This implied context is as much a part of the rule as the supposedly rational or internal principle of equality. In addition, each term of the idea implies a history and a differential value system. 'Equal' implies that unequal treatment is a real possibility in this particular social system, unless equality is guaranteed by law. 'Protection' similarly insinuates that danger exists against which protection is necessary. 'Before' suggests that subjects or citizens stand in a subordinate relation according to this spatial metaphor to the legal institution. And finally, 'the law' implies that law is separate and autonomous, an authority outside the field of social struggle implied in all the other words of the phrase. Each one of the elements of the standard of equal treatment is constituted discursively, differentially, or relationally; that is, its identity is the result of evocations, solicitations, productions, and determinations arising from the institutional context of the society and from the interrelation of the terms. And this legal rule can also be situated within a range of possible legal formulations that imply or summon forth other institutional or social contexts or realities, ones in which protection would not have to be guaranteed because there is no danger, no institutional or structural possibility of harm. In such contexts, equal would mean a substantive equality rather than a formal legal one, with the result that such formal guarantees would not need to be applied to people of unequal social substance, and the law would create a situation in which people would not have to stand before it as an authority but would constitute it as the embodiment of their agreements democratically arrived at under conditions of actual material equality.

The shift to rhetoric and discourse in understanding liberalism and in plotting its transcendence means that liberal concepts are no longer thought of as truths whose authority is self-evident or as principles (property) which must be guaranteed by legitimate sovereignty. Those concepts must be seen as discursive effects that are created through rhetorical means – analogy, parallel, metonymy, metaphor, and so on. Equal protection before the law exists because it is analogous to the kind of equal guarantees commercial contracts must guarantee if liberal capitalism is to work properly. And the alternative values that a post-liberal discourse proposes are themselves conceived materially as rhetorical constructs that posit and create alternative institutional possibilities. Rather than stand 'before' the law, people will stand 'in' the law. What this means is that the new values cannot be thought of as formal ideals like freedom that are dissociated from their material settings, their substantive contexts, their discursive relations, and their rhetorical formulations. By shifting focus to the discursive mechanisms that create social meaning, one also shifts to the necessary material underpinnings of those meanings. And this will mean that no standard like equal treatment can be isolated from the material and institutional setting or context of structural unequal treatment that calls it forth. Equal treatment in law will be inseparable from the legislation of material equality. Just as the ideas are indissociable from their discursive webs of relation, the institution itself will be inseparable from the material relations in which it exists.

The critique of the liberal subject displays the differential or discursive character of all the categories of liberalism. What is seen as projecting itself beyond liberalism is something that already inhabits liberalism as its own excluded yet contained other. It is something that is banished from liberalism because it threatens it but that is nevertheless internal to its system. That other is the process of differentiation whose linguistic embodiment is the connective devices of rhetoric, which, like its companion term democracy as seen from the point of view of liberalism, is represented as a threatening dispersion, the potential that fixed rules and authoritative laws will lose their meaning. What is really feared, of course, is that the pretence of self-evident truth or of sovereign authority by liberalism will be exposed as itself an act of rhetoric, just as what is feared from the threat of democracy is really that it will expose liberalism to be an unnecessary minoritarian form of republican rule. What rhetoric always implies is that other formulations are possible, other ways of arranging both the language of so-called self-evident truth and the supposed legitimate authority of political sovereignty. And what is perhaps most threatening is that if rhetoric and discourse describe what such truth is really like, then such truth is differential and contextual, an undecidable term situated at the crossing between conceptual discourse and social world – everything, in other words, that liberalism, in its adherence to values of identity, propriety, reason and authority, claims such truth is not.

A major consequence of the post-structuralist critique of the subject, therefore, is to set the stage for another social reality, which is to say, another discursive construction. The important terms of that critique are that the subject be replaced with a concept of differential boundary relations between self and context, and that the ideal of self-evident truth or sovereign authority give way to a notion of rhetorical construction and discursive figuration. These terms also supply the psychological, ethical, political, and economic principles of the alternative society projected from within liberalism. The liberal subject is already other than itself, given over to 'object-relations' which situate it as a nexus of emotional ties, psychological dependencies, and internalized representations. The liberal ideal of property right is already a systematic denial of the interrelational character of social wealth, the fact that appropriation is necessarily also an immediate expropriation. And the liberal ideal of political rights is already an acknowledgment of the fact that any claim to a right presupposes the denial of it by the institutional set-up of the society; rights are always transsubjective in the sense that they are elicited, produced, and sustained by situations and contexts that structurally threaten what rights seek to assure.

I will now review the post-structuralist critique of the subject more specifically in relation to the liberal doctrine of rights. I will then suggest some ways in which it generates a positive political theory of post-liberal rights.

Rhetorical aesthetics, like democracy, has always been either banished or denigrated by political authority grounded in instances of transcendence or authority like the subject because both aesthetics and democracy suggest the malleability of supposedly rationally grounded social institutions. This prejudice runs through so-called 'mainstream' discourse, which divides the world between 'hard' or scientific-realistic thought, which replicates the founding assumptions of the social system by confining knowledge to a computation of empirically perceivable facts, and 'soft' or imaginative literary thinking, which generally more democratically questions such assumptions. A post-structuralist or deconstructive argument usually proceeds by temporarily assuming the lower pole of such oppositions. I will therefore begin with literature and in particular with that literary mode that became dominant, either in fictional or documentary form, at the same time (the late seventeenth century) as the liberal ideal of personhood – autobiography. It is around the issues raised by literary critics' attempts to ground a 'theory' of autobiography that the post-structuralist critique of the subject can be elaborated.

Autobiography would seem at first glance to be a genre where subjective self-identity could be taken for granted. Indeed, there the self-evidence of personhood would seem to be established without question once and for all. An examination of a particularly liberal attempt to establish these truths suggests other conclusions. Phillipe Lejeune's *The Autobiographical Pact*[6] purports to provide a general theory of autobiography that would dispel any doubts or differences regarding the identity of the genre. This attempt at generic policing is based on certain assumptions regarding personal identity that are questionable, but eminently liberal, in that they take property for granted as an effaced metaphor defining personhood.

Lejeune defines autobiography as a more authentic genre than fiction because the identity and reality of the author of an autobiography can be verified and validated. The mark of authenticity is the proper name on the book, and it is supported by two social institutions – civil law and the publication contract. The author enters into a 'referential pact' with the reader guaranteeing that he will tell the truth, and this is substantiated by civil laws that guarantee that he is who he claims to be. The 'distinctive trait', the marker of generic identity, that distinguishes autobiography from fiction is, then, the authenticity of reference assured by the proper name.

But is the structure of writing in autobiography different from that in fiction? The referent of fiction seems absent; it cannot, like the writer of autobiography, be called forth in its presence to give evidence for the truth of fictional writing. But the referent of autobiography is in some regards very similar to the referent of fiction, which is ideal and conventional, not real. Even if the autobiographical writer stepped forward and gave evidence, that would simply be spoken evidence – another text as well as another set of representations. That presence would always somehow be mediated by language. Moreover, there is nothing in autobiographical writing that guarantees that it might not be read as fiction. Its veracity can only be ultimately guaranteed by law, the law that records the author's name in the record books. And such laws are themselves merely conventions, acts of rhetoric and representation. Where is the presence?

The proper name is so crucial to autobiography because it puts a mark of private ownership on a life. Without the name, Lejeune asks, how would one know it was 'my life'? Just so. One might not. The proper name establishes a boundary that excludes others and what is improper in general, but this suggests that the proper name can only arise in a field that includes as one of its possibilities a general anonymity in which no 'own' can be known. The possibility always exists that the removal of the proper name would render the subject of autobiography property-less. No one would know it was 'my' life. Anonymity or impropriety can thus be said to exist in a state of internal exclusion within the proper or self-identical in general.

The removal of the proper name may have so devastating an effect on proper self-identity because the constituents of the subject are the same for all and therefore equally, potentially anonymous for all. But if such anonymity is possible without a mere conventional tag of ownership like a proper name, then anonymity, the possibility of a radical non-identity of the subject, is not an accident, a secondary possibility attached to a more primary identity. It is rather the condition of such identity, the cloth from which its shape is cut. What this means is that the proper name is not really proper at all, in the sense that it does not name accurately what the subject really is. It is an improper name for the impropriety or non-self-identity that threatens to overwhelm subjectivity if the proper name is removed.

Is it really true then that there is an identity of an autobiographical subject? The possibility that its experiences could belong to anyone seems to trouble this assumption. But so does the fact that civil law is necessary to make certain this does not happen. The necessity of law implies that the constituents of subjective identity are external to that identity. Class, language, culture, legal system, and so on – the power of all of these instances is signalled by Lejeune's need to rely on the civil code as the ultimate guarantor of autobiographical identity and truth. What this means is that an autobiography can never be fully about what a life is really about; that is, it can never cover in their entirety all the impersonal constituents that make up the identity of a life.

This conclusion implies that an autobiographer cannot help but not tell the truth. His 'authentic reference' or meaning is a deformation of the impersonal forces and determinants of subjectivity. The immediacy of the subject is derived in relation to an impersonal historical and social field. Like writing, which can never be more primordial than the space on which it is deployed, autobiographic identity is inscribed on a space that is more primordial than its seemingly unmediated originality. Thus, the immediacy of the subject, the consciousness that gives it the sense of being primary and self-identical, is itself secondary and mediated. The subject's mode of thought, its language, its bodily behaviour – all are effects of histories none of which can be made available to the kind of immediate presence which authentic reference requires. The subject is a repository of effects whose causes are unavailable except through the mediation of other non-autobiographical discourses. Its identity is produced and simultaneously dislocated by the 'already there' of the historical field. Lejeune's entire undertaking represents a desire to foreclose this 'truth' of non-identity with a model of truth as self-identity. But what the deconstructive critique of this project suggests is that the seemingly private subject of autobiography is always public – constitutively opened out onto a socio-historical space that it can never fully possess as its 'own'.

This critique adds two things to discussions of the politics of rights. First, it implies that because the 'interiority' of subjective rights and the 'exteriority' of institutional contexts are indissociable, rights politics necessarily and logically lead to a politics of contextual institutional reconstruction. Second, the doctrine of formal rights in liberalism must be replaced with a substantive doctrine of exercisable rights. This second project requires a reformulation of the liberal concept of the subject that deconstructs the ideal of interiority that grounds it.

The critique of the subject suggests that the boundary demarcating psychological inside from institutional or interpersonal outside is a false one. The doctrine of rights assumes such a boundary demarcating an interiority where rights exist from an exteriority (the state, corporations, other people) that threatens them. The defensive and therefore differential character of rights means that every claim to a right posits an institutional reality that potentially negates the interest that right attempts to secure; otherwise, there would be no need to claim a right. Every claim to the right of free speech presupposes the institutionalized reality of forces that move to deprive people of the ability to exercise that freedom. Thus, rights, which seem to be grounded in an ideal of interiority and identity, a boundaried self whose integrity is taken for granted, are simultaneously the confirmation of institutional exteriorities that belie the ideal. The ideal of interiority simultaneously points toward a potentially negative exteriority that constitutes the affirmation of interiority by eliciting or calling it forth as a remedial response.

This, of course, puts in question a crucial value of the ideology of liberalism, which claims that liberal institutions (government, the market) operate according to the law of the subject, of respect for its identity as articulated in the doctrine of rights. It also deprives that ideal of interiority of its legitimacy as something sealed off from external institutions, since the 'interior' individual rights claim and the 'exterior' institutional denial are part of the same discursive or relational system. Attention is thereby also shifted away from rights toward institutions. The claim to a right is always an institutional claim, for even when it is a claim against another person, it is directed against the institutional set-up of society that is so constituted as to permit, even to promote the crossing of personal boundaries – economically, physically, politically, sexually, and so on. Rights therefore are not so much markers of identity or personhood as tokens of defence against the institutions (markets, property ownership, patriarchy, republican government, and the like) whose existence is sanctioned by the ideology of personhood.

Rights are also by virtue of this critique no longer dissociable from their exercise. Liberalism is distinguished by its claim that rights are internal properties of a subject that do not need to be exercised in order to exist. They are 'trumps' held in reserve. So the right to own property is not in liberalism the necessary right to actualize or exercise that right. But privately possessed rights vary according to their context and material situation, both of which determine whether rights will be exercisable. And these variations, rather than being secondary in relation to the primary substance of self-identity, affect the character of that identity in its very constitution.

The point of the analysis of the anonymous background of subjectivity, the improper ground of personal propriety or identity, in the theory of autobiography was to suggest that personal boundaries are always artificial and variable constructs, the results of conventional stabilizations promoted by the institutional framework of a social regime like liberalism. One's right as a corporate executive to own large quantities of property is sanctioned by an entire institutional set-up that is entirely external to the subjective interiority that grounds that right; it is no more a 'personal' right than the right to die of natural causes. Conversely, one's right as a black single mother on welfare or state support for one's children in the form of food stamps and housing for the homeless is shaped by an insitutional context that denies greater forms of security on a universal basis. The personal identity of the white male corporate executive, as of the black mother on welfare, is not something freely chosen or subjectively originated. It is externally given and elicited; the psychological attitudes of each subject position are scripted elsewhere.

Along with being a private agent whose thoughts are invisible to others, each subject is also institutionally or externally constituted, and the boundaries of its 'identity' are drawn as a line of institutional forces. What this means is that the boundaries of each subject contract or expand according to differences in institutional context. The white executive subject is expansive; it can lay claim as a right to any number of institutional possessions that widen its possibilities of action and expression, thus widening the boundaries of its identity and the range of its exercisable rights. The black woman subject has contracted boundaries; she can lay claim to many fewer exercisable rights, and consequently, her identity is abridged in comparison to that of the executive.

One of the conundrums of liberalism is that it is precisely the right to property, carried to an extreme in corporate ownership, the private accumulation of capital, and the claim on political power resulting from such ownership and such accumulation, that is most responsible for institutional curtailments of the rights of person. Property and person ultimately contradict each other, for the right to property, sanctioned by the metaphor of a subjective personhood whose identity encompasses even one's instruments, effects, or possessions, cannot be balanced with rights of person which are assumed to be exercisable independently of their instruments and effects, independently, that is, of property possessed.

The doctrine of property right in liberalism assumes that the interiority of subjectivity extends into the exteriority of objects and institutions (even at times of other persons – women, children, workers, slaves); the two realms are continuous. But the doctrine of personal rights assumes they are absolutely discontinuous. Although the right to property assumes that subjective self-identity extends into external effects, so that any encroachment on property is an abridgement of the right of personhood, under liberalism, rights of person are not related to property. Property remains external and disconnected as far as the internal constitution of such rights is concerned. Within the liberal framework, the right of person cannot depend in any way on the externality of property. Everyone has the same abstract right of speech or thought no matter what they own. But in regard to property, this is reversed: although for those with property, property right is an extension of their rights of person, for those without property, property is merely contingent in relation to their rights as persons. Their interiority as rights-bearing subjects with equal rights to own property is in no way dependent on whether or not they actually exercise their right to have property. And this creates the other great curiosity of liberalism: one can still be a 'free' subject even if one is entirely without possessions.

According to liberalism, then, a person without property has the same subjective rights as a person with property, even though a substantive deficiency implies an inability to exercise rights. This is why liberalism must think of the subject as a proper or self-identical interiority fixed within its boundaries, boundaries that are neither expanded nor contracted by such 'externalities' as actual property owned. Yet this formulation contradicts what liberalism claims regarding the extendability of subjective identity into property without break or artificial addition, the very concept that grounds the right to property. If subjectivity is extendable into things, then it is not the pure interiority liberalism claims. Yet liberalism must make this claim when it seeks to separate the actual exercise of the right of property ownership from rights of person in order to prevent the right of person from being an actual(izable) claim on substantive property ownership. The logic defining the connection between person and property abuts in an aporia, an irresolvable contradiction between mutually exclusive yet mutually sustaining propositions. The right to property is determined as an extension of the right to personal identity on the one hand, but an exercisable right to property is denied by the claim that personal identity has nothing to do with an externality like property.[7]

From a post-structuralist (and post-liberal) perspective, the subject is conceived as an elastic and indeterminate entity whose interiority can expand or contract depending on its power to exercise its rights in an institutional context that is not deemed external to subjectivity. In this framework, subjective interiority loses the firmness of its boundary as well as the presumption of its primordiality and is instead defined as in necessary relation to externals like property. One cannot be 'free' and not own anything. The post-structuralist argument that external representations or instruments are not contingent attachments to a more primordial and essential subjective interiority, but are instead retroactive constitutents of that putative ground, takes the form here of insisting that institutions like property, which are supposedly the derivative, external terms in relation to person, play a constitutive role in the construction of subjectivity. What one owns determines what one is.

The erosion of boundaries promoted in this critique does not sacrifice the idea of identity entirely. It removes it from a position that transcends relations with other parts of the social field. And it suggests that identity will cease to be an ideological category only when the material contexts that now make it ideological are reconstructed. There can be no identity of subjectivity when such externals as differences in wealth play so powerful a role in determining the content of subjectivity.

This undermining of transcendence also deprives law of its formality, its ability to remain an abstract formulation of equal opportunities. A post-structuralist revision of the liberal doctrine of rights prescribes the necessity of transforming merely formal rights (the potential but not the actual claim to own property) into exercisable or actualized rights. Rights would no longer be construed as the formal possibility of doing something; they become the claim on the exercise, or the actual realization, of that potential.[8] That everyone has the right to own property must mean that everyone not only has the ideal or unrealized potential to do such a thing. It must be the actual case. This, needless to say, would be both the fulfilment as well as the end of liberalism.

9 Post-Structuralism and Law

Liberal law polices the social universe as much by policing meaning as by making certain that those who do not benefit greatly from liberal capitalism do not get out of hand. Liberal law polices meaning by making certain that concepts like equality and fairness are limited to understandings that do not disturb the basic structure of liberal society, a structure characterized by a high degree of material inequality and practical unfairness. Hence, equality, for example, shall mean equal treatment by government rather than a redistribution of wealth or a levelling of power. Those other meanings or references exist in potential form in the liberal conceptual scheme, but they are held in place by a version of the same distinction that holds workers and managers, non-owners and owners apart in capitalism. The right meaning is thought to be the one most detached from materiality, from the world of empirical contingency and difference. It is ideal and formal, and as a result, it is more general and universal. It can be applied equally to all, like equality itself. Another way of putting this is to say that the right meaning is one that transcends situation as well as representation. It is not bound to any specific context or material site, and it rises above the material vehicles of thought, as formal principles are always said to exist outside language particularly. Implicit in this model of meaning, one that privileges the semantic realm over the syntactic, ideality over materiality, is a mechanism of control. Under this regime, equality cannot mean just any old thing. Its references are held to an understanding that favours a universality of application. It cannot seem to favour any one group over another through, say, a programme of redistribution. Thus, semantic control and social control intersect.

Liberal rational unversalism must privilege ideal principle over empirical contingency, semantics over syntax, because it requires meanings that are stable and consistent over time and across space. The materiality of representation, its anchoring in specific situations and in linguistic forms, is necessary for the embodiment of any meaning, but it also contravenes semantic stability. Nothing in the word 'equality' prevents it from meaning redistribution. Indeed, in certain situations on the lower or material end of a society divided unequally between a managerial élite secure behind the protection of an ideal of equal treatment and an exploited, working majority, the word would immediately have that particular meaning. Because these differences of situation introduce differences of meaning, they must be kept at bay. And because the materiality of words can in their empirical literality mean just about anything, they too must be purged if the rational universalism of liberal law is to secure the controlled meanings it requires.

Post-structuralism is notorious for troubling such pretensions. It focuses on the materiality of representation, the inextricability of situation from meaning, and the irrecuperable spread of reference beyond all semantic limitations. The meaning of a concept like equality cannot be held to the kind of formal or ideal sense that liberalism requires of it. Rather, the references generated by the term can be pursued to the full extent of the material connections into which it enters, and those are endless. They map out a social terrain as much as a conceptual one, since from the post-structuralist perspective, meaning is inseparable from the webs of reference into situation and context that any representation like the word 'equality' generates. Under such an analysis, an ideal rational understanding of principles like freedom or equality cannot function as dams that hold reference back from spreading further. Indeed, they themselves come to be seen as representatives of further meanings, further referential possibilities. They no longer appear as grounds where reference stops and is absorbed into a formal or ideal truth; rather, they are effects of other causes, representatives of other meanings that are less ideal and formal than material, historical, and situational. Indeed, in this light, all meaning is seen as irremediably material, a matter of representational vehicles tied directly to social situations. To use the vocabulary I have relied on already in this book, post-structuralism draws attention to the way a metonymic process of reference undermines the metaphoric pretensions of liberal legality.

I will use this post-structuralist argument – that reference spreads, undermining the grounds of liberal legality and showing them to be effects either of social situations or of the very representations to which they supposedly gave rise – to critique several recent schools of legal theory. I will then suggest some ways in which the post-structuralist argument might aid the construction of an alternative legal system.[1]

According to post-structuralism, concepts are inseparable from representation; no transcendent ideals exist apart from the material processes that communicate them; semantics never fully eludes syntax, the shapes and forms thought is given by the very material vehicles of representation that are supposedly appended to an already constituted mental world in the metaphysical version of things. All the concepts of legal reason exist in discourse, and such discourse is material, historical, and social. What this means is that meaning must be understood as a function of the particular relation of social forces that brought a word/concept into being. For example, a concept like equality acquires its modern sense because of a particular historical and social situation to which it is a response. Early liberals required a principle of equal treatment as a means of dealing with invested aristocratic power, but because they also required a defence against the working class their commercial enterprises was bringing into existence, they limited the meaning of the term to formal equality of treatment by government. It cannot, therefore, be understood as having a meaning apart from that situation. More generally, the liberal ideal of equal treatment of citizens by government presupposes a neutralization of direct democracy by republican representational forms, and it presupposes an economic and social regime of unequal resource and power distribution. No one would need to be treated equally, that meaning would not have to exist in the form that it takes under liberalism, if inequality did not reign in the surrounding society. The principle and meaning of equality that liberalism sustains presupposes a situation of inequality that calls the liberal meaning forth and makes it necessary as a response to some of the more negative outcomes of structural inequality. Consequently, meaning does not consist of stable and consistent unities whose contours are given by an internal content so much as of differential relations between terms or between those terms and the situations in which they exist and to which they respond. Such relations take the shape of rhetorical tropes in that they consist of negations, inversions, displace-ments, substitutions, and the like. They define processional relations of force, rather than simple identities.

In this discussion, I will concentrate on the trope of metalepsis, the reversal of cause and effect, whereby an effect is mistaken for a cause. Metalepsis occurs when the meaning of legal concepts like equality is detached from their determining situation and elevated above the material world of representation in liberal legality. This process of extraction creates the impression that the term's meaning can and should be limited to an ideal rational understanding of equality as a formal principle of equal treatment, regardless of empirical specifici-ties and differences of station and status. The ideal of equality can then be said to arise from reason, from the principles of rational justice that are developed apart from any concern for the actual material situation of the social world, which in this framework is seen simply as external interference. The ideal of equal treatment then becomes a means of justifying the existence of that particular social situation. If all are treated equally by the law, then the empirical specificities of social inequality can be made to seem legitimate. They are the result of fair play regulated by fair rules or principles. In this scheme, then, the rational principle of equality is the cause of law, and social inequality, rather than being seen as the cause that calls forth the principle of equal treatment as a response, comes to be seen as a secondary effect, an accidental result of essentially fair rules. As I have suggested, the deconstructive reversal of this metaleptic mistaking of an effect (the principle of equal treatment) for a cause (the law that justifies social inequality because all are treated fairly) would point to the fact that the liberal concept of equality is the effect of the very social situation of inequality for which it seems to provide cause or reason or justification.

In liberal thinking, social inequality cannot be acknowledged as the real cause of liberalism's supposed first principles. It is for this reason that meaning must be conceived of as an inherent property of categories like equality and freedom. Context and situation cannot be granted any power, nor can representation be seen as anything more than a dispensable vehicle of communication without powers of its own, powers of reference that are seen as troublesome interference that must be controlled so that the communication of the inherent meaning of the legal categories and principles can occur properly and efficiently.

Another way of speaking of metaleptic reversal in liberal law is to say that re esentations do not so much express or depict existing social categories as create or construct those very things. The liberal discourse of rights thus constructs our perceptions in such a way that we see the world in terms of the categories of the discourse. What this means generally is that we see identitites of meaning – the right to free speech, for example – rather than the relations between terms or between terms and situations that actually give rise to those apparent identities. We see 'right' rather than a situation that makes the assertion of right necessary as a response to that situation, for example, or rather than a relational distribution of power that makes certain people more susceptible than others to a deprivation of the capacity of speach. If rights are always situations, they are also always responses to those situations. Post-structuralism draws our attention to the way our categorical representations occlude these complex social rhetorical processes of construction in favour of semantic identities that appear underived or non-relational. They seem to be causes or reasons for legal institutions rather than effects of social situations.

By pointing out the representational character of legal categories, post-structuralism also suggests that such categories are the products of social struggles and that the expansion or contraction of the semantic boundaries of such categories is a crucial issue of such struggles. The limitation of meaning is also the curtailment of social possibilities or the elimination of potential political alternatives. The struggle to expand the meaning of such categories as freedom and equality, therefore, which requires the expansion of such categories as causality and restitution – the broad determination of the reasons for things like poverty and crime that leads to a redefinition of what it means to make people whole once again – is inseparable from fights over the arrangement of institutions and the distribution of resources.

Consequently, liberalism cannot acknowledge the materiality of its categories, the way in which they are anchored in representation and discourse, without putting in question the social regime it safeguards. To do so would be to take such categories as equality and freedom out of the ether of transcendent abstraction, where the range of their meanings is limited to formal possibilities, and to situate them in the material universe. Their meaning would no longer consists of a semantic ideal whose identity is guaranteed by its immunity to divergent interpretations that are motivated by 'merely' material interests which stand at odds with the liberal rational ideal of formal purity. Rather, that very meaning would be seen as very much the product of dominant interpretations that have emerged as the result of successful struggles for social power. And the categories would become susceptible to expansive reinterpretations. Removed from the security provided by the ideal of semantic identity or formality, they begin to move and to change shape, depending on who is using them and in what situation. They cease to mean, in the sense of having a truth as their origin that they express or re-present, and begin to perform, in the sense of giving rise to meanings whose potential range is impossible to determine in advance.

The post-structuralist critique thus has two negative effects on liberal legal theory, and those effects give rise to one proto-utopian possibility. The two negative effects are, first, the anchoring of legal categories in material discourses that are available for struggle and, second, the unhinging of those categories from any determinate, inherent meaning that is expressed in, rather than constructed by, those categories (which is to say, those discursive representations). The proto-utopian possibility is that the meaning of such categories as freedom and equality and causality cannot be limited. Once meaning is disarticulated from supposedly expressive truths that transcend mere materiality (the social struggle over meaning and power), it becomes impossible to set boundaries on what meaning can mean. Reference spreads, and no transcendent rationale can hold it in place. If everything is material, then only power can relieve the indeterminacy of the categories. And such indeterminacy is as unlimited as materiality itself.

Equality can no longer be restrained by a meaning that limits it to being a formal principle of equal treatment. Such meaning is supposedly ideal rather than material, and it therefore automatically limits the expanse of the category to what respects the requirements of ideal meaning – transcendence and formality. From a post-structuralist perspective, equality is limited only by the exhaustion of the material possibilities for the creation of further equality. The possible meanings of the term are in fact therefore inexhaustible, and no ideal or formal principle of identity that establishes boundaries which limit the possible expansion of the category in advance can restrain their material force. That force works as the formation of ever different varieties of the category. The demolition of the semantic identity of the category by anchoring it in the materiality of representation, therefore, sets loose these social possibilities.

I will argue that the post-structuralist critique of liberal law imposes on radicals a programme of substantive or material justice that is open-ended. That is, rather than set an agenda for limited equalization according to a logic of rights still beholden to an identitarian understanding of the world (with identitarian having the economic meaning of market entrepreneurialism, the psychological meaning of subjective identity, and the linguistic philosophical meaning of semantic unity), the radical project must respect the indeterminacy that has been its ally in dismantling the rationale for liberal legality. And it can only do so through a programme that unprogrammes itself as soon as it sets itself up. This is done by creating the mechanism for the further elaboration of projects of equalization that respect no one perspective's limited understanding of what equality means. Radical responsibility in this sense means not trying to cover all the bases oneself in some deluded dream of totality, but rather leaving oneself open to accepting what others decide is best for themselves, responding to what is not yet known or what has not yet been created rather than trying to determine in advance what those things will be, and allowing the possibilities of meaning to expand beyond what any one of us can determine as the truth of categories like freedom and equality.

I will now turn to three legal theories that operate within the general liberal tradition. I will criticize all three in the post-structuralist terms laid out above.

'Law and economics' promotes the view that law should operate in terms of the goal of economic efficiency, with efficiency being defined in strictly pro-business terms.[2] This legal theory developed in response to the liberal reforms of the 1960s, reforms touching on the regulation of business particularly. Such regulations ordered business to pay the costs of such things as cleaning up the environment. Conservatives argued that this hampered efficiency by placing too large a financial burden on business. They responded with the idea that trade-offs could be worked out between businesses and those affected by such things as pollution. These transactions would determine which cost less – preventing pollution or allowing pollution and paying compensation. Those affected by pollution might decide that they would accept compensation for tolerating it, and this transaction would replace government regulation. The cost of regulation would be eliminated, and the cost to business of preventing pollution in the first place would also be reduced.

The economic market would thus come to act as an intermediary between business and the surrounding community, replacing government regulation and promoting greater efficiency. For this reason, law and economics theorists argue that adjudication should as much as possible strive to imitate the market. In making decisions, judges should determine which result would be most efficient or which would be the case in a perfectly operating market.

Critics point out that if law goes to the highest bidder, only those with economic power will benefit, and it will be at the expense of those less privileged. Moreover, the market varies from region to region, and it is not what conservative economists claim it is – that is, a fair and neutral arbiter of economic interaction. Those with the power to demand higher prices do so, regardless of what a fair market price would be. And even the idea of a fair market price ignores the history of power lying behind this supposedly value neutral mechanism.[3]

These critiques tend to be moral and political, rather than methodological or discursive. They do not target what is wrong with the way of thinking (and representing) that underlies the theory. From a post-structuralist perspective, law and economics can be said to be founded on metaphysical assumptions regarding interiority. Its norm is the market, especially the assumption that the market, acting alone and without interference from without, is a mechanism sufficient unto itself for resolving social problems. The metaphysical ideal of interiority or self-identity is implicit in this assumption. Questions of morality, political regulation, social consequence, and so on are all considered to be external to the supposedly self-identical market. That ideal implies two things – first, the market is a machine that is independent, proper to itself and not in need of additional or external supplementation or assistance, and second, it constitutes a scientifically objective and neutral measure that is not skewed by interests, emotions, representations, or other subjective criteria. The market is like a pure indubitable idea that transcends the vagaries of contingent representation and rhetorical debate. It provides a sense of authority, and it reproduces a separation between ideality and materiality by suggesting a rational ideal that is akin to a natural or scientific law.

The argument in law and economics that adjudication should as much as possible seek to mimic the marketplace draws attention to a boundary dilemma of the theory. If we think of law as operating within a general system of representation that regulates social behaviour, then law, from a law and economics perspective, is a supplemental representation of the market that is added onto the real market. Law behaves *like* the market in order to accomplish what the market itself could not do. What is curious about this argument is that the market is not supposed to need such external supplementation. The reason for its use as a norm for adjudication is that it is an entirely self-sufficient mechanism for mediating economic and social disputes. But if the market needs external legal supplementation, it is not a self-regulating, purely internal system. And it loses the value that qualified it as the model or norm of legal action. Thus, law should mimic the market, but the necessity of the law to the market signals a deficiency that disqualifies the market as an ideal of perfect self-sufficiency. The value of interiority is not sustainable because what seems self-identical, organic, and natural turns out to be dependent on an external legal supplement with which it exists in differential interrelation.

Law and economics also creates a sense of self-sufficiency through the use of scientific representations (optimality equations, graphs). A semblance of meta-representational, non-contingent objectivity is created by associating the theory with the scientific rationalist ideal of deducing and following laws that are beyond doubt or negotiation. The theory relies on mathematical calculation and on such standards as Pareto Optimality, which is a measure of cost efficiency. This particular form or style of reasoning and of calculating is chosen because it seems to exclude neutrality-invalidating interests and to guarantee an unquestionable authority for the results attained.

But the literature of law and economics also relies on exemplary narratives, representations that concretize the ideas in question. The most famous concerns a dispute between a railroad and a farmer whose fields of wheat are burned by fires set by sparks from passing locomotives. The railroad offers to pay the farmer a certain amount of money as compensation, and that amount is less than what it would cost to change the path of the locomotives or to modify them so that they do not emit sparks. This is the classic example of a market transaction replacing government regulation. In essence, the railroad buys on the free market the right to inflict harm, and the farmer accepts this harm because the money he receives in compensation is more than what his loss in burnt wheat amounts to. This is a situation of Pareto optimality. Each side either gets more or pays less than it would otherwise by relying on non-market remedies such as litigation.

What is peculiar and interesting about this little narrative (and it is recounted as a story in Posner's *The Economic Analysis of Law*)[4] is that it makes clear the interests that lie behind this legal theory, while also thereby betraying its pretense to scientific objectivity. The narrative is a representation, and usually, at least in the scientistic ideology of the sort relied on in law and economics, one thinks of such representations as mere secondary appendages to a more central, self-sufficient conceptual argument. They exist at the frontier or margin of the conceptual system, interesting but ultimately dispensible illustrations. But this particular representational illustration is more than that. It embodies certain crucial values that lie at the heart of law and economics theory. The most important value is nature. In a society and in a climate of legal debate marked by its urban, modern, technological character, the story is striking for its rural aura and setting. This reinforces the sense that the market is closer to the natural order of things, and indeed, the conservative argument in favour of following the market is that it constitutes a way of letting things fall into place as they would in nature, without human interference.

But the story is more than merely rural; it is rural in a pre-modern manner – it includes a locomotive that emits sparks, and image that evokes the period in the late nineteenth century known as the era of 'freedom of contract' prior to the onset of government regulation of business. Not surprisingly, the narrative is enacted on the frontier, at the edge or margin of civilized, that is to say, legal society. It embeds a topographical and historical image of escape from the constraints of modern legality. Thus, the narrative betrays the fundamental and inherent interest of law and economics, which is not to make law, but to escape it. The call for market mimicry is in effect a call to neutralize that dimension of law which has since the nineteenth century reduced the 'freedom' of capitalists to do harm without being held accountable to the social context.

That so historically regressive a narrative should be appended to an argument that gives itself out to be a progressively scientistic, replete with graphs and optimality equations, may seem surprising, but in fact, the narrative of historical regression evidences a desire for rural simplicity that is in keeping with the desire for enforceable order, unavoidable in its necessary results, implied in law and economic's scientism. In right-wing ideology, the myth of rural simplicity has always connoted an ideal of a self-regulating nature immune to urban, liberal reconstruction, and it has always also suggested an unavoidable, organic order in things that could be transferred onto society in the form of the sanctification of authority, hierarchical positioning, and corporatist bonding.

Something of the same sort is at work in law and economics. Its inconography combines an ideal of pre-liberal, pre-urban rural life, which is organically self-sustaining and not in need of supplemental rectification by government, with an ideal of scientific order, enforced mathematically. Both ideals imply something that cannot be contravened, whose force is so great that it leads to inevitable results. Market calculation can thus be seen to the modern right-wing equivalent of what the ideology of discipline was to earlier reactionary movements. Both imply obedience, but they do so not in terms of submission to liberal statism, but in terms of an alliance with an ideal of self-regulation lodged in nature, especially a rural American version of nature. The exemplary narrative of law and economics gives this away, even as the theory presents itself as the height of modern scientific achievement. It is in fact a version of right-wing ruralist ideology, the token of a folksy world where traditional beliefs are passed on through anecdotes.

The supposedly ancillary story or representation thus turns out to be more than a mere supplement to the more important conceptual argument. If anything, that story displays a core truth of law and economics theory that could not be found in any other place in its conceptual system. And it displays the anchoring of that putatively independent and autonomously operating scientific calculus of marketplace efficiency in both cultural representations and in unscientific, merely subjective desires and interests.

Post-structuralism is threatening to right-wing legal theory because it calls into question the idea of an institutional identity of law that has its own appropriate standards and rules, its own singular paternal instance of adjudicative authority that transcends all participants and is impartial. From a deconstructive perspective, the separate existence of law as an institution with supposedly internal doctrines or coherent mathematical rules in contemporary society is itself a symptom of that society's pathology. The desire for legal autonomy expresses desires and needs for authority that are themselves produced by the systemic instability of social capitalism. A patriarchal society of competing unequal subjects makes a paternal arbiter seem a logical and natural necessity. The effect of a competitive, patriarchal social arrangement thus comes to seem its justification or cause. The paternalism that results from social instability becomes an excuse for preserving it.

If there is a law of post-structuralism, it is that context inheres, what seems supplemental is in fact essential. Consequently, law must be seen as a response to a situation, an act of discourse elicited or called forth by a problematic social context that requires remedy. Law's identity is given by the differences it addresses, and those differences are not external to what it is. All law is attached to a situation from which it could not be extracted without depriving it of its reason for being and of the forces that give it meaning. Thus, one can say that the paternal instance advertised in conservative legal theory as a solution to society is itself a symptom of that society. The transcendental legal arbiter, the authority removed from the field of contention and debate, whose decisions provide order to what cannot give order to itself, is itself a means of preventing self-generated order. Both sides of the equation – legal arbiter, unstable market society – are pathological and both sustain each other. They are pathological because they imply a system of material inequality and domination that makes the removal of the causes of harm impossible without external authority. And they are mutually sustaining because the fixing of an external authority in law precludes the development of a process of social and legal mediation in a context of material equality that would make such an external instance unnecessary. The pathologies of inequality and domination call that instance of legal authority forth as a remedy, and the continuing use of that legal instance helps maintain society in a state of underdevelopment that merely reproduces the need for an external arbiter. One can speak, therefore, of right-wing legal theory as operating on the basis of a metelepsis. It offers as a cause or reason behind law – the indubitable ideal of an arbiter who follows market science – something that is an effect of a society legally structured in such a way as to make that ideal seem necessary.

The liberal legal theory of Ronald Dworkin is on the whole more sophisticated and benign than the simplistic calculus of monetary gain proposed by law and economics as a model for adjudication. But Dworkin's great strength while contending with conservative theory – the idea that law should be guided by principles rather than utilitarian policies – is his great weakness from the perspective of a post-structuralist critique that points in the direction of a legal system that would not be an excuse for inequality and power.

In *Taking Rights Seriously*, Dworkin argues that adjudication should be guided not by strict legal rules but rather by the principles embedded in those rules.[5] Judges should follow the principles of fairness and equality that a community has built into its legal system, and they should seek to determine and respect in each case what the rights of citizens are. Arguing against positivism, which holds that rights are created by legislation and have no prior existence, Dworkin contends that rights exist apart from legislation and must sometimes take precedence to legal rules. Although this would seem to threaten the ideal of the rule of law, Dworkin argues that the gravitational force of principle limits the interpretation of law to a certain range that does not betray the ideal of precedent.

A post-structuralist reading of Dworkin's claims in this book would invert certain of his premises by pursuing their references in the direction of the material situations his abstract principles presuppose yet also attempt to deny. The very idea of appealing to principles of fairness and equal treatment, for example, points to a material reality of unfairness and inequality that calls those principles forth, and because the principles summoned to address the results of that situation are legal and formal, rather than substantive and economic, they cannot redress that inequality. Indeed, the very idea of a principle, defined as something abstract and without any specific content, suits perfectly a legal theory that assumes that its own social context is normative. Dworkin can therefore speak of 'those in power' even as he discusses the ideal of equality (p. 357). The operations and assumptions of that social system are presumed not to contradict the ideals of the legal theory. Indeed, they are presumed to belong to a realm outside the domain of legal principle altogether.

But can this be the case? If one pursues the references necessarily implied in the theory, it becomes evident that they imply an embedded reality of inequality at odds with the principles the theory supposedly respects. In other words, the theory cannot be detached from the reality that is its constitutive context, that without which its existence would not be necessary. Inequality is the reason or cause of the liberal principle of equal treatment. Social inequality cannot therefore be declared external to legal equality. The liberal principle of equal treatment, by limiting its range of reference to formal concerns that abstract from empirical realities, is, curiously, a way of maintaining an unfair social system.

Social inequality is not only an outer limit that must go unbroached by liberal legality as Dworkin formulates it. The realities of unequal power also undermine the principled character of Dworkin's principles. A principle is distinguished from a policy in that it serves no immediate concrete end. Rather, it names an ideal form that can accommodate any specific content. It is universal and therefore equal in its implications. But the extent of such principles as fairness is limited by liberal allegiance to the rules and policies that maintain the fundamental structures of social and economic power. Legal fairness cannot touch on such matters as the inequalities of wealth that seem to persist despite an individualist social economic ideology, but as a result, fairness cannot be a universal principle. It must limit its range of reference to applications that assume the normativity of the contextual causes of the problems it addresses. Fair treatment will be awarded to people whose lives reflect the effects of the fundamental rules of economic and social inequality, people who would not require fair treatment if those rules were not in effect. But the principle of fairness cannot touch those rules. The embedded policy decision of even the most principled application of Dworkin's liberal ideas is that the social system as constituted cannot be modified by law. Its rules shall not be broken or even questioned. One could say therefore that liberal legality never succeeds in demarcating principle from policy. What it does is apply principle to sustain a particular kind of policy, one that goes unacknowledged as such.

Within Dworkin's theory, therefore, one encounters a metalepsis or reversal of cause and effect. Principles supposedly are prior to policies,

but principles can be shown to rest on policy choices. Those choice
limit the material references that even the most self-containe
principled decision generates, references to the social context tha
makes that very kind of principled decision necessary in the first place
What results is what could be called a normativization of context. Th
liberal theorist assumes the moral justifiability of his own socia
situation, and this permits him to limit the meaning of principles lik
fairness to a rather narrow notion of legal equality of treatment. Bu
the very fact that such principles have to be mustered at all to deal witl
situations that beg for the external application of such principle
constitutes a reference that cannot be quelled. It is what constitutes th
ground or reason for liberal legality as well as the loose string tha
undoes the boundary of its institutional identity.

Similar problems arise in Dworkin's second book, *A Matter o
Principle*.[6] There he argues that judges' decisions should be in keepin
with the established political morality of the community. In confront
ing hard cases, judges should seek to determine what the implici
principles of the community are, the political theory implied by it
rules. Principles are based in rights rather than in policy goals, an
legal rules should be seen as the community's attempt to capture mora
rights that pre-exist all legislation. The creation of new rights by judge
should be limited to already established community standards.

Like all liberals, Dworkin assumes that communities founded o
liberal economic and political principles are free from coercion
People enter into them voluntarily. Moreover, those principles ar
morally justifiable; they even constitute a normative theory that can b
the basis for adjudication. Consequently, all judges have to do is figur
out the coherent political theory lying behind the US Constitution, fo
example, in order to arrive at good decisions. But all of this changes i
legal principles are seen as excuses for social policies that requir
coercion and an unequal distribution of power in order to functio
successfully. Such is one description, at least, of a liberal capitalis
society that requires a docile workforce which trades energy fo
unequal remuneration and which is excluded systematically from th
power to determine the rules of the economy. In this light, decisions o
principle that are in keeping with the established political morality o
the community are themselves policy decisions. Crucial in this critica
reformulation of the liberal position is the question of the limits o
expansion of rights by judges to already established communit
standards. If the community is one in which the standard of coerce
labour is taken for granted, then rights will have to be fairly severel

imited to those that do not disturb the power of employers over
workers. There will be no right to be free from workplace domination
or to be able to live fully and freely without have to trade labour for
wages or without suffering the implicit coercion of a supposedly free
economic system. Dworkin's apparently marginal remarks regarding
he anomalous possibility that an anarchist or marxist judge might
elect to redistribute wealth are thus quite telling. They point out the
real limit of liberal theory and the very powerful assent it gives a
particular form of community whose inequalities it defends on
principle'.

Given this, it is probably appropriate that the title of Dworkin's
most recent book is *Law's Empire*, since what seems at issue in his legal
theory is a kind of domestic imperialism that is sanctioned by liberal
law.[7] Dworkin argues for an ideal of integrity that would adjudicate in
a way that would make law more coherent in principle. Law from this
perspective constitutes a kind of literary narrative, and legal decisions
must try to justify the story as a whole by operating from the point of
view of the best interpretation of the legal process as a whole. If law is a
matter of interpretation, then the crucial issue is the determination of
the meaning of statutes for borderline cases. Dworkin takes what
might be called a cognitivist position in that he sees the issue as a
question of how we can know law. He integrates the literary critical
idea of an interpretive community whose language would be consistent
for all its members. Legal interpretation would thus determine the
principles at work in law, and in this way, interpretation would take
precedence over the invention of new law by judges. He uses the
example of an imaginary regime of Courtesy whose new rules would
become evident to interpreters who respect the implicit principles of
the courteous community. What Dworkin calls 'law as integrity' thus
embodies or personifies a community by proposing an ideal of unity in
adjudication that further flushes out the coherence already embedded
in law.

Dworkin's ideal of a legal narrative implies a standard of unity and
completeness that law can never meet. By acknowledging the anchoring of law in the material processes of interpretation and language,
Dworkin sabotages any possibility that law could ever attain a
narrative completeness sealed off entirely against contextual constituents whose unassimilability to the legal narrative testifies to a radical
disunity at the heart of the supposedly unified liberal legal enterprise.
Once again, the issue is one of material limits that betray the principled
character of Dworkin's principles and of internal fissures that reveal

the implicit assent to power that respect for those material limits
entails. Interpretation of the Constitution, for example, is limited by
the range of implicit principles in the document, but it is also limited by
the requirements of the system of economic domination the Constitution is designed to meet. Interpretation is not merely, therefore, an
issue of cognition, of knowing what law means; rather, it is a matter of
respecting social material limits on possible departures from certain
extra-legal economic rules that law must respect. If the Constitution as
a meaningful document is anchored in a social situation in such a way
that the meaning of its terms are indissociable from social imperatives
so also its interpretation is similarly anchored situationally. No
determination of meaning can detach itself from a context without
which there could be no meaning. Legal meaning, as much as literary
meaning, cannot be a matter of intention alone; it is a matter of address
and of the dialogic social situation implied by any address. It is a matter
of a social network that permits certain words to mean certain things –
'right' or 'freedom', for example, neither of which could mean
anything without material points of reference in society that give them
substance and shape their semantic content. Moreover, as I have
already noted in different terms, an interpretation that takes the social
system for granted as normative or at least neutral from the perspective of justice is not one that can claim to be purged entirely of
interested, policy-oriented prejudices. Indeed, the very dream of a
purely cognitivist interpretation, one without social residues or
contextual determinants, is one that must posit the social situation in
which it occurs as irrelevant, and in so doing, it defines itself as a highly
interested political act.

Legal interpretation, therefore, can never be simply a matter of
principle or of respect for the integrity of the community's implicit
legal theory. That formulation already betrays the habit of abstraction
that permits liberals like Dworkin to use a world like 'community' to
name a highly contentious, class-, gender-, and race-divided society in
which power and resources are unequally allocated and in which those
inequalities are enforced by the legal system. The unity of communities of interpretation of the kind Dworkin's theory requires is always a
coerced unity that attempts to ignore the fact that divided societies give
rise to divided languages of interpretation. There can be no common
language of the kind required in 'law as integrity', and it is doubtful
that Dworkin's concept of 'community', general and abstract as it is,
would have meaning for urban underclass blacks in the US, say, for
whom the word generally means the local black world that stands at
odds with the white world outside.

Social differences and situations of this kind can never be assimilated to the cognitivist model of legal interpretation that Dworkin proposes. They resist integration into a model of adjudication that limits itself to the determination of the unified meaning of a community's principles conceived as a narrative, the 'story as a whole'. The liberal legal ideals of integrity and fairness imply a social reality of unfairness and disintegrity because they would not be necessary if the social world were structured differently – as a scene of principled, which is to say, universal material equality, for example. But we have already noticed more than once that liberal theory cannot take that determining social situation into account without betraying an allegiance to its maintenance. Liberal principle would cease to be principle and become policy if it tried to modify its social context. This is why Dworkin's choice of the example of Courtesy as deference to authority and power is so telling; it sums up the liberal theory of law.

Consequently, the liberal ideal of adjudication as the best interpretation of the legal process as a whole, in such a way as to justify the community's legal story as a whole, cannot help but fail to live up to its pretensions. It remains necessarily incomplete. Simultaneously and contradictorily it requires both the expulsion of material or social contextual concerns from its cognitivist description of legal meaning as legal principle and the summoning forth of those material situational concerns. The very evocation of principles such as fairness and equality of treatment point beyond the realm of cognitively derived or interpreted principles to a social reality which calls them forth and which the liberal legal theorist cannot afford to acknowledge. The story can never, as a result, be complete. Only an application of the liberal principles of fairness and equality to the substantive social context that now limits and shapes them would even approximate that dream. But one suspects that one aspect of that application would be the abandonment of the dream of completeness, of a unified narrative or of law as integrity. Completeness, at least in its liberal formulation, seems to imply severing disturbing connections between law and social context, so that law's integrity as a set of coherent principles can be maintained in the face of systemic social violence. Once those connections are allowed to occur, legal completeness comes to depend less on principled coherence and more on the rectification of the sources of social violence that make the principled application of legal fairness necessary – inequality, power, systemic unfairness, and so on. That work is necessarily an open-ended endeavour that can never by definition rest with an illusion of merely cognitive completeness.

Versions of a post-structuralist critique of liberal legal theory are evident in radical work being done by scholars in the Critical Legal Studies Movement.[8] Yet that movement is quite diverse, and some of its leading voices, Roberto Unger particularly, continue to work within liberal categories that are susceptible to post-structuralist revision.

In *Politics, A Work in Constructive Social Theory.* Unger polemicizes against the Second International or stalinist interpretation of marxism, which sees history as moving along a course of necessary evolution from feudalism to capitalism to communism.[9] Rather than remain bound by necessity, Unger argues, we should see history as a discontinuous series of struggles. The losers in such struggles were not the victims of a necessary logical evolution of society from stage to stage; rather, they lost out by virtue of the accidents of political chance. His alternative to marxism as a theory of society is a model of contingency that is an important antidote to the excessive necessitarianism of the stalinist tradition, but Unger recuperates this potentially innovative model to a left liberal political ideal that would tolerate the preservation of inequality. His alternative favours a mixture of modernist context-smashing and petty bourgeois small capitalist production. The modernist approach emphasizes our power to break away from rigid roles and hierarchies. Against absolute property right, which he sees as one of the primary obstacles to progress, Unger suggests the idea of a rotating capital fund that would be available to teams of entrepreneurs, technicians, and workers. A programme of rights (immunity, welfare, destabilization, and so on) would assure that basic security would be guaranteed and that the capacity to revise the institutional framework of society would become a permanent feature of our lives. The political arrangement of society would consist of a representational democracy with 'central reformers' operating from a locus of governmental power that would nonetheless be more flexible than anything liberals have so far envisioned. The right to decide things would occasionally 'devolve' to the populace, but essentially, the republican structure of political representation now prevalent under liberalism would be maintained. Flexibility and freedom are core values for Unger, and he argues against the ideals of radical popular democracy and absolute equality that have been at the forefront of post-liberal radicalism. He is more concerned with developing flexible institutions that would permit a maximum of decentralized economic activity. Democracy and markets are, he argues, essential to each other.

Unger does not do great justice to marxism. He fails to give its due to western marxism particularly, which noticed the failings of the stalinist evolutionary model some time ago, and by limiting the definition of marxism to that historical model, he neutralizes a major critical impulse of marxism that also troubles his own theory of history. According to the marxist account, social struggles always occur between parties with real material interests; otherwise, there would not have been any struggles for power. Unger is right to point to the accidental quality of most struggles, the variability and unpredictability of many of their outcomes. But it is symptomatic of his theological and metaphysical presuppositions that he ignores the weight of materiality in motivating such struggles and in determining their stakes. If certain groups won, it was generally because their greater economic power could be parlayed into more material military power in the search for markets, raw materials, and wider productive capacities. The Africans who were enslaved for colonial labour did not lose by virtue of an accident; they were simply outgunned. Moreover, by flattening marxism out into a 'deep-structure theory' of historical change, Unger leaves out the tremendous amount of work in marxist cultural studies, from Gramsci and the Frankfurt School to Althusser and the Birmingham School, which emphasizes the determining role of cultural and social institutions in shaping material life. In Unger's hands, marxism is less a straw man than a dummy who is not allowed to speak.

More crucial to my concerns here is the fact that a post-structuralist critique would note that a metaphysical-theological mode of understanding fuels Unger's social theory and accounts for its evident limitations. His entire programme of modernist context-smashing, visionary leadership, and entrepreneurial innovation in a decentralized market society rests on highly questionable assumptions about the possibility of transcending materiality and about the priority of interiority over exteriority. In this perspective, materiality is what is external, and interiority is what is subjective. Subjectivity is seen as a repository of spiritual truth that exceeds the limits of all constraining or determining contexts. It will seem odd to say that Unger is an anti-contextualist, since he uses the word context so much to name social formations. But his primary value is the capacity of men (no sic, he means men) to be free from the rigidities and constraints that determining social contexts impose. This ideal ignores the extent to which everyone in a society internalizes social figure and external relations in their so-called identity. Context constitutes subjective interiority. The same can be said of the social determinants that shape so-called entrepreneurial market capitalism. The interiority of the entrepreneur's free flexibility, the triumphant will Unger finds so potentially progressive, is determined by the external situation and the material constituents – most importantly, the situation of policed labour in a structure of unequal and restricted resource allocation – that make entrepreneurialism possible.

The origin of these oversights is located in Unger's initial animus against materiality, exteriority, and contextual determination. Because his theologically based sights are set so high above materiality, Unger fails to take into account the actual material and external determinants of the ideals he privileges. For example, when he elaborates a theory of rights that would make certain that security, welfare, and institutional revision would be guaranteed in his version of republican capitalism, he fails to note that the very concept of right presupposes situations or contexts of potential deprivation, structural social threats that make rights necessary as defences against them. Consequently, where a perspective that focuses on the materiality of representation and of social life would see power, Unger sees an acceptable situation that he shrouds in such mataphorical mystifications as the word 'economy' and the term 'economic rationality'. And where the same perspective would see situations or structures that should be reconstructed so that it would be unnecessary to guarantee safety through rights because there would no longer be any situational threats to such things as physical security, freedom from domination, the desire for need fulfillment, and the aspiration for equality, Unger sees individuals striving conflictually with each other in a situation not in the least purged of the threats that make rights necessary in the first place. Indeed, his very programme of individual conflict modelled on male psycho-sexual development would guarantee the preservation of those endangering situations.

The prevalence of mystificatory metaphors in Unger's theory can be traced back to his metaphysical concept of truth and of language. Unger believes that society can transcend its material limitations in the same way that truth supposedly exceeds the vehicles of discourse that communicate it. But such social transendence is always merely the further rearrangement of material terms, the making of more goods, for example, or the selection of more equal techniques or instruments of distribution. Similarly, 'truth', which is to say, semantic content or meaning, never outruns the vehicles of discourse. If it seems to, it is only as further vehicles, additional representations. Unger's metaphysics inheres most tellingly in his belief that ideational content actually substitutes at some point for a material representational vehicle, that syntax, the articulation of representational techniques, stops, and semantics, conceived in spiritualist terms as an ideal form of truth, takes over. This substitution of something ideal for something material, of something endowed with spiritual presence for a wordly technique, is associated in the philosophical tradition with a privileging of the subject over the material world. The subject or logos is the site of a cognition supposedly liberated from representational techniques entirely, an interiority subtracted from the exteriority of mechanics, materiality, and representation. It is therefore the site of truth conceived in spiritual terms as a non-material thing. From this metaphysical set of beliefs can be derived most of Unger's social values.

The values that derive from the base metaphysics include his locating of governmental authority in a central 'decisional' instance, his assumption that freedom is a more important value than equality, the accent given to the breaking free of a subject from all constraining contexts, the holding to entrepreneurialism in small commodity production as a primary goal of economic life more important than redistribution, his privileging of conflict over co-operation, the centring of his programme on rights rather on a reconstruction of the situations or structures of potential duress that makes rights necessary, and his assertion that the triumph of the modernist will over all material necessity is the essential operator of 'revolutionary reform'. All of these values in some way connect back to the belief that truth, grasped in the spiritual realm of a pure subjectivity, somehow transcends representation. Each one of the values privileges substitution, the replacement of something associated with materiality and social determination or contextual limitation by something defined by the purity of its interiority, its subtraction from contextual determinants and material limitations. That internal source, be it the individual or the triumphant will or the modernist desire to break free, is considered to be at some point beyond all other-relations, all ties to related, contextual terms or concerns. It knows no limits.

What I am describing, of course, is also male sexual identity as it is defined by the breaking away from 'female', emotional bonds and relations associated with the mother, whose power over the male child threatens to limit its quest for an identity apart from the female one with which he is born. That urge toward separation also tends to require a move toward substitution, the replacement of determination by a surrounding female context by an identity predicated on a paternal principle of social authority, one that the male can attain only by severing himself from his initial connection to the mother. That new identity thus comes to have the sense of a freedom from all contextual or material determination in a mythic separation or independence. The substitution of a subjective interiority (will, entrepreneur, decisional centre, leader visionary, freedom and rights rather than equality and structural redistribution) for materiality and context can thus be read off an earlier process of separation and substitution that replaces mothers with fathers, the constraints of a 'foreordained' necessity and predetermined 'script' with an ideal of subjective action against all limitations.

Moreover, that substitution occurs through idealizing metaphoric representations that seem to negate the power of materiality by privileging a spiritualistic truth or ideal meaning. Such meaning comes to seem the possession of a subject who can grasp its semantic unity without being dependent on others to supply further references. A term like 'entrepreneur' or 'worker' thus comes to seem to mean something in itself, without referring beyond, metonymically, to external determinants. Its potential references are bound by a singular meaning whose truth it expresses. This process of representation is crucial to the sense of male singularity that imbues Unger's work. Male psychosexual identity is predicated on the capacity to separate from the mother, and that separation occurs through the development of a capacity of mental representation that permits the child to exist apart from the mother. He retains her image as a substitute. An extreme separation, arising from the need not to be mistaken for a female, gives rise to extreme forms of substitution that excessively privilege the ideational over the material, the semantic over the syntactic, truth over discourse. This in part explains why misogyny seems endemic to the great male tradition of idealist philosophy.

The political consequences of this representational practice are also enormous. Rather than speak of the economy as a site of domination and exploitation, the marxist gesture, Unger speaks of possibly greater 'innovation' and 'efficiency'. These terms are idealized substitute descriptions of what a more materially-oriented vocabulary would describe in terms of the relations of power that obtain between participants in the so-called 'economy'. It is as if by leaving behind a materialist perspective altogether, Unger also leaves behind the possibility of seeing the site of material production in any way other than through highly metaphoric categories that keep its offensive materiality at bay. It is this perhaps that accounts for the economic programme he promotes which seems to accept that so-called 'workers' are and will be 'workers'. By accepting the liberal substitutions that replace the issue of power and domination with a concern for markets and entrepreneurialism, Unger also accepts the justness of an unequal division of labour. His utopia will still preserve a division between 'entrepreneurs' and 'workers'. The goal of economic reform is not the equalization of power or access to resources, but rather the freeing up of rigid roles and hierarchies through envigorated entrepreneurialism. If the privileging of semantics over representational materiality seems to preserve social divisions that favour a centralization of male-socialized subjectivity in the form of the economic entrepreneur, it also relates to the centralized political model Unger proposes. It is clear from his exposition that he envisions a professional class of reformers like himself occupying governmental power and determining the shape of social life. If the masses participate, it will be through mobilization and in ground-level administrative positions. This political programme is not surprisingly also founded on a process of substitution. Political representatives will be substituted for the electorate, just as economic entrepreneurs will stand in for teams of workers and be their directors. The same metaphysical distinction between a more privileged spiritual or cognitive level and a degraded physical or material level obtains.

A programme that gives priority to the concerns of those stuck on the bottom of society in positions of domination as 'workers' would be one that would necessarily have to begin from a more materialist conception of the world as well as with a greater attentiveness to the materiality of its own representational or discursive instruments. It would have to give priority to necessity, to the material needs of people, and to equality, the desires of people for fair distribution. It would not accept the substitution of terms that connote a higher meaning ('economic rationality') for terms that are directly connected to that level of material need. By giving priority to materiality over the spirituality of 'truth' conceived as what transcends representation, one would make it impossible to develop a political programme that does not privilege the desires and preferences of those on the material underside of society. If truth can no longer stand in for material representation, so also 'central reformers' can no longer stand in for the populace and make decisions for them, including the decision already made in advance that inequality is necessary. Equality and an end to domination move necessarily to centre stage, as does direct participatory democracy because it would in all likelihood (and the risk of its indeterminacy is that one could not determine the outcome in advance) eliminate inequality along with the structures that produce it.

If the metaphysical perspective privileges subjectivity over materiality and thereby fuels a liberal politics that favours freedom over equality, the materialist perspective (which is also the post-structuralist perspective in that the latter's emphasis on the materiality of representation ties it immediately to a broader social materialism) emphasizes the materiality of subjectivity, its inseparability from what lies outside its supposed interiority. From the point of view of material need, no ideal rational logic predicated on the privileging of subjectivity over materiality can justify inequality. Indeed, on the level of materiality, all are equal: all share the same desires: and all suffer the same limitations regardless of station. The principle that prevails here is not subjective freedom or the higher truth of logics like 'economic rationality' that require the preservation of material inequality and domination, but rather the rule of material need that what one person has, no other should be denied. On the plane of materiality, no logic can restrain that trope of equalization. It spreads beyond all the limits that a rationale of substitution would seek to impose.

Such a hypothetical change in programme would require a transformation in every dimension of Unger's theoretical and representational practice – as well as a change in sexual orientation away from the napoleonic male who smashes all 'female' ties and contextual constraints to a somewhat less boundary-anxious character. It would see the goal of the economic programme not as innovation in the hands of petty bourgeois entrepreneurs but rather as a fundamental questioning of what the basic social reasons are for an economy. Is it to supply needs through equal distribution and to provide interesting and rewarding activity? Or is it to mortgage social life to such mystifications as 'growth' and 'efficiency'? Is it to dismantle all inequality and all power relations that bring suffering, or is it to set up an apparatus for constantly revising institutions according to a modernist imperative for innovation that merely changes the configurations of power?

Such a change would also impose a different representational practice, one that would not assume the existence of semantic unities that are not debatable constructs. If society is an artifact, as Unger puts it, so also are all our categories for talking about society. Thus representations like 'the market' and 'economic development' need to be broken down into their material constituents and replaced by representations that name the actuality of power, exploitation, and inequality. Once this is done, it becomes impossible to propose programme like the rotating capital fund that would be used by teams of entrepreneurs and workers, since the very categories 'entrepreneur' and 'worker' would be under interrogation. The idea that there is such a thing as a 'worker', that is, someone with the ontological quality of being a worker and of spending her life performing tasks for 'entrepreneurs', comes into question.

I will close this section with a more concrete example of the supersession of representational technique over substitute spiritual meanings that post-structuralism sees as undermining this kind of metaphysics. I have suggested that Unger is given to substituting such meanings or representations for more material accounts. At the end of the second volume of his book, when he praises Gance's *Napoleon*, he also describes nineteenth century photographs of Asians that seem to capture the same wild, piercing look in the eye that one notices in the cinematic Napoleon. Unger has just described Napoleon as the 'context smasher [who] puts himself into situations that others would regard as ridiculous and demeaning (e.g. Napoleon's awkward and self-deceiving pursuit of the philanderer Josephine). He doesn't feel tainted; he just doesn't give a damn'. Of the photographs, Unger writes that the subject 'looks into the camera with the same crazed expression [as Napoleon]. Perhaps his disquiet comes from the unfamiliarity of the camera . . . The fierce-eyed subjects . . . look as if they had seen beyond the photographer and their circumstances to a reality previously hidden from their eyes. They had seen something of the God who says, No man sees me and lives'.

The substitute meaning is quite ideal and transcendental; it privileges the notion of the great leader who stands out from and above 'ordinary' humans. The privilege of the individual subject acquires here a quite overt theological reference, and its basis in a spurious spirituality is quite clear. But anyone familiar with the actual material mechanics of nineteenth-century photography knows that the subject had to stare into the open iris for quite a long time without blinking. Otherwise the eyes in the photograph would be closed. This, not going eyeball to eyeball with divinity, is the origin of the crazed look. And I suspect one could carry out the same materializing deconstructive operation with all of the ideological substitutes Unger deploys, from the entrepreneur to the visionary leader to truth. The result would necessarily be a much more democratic, more radically egalitarian politics, one that, instead of lingering with early twentieth-century modernism, moves as much contemporary radical social and political theory already has, through and beyond post-modernism, the insight into the representationally constructed and materially or contextually anchored and situationally defined character of all of our categories.

A post-structuralist legal model would situate the subject as already part of larger chains of relations, and this imposes a different ideal of legal order, one that privileged the reduction and elimination of effects like harm over a privileging of self-assertion, that promoted symmetry of economic condition rather than entrepreneurial flexibility, that sought to rectify the transpersonal structures that produced supposedly individual actions that require legal address rather than privileging a subjectivist vision of rights. And it would question the ideals of subjective interiority and state authority that define rights discourse by offering the alternative of contextual reconstruction, one that would so remedy the situations in which people act freely that harm would not be possible and external arbitration would not be necessary, and of intersubjective ethics, one that would make what law accomplishes an internal feature of a lived culture of educated interaction in an egalitarian context. The undertaking of legal theory thus necessarily extends into the social context whose elimination from view in the liberal humanist discourse of right allows law to be reduced to either a positivist correlation of statutes and facts or a liberalist application of a paternalist authority to a decontextualized model of individual action.

If one assumes the dialogic character of law, the way it responds to the situations it addresses and to the differences it attempts to rectify, can there be an 'internal' critique of law as some CLS thinkers claim? Or is legal criticism necessarily turned toward such things as the structuring of social differences in a way that make those contextual issues essential to even a doctrinal critique? If legal doctrine is itself a paternal instance, a way of maintaining a populace in a state of dependency on a patriarchal form of authority that is supposedly external, necessarily, to its control or its direct democratic determination, then a critique that respects the ideological identity of law by working within the boundaries it gives itself runs the risk of reproducing the separation between the paternal institution and the paternalized society. Those boundaries and that separation begin to lose some of their rationalizing power when one attends to the level of legal representation. There, in the materiality of law, its empirical existence as strategies of representation that structure reality in a particular way, a deconstruction of law's identity becomes possible. On the level of representation, law ceases to seem to be a theory, a doctrine, a standard apart from the contingencies of materiality. Its being as a particular formulation of society, a particular inflection of a patriarchal substitutional mode of rhetoric, becomes unavoidably evident. There too, moreover, the tendency of representation to spread references beyond the limits of liberal truth becomes powerfully striking. And it is on the basis of that dissemination of reference that alternative legal theories and alternative social worlds can be built.

I will look at the representational dynamics of two legal decisions from a deconstructive perspective.[10] My argument in each instance will be that the identity of legal rationality is founded on the denial of social difference and that legal ideas cannot be separated from rhetorical representations. My conclusion will be that this argument has disabling consequences for the authoritative identities (of law, person, property) seemingly assured in each case.

The first concerns a petition by the National Labor Relations Board for enforcement of a statute forbidding strikes without due notice against a union, the United Electrical Workers, in 1987. The petition for enforcement was granted. The meaning or truth of this decision as an act of law would begin with a description of the NLRB at the time; comprised primarily of conservative appointees, it tended to operate as much as possible in favour of business. The very petition itself, therefore, emerged out of a context that gave it meaning as an anti-union action, one part of a larger offensive during the Reagan era against labour. Its meaning cannot be confined to textual interpretation alone, but can only be understood as fitting into a wider texture of references that extend beyond the bounds of the case. Nevertheless, one function of the decision's rhetoric is to limit the possible references and meanings to which the case can give rise.

The dominant rhetoric of the decision is metaphoric; its substitutes identities ('loss of status') for differences of power (the act of being fired). The wording of the decision presupposes discrete categories and identitites whose existence must be taken for granted in order for this operation of substitution to succeed. 'Pure speech' (what the judges decide the union was not exercising) is probably the clearest example, though any category from the decision would do, from 'employer' to 'public interest'. The judges refuse to categorize the union's threat to strike as an exercise of free speech because it is not pure, that is, it is not detached from a threat of force. This interpretation presupposes that the meaning of a strike is determinable apart from the difference of power between workers and owners, differences that the judges refuse to evoke. Consequently, one could say that the ideal of pure speech is mirrored in an implicit ideal of pure meaning that is not shaped by context and circumstance. What seems to be at stake in the case is the establishment of a certain kind of meaning as normative in such decisions, a meaning that substitutes ideal statements for material actualities. Needless to say, that ideal of meaning is one that would make the evocation of 'external' issues such as actual power unnecessary.

Similarly, the 'facts' of the case are represented through a process of metaphoric substitution that works to limit an understanding of the events at issue. For example, the first sentence under 'FACTS' reads: 'Burroughs was a corporation engaged in the manufacture and sale of computers'. This simple, apparently literal statement is metaphoric in that the corporation is substituted for the employees, those actually engaged in the act of manufacture. The positioning of Burroughs as the subject of action, especially the action of 'manufacture and sale', establishes a frame of reference that precludes an understanding of the workers' position as anything but an interference with the corporate subject's free intentions and actions. In that one metaphoric device is summed up an entire history of ideological occlusion whereby the real subjects of production are displaced from the scene of legal reflection and substituted for by corporate entities, entities that in fact represent only one part of the process of 'manufacture and sale'. Through metalepsis, an effect – the power of Burroughs to sell goods – comes to stand in as a cause – the actual production of those goods, and as a result, the level of material connections or references that would have made the issue of who actually does the production unavoidable is subsumed to a more ideal, stable, and self-contained description.

The decision also presents itself as a merely formal exercise of the application of statutes to facts. The metaphoric style of the case creates an impression of formality that is necessary to the pretense that statutes belong to a different order of discourse than the facts, a pretense that assumes that the statutory discourse substitutes for the merely contingent discourse of fact description in the narrative of the decision, thus conferring rationality and order upon mere contingencies. But if the facts are artifacts, figures of subjectivity ('Burroughs was . . .') constructed through a particular representation of the world, then the distinction between the literality of the facts and the figurality of the statutes, the social cause and the legal statutory effect, is troubled. By merely citing precedents, the decision portrays the facts as being themselves the results of previous acts of legal discourse. The citation of previous statutes and decisions thus points to the artifactual character of the supposedly literal world of facts and identifies them as the effects of previous acts of legal figuration.

The two levels of discourse – the descriptive and the prescriptive, the literal and the figural, the factual and the statutory – thus cannot be rigorously distinguished, yet the decision (and liberal legality as a whole) depends on their exteriority to each other. What this analysis suggests is that liberal law works by making the constructed character of the social world (that it is figured or arranged in certain ways) seem literal, a matter of simple facts. A boundary is thereby created between the world of objects or pre-figural facts and the discourse of statutes, which presents itself as a metaphoric substitution of legal standards and precedents for those facts. That substitution resolves the facts into an identity that is the meaning of the decision. The boundary between the literal and the figural, the facts and the statutory decision, allows the subject of law, the empirical judge, but also the transcendental subject implied in a judicial instance charged with the power to decide as if he stood outside the social scene, to come into being. At stake, then, in the troubling of that boundary by the confusion of literal and figural registers in the decision is the very reason of law, its necessity as a transcendental instance of judicial authority.

By putting the metaphoric and figural process of judicial stabilization on display to the extent that it does, the decision also draws attention to the way the decision curtails the material references, the metonymic connections that elude the identity of meaning the metaphoric style seeks to impose. The decision posits Burroughs as the subject of production, but at the same time, it must literally point to the fact that people who work in production are threatening to stop that operation by refusing to produce. The decision cannot take that seeming contradiction into account and still promote its version of reality. Moreover, the very fact that the rhetorical mode of the decision is to 'stay' an action on the part of those workers that threatens production, suggests the highly contingent and unstable character of social reality, a contingency and instability that explains why the decision mobilizes a metaphoric mode of meaning as a stabilizing device. By pointing to the metonymic and contingent character of social reality, the decision suggests that social reality must be held in place by metaphors that translate the instabilities of power into enforceable stabilities of meaning. The violence of firing must become 'loss of status' if those contingencies are not to be exacerbated. The forcing of others to work for one's profit must become the metaphorical positing of corporate subjects of production: 'Burroughs was a corporation engaged in . . .' But by successfully holding that figural and contingent reality in place, the decision also displays its vulnerability. Without law, no capitalism; without the power of a republican form of adjudication that mirrors capitalist hierarchies (with the judicial instance standing above the field of difference in the same way that the capitalist stands above his workers), no pacification of the radical differences of inequality. Without a metaphoric mode of judicial description to legitimate enforcement, no acceptable social order that can withstand the metonymic and material forces that constitute the instability and contingency of that social world.

Legal rhetoric must therefore be read as a defensive operation. The decision is as important for what it implicitly prevents from being said as for what it says explicitly. And the prevalence of defensive metaphoric descriptions in the decision points to threatening forces that must be quelled, either by meaning or by the police, if the order of substitution, whereby Burroughs stands in for workers, judges stand in for society, and the equalization of terms carried out in legal metaphors stands in for actual social equality, is to be maintained.

My second case concerns a suit against Aetna Insurance Company regarding A. H. Robins Company, the manufacturer of the dalkon shield, an intrauterine contraceptive device alleged to have caused damage to women. The decision was to stay or hold off action holding Aetna liable. The reason was that such a suit would necessarily affect the managers of Robins, who were undergoing bankruptcy reorganization as a way of forestalling the massive claims levelled against the company by the women in question. Another Reagan era decision, it clearly served the interests of the business community at the expense of the consumer. Although Aetna had participated in the cover-up of evidence against Robins, the judges decided that action against the insurance company would inevitably entail action against the dalkon manufacturer, Robins, 'thus implicating the debtor's property' and upsetting bankruptcy reorganization, 'which would exhaust [the Robins' company directors'] energies', causing them 'harm'.

Many of the same things said about the previous case also apply to this one. The facts are artifacts; they summon forth entire histories of practices involving sexuality, the control of women's bodies, the constructed necessity of relying on profit-oriented organizations to provide health care, the structural instability of capitalism that makes insurance companies necessary, and so on. It is a case with many strands of reference leading away from it toward the power dynamics of patriarchy as well as capitalism. Any 'true' decision in the matter would require addressing a broad range of supposedly contexual issues that are not really contextual at all because they impinge very directly on what is at issue in the case. Once again, however, the references that tie the case to those issues must be occluded if the legal process is to function efficiently as an application of statutes to facts. A judge, constrained by the forces at work in the legal and social context shaping her decision, cannot ask; 'Why does this insurance company have this much power in the first place?' or 'Why should this company be permitted to be protected by bankruptcy law?' It is the very absence of such questions, the absence of the possibility of posing such questions, that constitutes an alterity or otherness that shadows the discourse of such a decision, pointing to an alternate set of statements that are as much ruled out by the decision as any legal action against Aetna.

The crucial logical turn in the case for the judges is the 'identity' of Aetna and Robins that implies that Robins' property will be at issue if the suit against Aetna is allowed to continue: 'We found that a stay was authorized . . . because there was such *identity* between the debtor (Robins) and the third-party defendant (Aetna) that a judgement against Aetna would in effect be a judgement against Robins' [my italics]. In bankruptcy law, the property of the defendant, Robins, must be protected from such suits, and the plaintiffs had sought instead to seek restitution from Aetna, Robin's insurer.

By positing an identity of the two different entities, however, the judges posit real connections of reference that demonstrate the elasticity of the boundaries of identity of each corporation. In doing so, the judges put at issue the very values their judgement sustains – the identity of property, most notably, but also the identity of the corporation that must be protected through bankruptcy law. Aetna cannot be sued, the judges contend, because 'Aetna's primary defense logically will be that Robins – not Aetna – is responsible for the injuries suffered by the plaintiffs, and therefore any detrimental actions taken by Aetna were on behalf or at the direction of Robins'. It is a matter of 'relative fault', then, and in any attempt to determine Aetna's fault, 'Robins will inexorably be drawn into this litigation' – thus interfering with its bankruptcy reorganization.

The case draws attention to the intermediated or differentially related character of the supposedly self-identical entities of capitalist economic and social life, yet it describes this relationship of contiguous connection in a metaphoric vocabulary of identity that implies that Aetna and Robins are intersubstitutable. If 'there was such identity between the debtor (Robins) and the third party defendant (Aetna)', it was because Robins had bought insurance from Aetna. But if the identity of the two is predicated on purchase, this logic would seem to imply that the same can be said of the plaintiffs and the defendant – that their purchase of dalkon shields from Robins creates a similar 'identity' between them and Robins. Nothing in the explicit logic of the decision prevents such a conclusion. Indeed, by pointing to the boundary indeterminacy of the companies in an interreferring economic system, the decision encourages further relays of reference, further explorations of how far identity extends as it ceases to be the identity of one thing and becomes the differential interreferencing of many contractually related things.

But the decision forbids the tracing of such referential connections as much as it forbids legal action against the companies. By positing their relationship as an 'identity', a metaphoric description that substitutes a figural and ideal description for the actual metonymic relation, one that is quite literally material in that it arises from contract and purchase, words and money, the rhetoric of the decision establishes a new boundary between the companies and the harmed consumers. The positing of the corporate identity implies a non-identity between corporations and consumers. Yet the metonymic connections underlying the identity posited by the judges cannot be annulled. They resist the closure of the decision by pointing beyond its limits. Indeed, in the form of the harm done to the women's bodies, which constitutes a very real material connection, the metonymic references that seem curtailed by the metaphoric rhetoric of the decision affirm their power. For they are the real cause of that metaphoric corporate identity. Aetna and Robins would not need to be identified metaphorically if that material connection were not operative. Thus, if Robins' interest includes Aetna's, it also pertains to a network that includes the women's lives.

The decision thus cannot be extracted from references and relations that deny it a simple unity of meaning. The decision secures its ends, but it also leaves them open. By arguing for an identity between Aetna and Robins, one that implies that a suit against Aetna is a suit against Robins (and thus enjoinable), the judges make possible further analogies, perhaps most powerfully, the analogy between the women affected by Robins and Robins itself. Their lives now include the company's life. The judges' logic, equating harm with the endangered energies of the company directors, can be made to imply that the energies of the women spent in protecting the property of their bodies makes them equal with those directors. They have a shared interest with the company in that their property is as much at stake or at issue in the suit over Robins' property. This logic of reference brings into question the boundary representation that establishes a self-identity of property that would permit the interests of Aetna and Robins to be equated, while the interests of the women affected and the company's are dissociated. If Aetna refers to Robins, and is therefore identical with it, so also, Robins refers to the women victims, and its identity or interest or property cannot, according to the logic operative in the judgement, be dissociated rationally or justifiably from them.

The case thus points to, by occluding, a hidden decision that is the real decision at work in the case – the decision to identify corporate interests and not to identify corporate and consumer interests. And that decision is not entirely conceptual; it has to do with rhetoric, with a judgement against permitting reference or analogy to operate freely and in favour of restraining it. This judgement itself obeys a certain law or boundary principle. For if Robins and the women were allowed to be equated in the same way that Aetna and Robins are, it would be impossible to dissociate corporate interests from consumer interests in any 'rational' way (that is, in a way that preserves proprieties that are ultimately metaphors of property power). The real metonymic connections that are the basis of the identity posited between Aetna and Robins and that link Robins to the women would manifest themselves as more material and more powerful than the metaphoric analogies of identity hat legal rationalism employs as a way of deflecting and occluding those metonymic connections.

The necessity of a metaphoric rhetoric in legal decisions is thus made all the more striking by the insight that the case both makes possible and conceals. For the move from Aetna to Robins to the consumers is a metonymic association of the kind that undermines metaphor, and it is such association as much as the suit that must be 'stayed'. This particular way of thinking (following the lines of metonymic connection rather than respecting the metaphoric rationale of the decision) points to a threat that the decision in part waylays. The threat is that the metonymic connection will prove to be more powerful than the metaphoric identities summoned forth to neutralize its force, that the women's plea will assume the form of a right of power over the company that harmed them. The decision thus points to an alternative way of conceiving things that represents the possibility of an alternative economic reality, another way of structuring economic life. It would, for example, give women control over the corporations that manufacture goods for their bodies because they are the ones directly connected to and directly affected by such manufacture. Those affected, which is to say, those connected materially, should be the ones who determine the forms of control and production, forms that could no longer operate as metaphoric substitutions of things not at all materially connected (with Robins standing in for the women's own self-determination and the judges standing in for Robins). Men could no longer produce for women, and men could no longer adjudicate women's lives.

The kind of deconstructive analysis I've proposed should not therefore stand simply as a question posed to the assumptions regarding identity underlying legal practice; it should be the basis for developing conceptual and institutional alternatives.[11] In this instance, the argument regarding the metonymic undermining of metaphoric identity implies that Robins has now come to include those women as part of its 'identity'. As part of us remains with those we harm, so in this larger economic instance, the corporation has extended its boundary into others' lives, and they should now control what happens to 'their' mutual existence. Another way of putting this would be to say that the exercise of power should be compensated by a proportional redistribution of power. The remedy should address the differential situation, not the immediate identity of 'fact'. It should internalize the unstated 'external' premises referenced by the case. And in this way, out of the occluded alterities of legal discourse, alternatives emerge, for it is in the silences, the repressed statements, that everywhere shadow legal language, that alternate possibilities exist in potential form. Whatever power does not allow to speak should be spoken. Only then will what law does not allow to occur take place.

Implied in a deconstructive critique of law, therefore, is an alternative legal system, which, following the references that can no longer be limited by ideal substitutes, must also be an alternative economic and social system. New constitutions need to be written; new words forged that construct different realitites. From our analysis of the prevailing legal theories and of the rhetoric of adjudication, we can begin to construct some of the necessary first principles and rules of such an alternative legality:

(1) No one shall be obliged to submit to the power of another for whatever reason.
(2) No one shall be obliged to work in a situation that requires accepting commands from others.
(3) No economic activity is allowed that requires that others trade their life energy for monetary remuneration.

(4) All productive organizations must be controlled equally by all participants, and all benefits derived must be shared equally.

(5) No production of any good shall take place without submitting the process of production to review by all those likely to be affected by that good.

(6) The satisfaction of human needs, from the material to the social, shall be guaranteed at levels that no one in the society could imagine not accepting.

(7) Decisions affecting people's lives shall be made by those whose lives are affected.

(8) The goal of law shall be to remedy the causes of injustice.

10 Working Hypotheses for A Post-Revolutionary Society

My argument has been that the logic of justice can come into being only as material or practical forms and procedures, only as a rhetoric of justice. In addition to formulating rationalist procedures, *á la* Habermas, for deriving the principles of a just society, we must also rework the modes and procedures of social life and the cultural forms and languages we use to name and construct it. A rational society may be as much dependent on the reshaping of family power relations so that domination and violence are neutralized and so that those relations create rational agents capable of reasoning without neurosis as it is on valid ideas.

Yet although such social institutions and cultural practices as the family and education are necessary preconditions of rational univerality, material form is usually considered to be subordinate or secondary in relation to the more essential content of reason. Validity, not a new texture of family relations purged of power and violence, is the reasonable ground of justice. The formal or external problem of how to shape non-violent psychologies, or non-neurotic family life, or non-exploitative work relations, or non-republican procedures of democracy is important only in so much as it either derives from a rational ideal or aims at its realization. Within the circle that moves from reason to form to reason, form is a merely intermediate term.

It has often been noted that rationalism results in ideology, a discrepancy between ideal and actuality, because rationalist ideals are belied by material inequalities that are stabilized, rather than forced toward amelioration, by those ideals. Like social form, such inequalities are also considered to be secondary accidents that in no way touch on the rational or modern essence of society. The fundamental structure of domination through the imposition of work that is capitalism is described as a merely regional pathology, if it is perceived at all. The goal of modernization is the maintenance of an identity or unity that is presumed to exist already as an implicit social contract or set of rational social rules, often located in the market. This is another version of the circle of representation, whereby the forms of life under liberal capitalism merely re-present or embody a content of social order or identity that supplies them with rational meaning.

Post-structuralism in part calls for a materialization of thought, a shift toward attending to the way the supposedly merely external forms and formulae of our thinking construct the content of our ideas, as an antidote to such ideology. By focusing on the material forms of our own ways of thinking, we anchor ourselves in the empirical world. Our philosophizing loses its abstract identity by acknowledging its immersion in the contingent and metonymic processes of language, and our language ceases to permit the construction of safe and secure boundaries of exclusion that can be the basis for rationalist (and ideological) ideals. We begin to see our thinking as a form of discoursing with others, as something knitted into the social worlds we inhabit, and as a process with a history that is the social history of language.

The individualist boundaries of rationalism begin to break down, boundaries that posit a separate field of objectivity and transcendentalize a subject of knowledge. It becomes less possible to speak of rational universals like validity without speaking immediately of the material forms of representational embodiment that are in this perspective not merely the representations of such universals but rather the very instruments of their construction, or of the material social forms that are the necessary precondition of unversality. And it quickly becomes evident that the contents of reason are not sufficient for justice, since they themselves are never sufficient unto themselves. If equality or freedom or security have no identity apart from the representational frames that construct them, and if they cannot exist apart from the material discourses that knit world and thought together, then they can be brought to existence as realized ideals only when we re-form and perform the material procedures of our lives, our social practices, our modes of discourse, and our cultural institutions in certain ways.

To talk about a rational ideal of justice thus necessarily entails talking about the figures and the forms in which that ideal will be acted out. It is as much a matter of the formal texture of life practice as it is a matter of offering reasons and agreeing on them. Privileged in this undertaking is a certain tactical disarticulation of identity, the adoption of a non-transcendable situatedness, a necessary inclusion of personal reconstruction to the project, and a focus on representation as something more than a mere adjunct to meaning or substance. We are where we are, working with the figural instruments at our disposal, stitched into rhetorical relations of desire and violence, outside the heaven of reason. We live through life forms even as we try to change them, and the rationalization of our world, which for me means the realization of material equality, entails work on multiple material sites, from politics, to personal relations, to one's own psychology and language, to the modes of cultural representation that construct us even as we speak or think. Reason is available only in those external forms, and it is only by reformulating them that something called reason will be possible as a social norm.

Not to acknowledge the necessarily fragmented and differential character of this undertaking would itself be ideological. Reason, that thing which supposedly marks personal and philosophical identity, is most reasonable when it accepts its own never fully masterable materiality. And in materiality, the boundaries of identity must be seen as constituted through differential relations. From a post-structuralist perspective, what is at stake in the formulation of a common and equal reality is precisely the risk of a loss of identity, an over-riding of those boundaries that maintain the rational self in exquisite isolation, detached from the field of 'objectivity', bolstered by foundation categories like validity that are exempt from debate and that seal it off in a delusory self-sufficiency of reason. We must be willing to accept the fear, the wager, and the hope that lies beyond the boundary secured by such transcendental exceptionalism. Outside the tidy world of universal reason is the messy world of politics and culture, where images are as important as arguments and where the perplexing reality of violence and of material desire must be confronted with as much care as we devote to getting our ideas right.

For these reasons, our work in this arena has to be multiple, relational, partial, and incomplete. The word partial comes from Martha Minow, and that debt signals an important consequence of a shift to a focus on social rhetoric and cultural form: the emphasis on connections between things and between people, connections that are contingent, embedded in the random interactions of speech and circumstance, and grounded in the supposedly pre-rational materialities of everyday life. It underscores the interactive quality of our work considered as a mutual endeavour at constructing knowledge and at constructing the possibility of an alternative world. No single subject, a secular kantian divinity charged with oracular powers, is privileged as declaring the total truth of a supposedly coherent social universe.

The emphasis on connection is both personal and theoretical, and it works across the line separating the personal from the theoretical. It marks as especially important the connections between such things as economic structure, sexual interaction, political institutionality, psychological formation, cultural representation, and so on. The interrelations between the way many people guilty of child and spouse abuse are shaped by cultural images, the displacement of violence from the public to the private realm, the formation of sexual identity in terms of boundary vulnerability, a structural limitation of self-worth to the domestic arena, a political system that neutralizes active self-governance and community life, the normalization of shame as a procedure of family socialization, and that abuse itself are clear. Similar connections emerge when one follows out the references of any single social problem or issue.

One cannot see those referential connections from the pinnacle of rationalist theory. One must assume a fallen rhetorical perspective that conceives of textures of references operating along material lines of determination, textures whose movements are often as much contingent and indeterminate, as they are logical and necessary. And their logic is not of argumentation but of social forces playing off each other, producing necessary material consequences rather than ideational ones. Moreover, although the ultimate remedy for such practices as domestic abuse is the application of our most rational model of psychological well-being and ethical interaction in a social context purged of material inequalities, it remains that the goal of that endeavour is new forms of life practice, new modes of self-representation and self-construction, new styles of being, feeling, and interacting whose motives and goals are situated not in the heights of reason but in the wells of desire.

Mainstream discourse usually assumes a boundary where the scientific or rational-logical determination of the truth of social existence is distinguished from accounts of the lived reality, the empirical detail, of that existence. To a certain extent, it is a boundary of paradox where incommensurate truths – that the rational must be material, yet the rational cannot include the material as such – meet and repel each other. I situate my concluding remarks along that boundary, as much attempting to import science into the project of the imagination and construction of a post-ideological world as attempting to remedy the deficiencies of rationalist abstraction with a sense of the lived forms and textures of experience. What a shift to a rhetorical understanding of the dependence of social content on form or style entails is not a disablement of reason but an ideal of a multivalent reason: one that connects together disparate discourses as well as different strategies of reconstruction; one that sees that a number of different true things can be said about the same thing; one that sees that the discourse of truth need not be limited to what is logical but can also follow the lines of experiential contingency, and that sees in the securing of an identity of means (equality) the creation of possibilities of difference (freedom).

I will describe certain political projects, personal experiences, and imagined possibilities that attempt to form bridges between logic and rhetoric, reason and emotion, science and imagination, the public and the private, the ideal and the corporeal, politics and culture. These pieces are not meant to be exemplary; they do not embody ideals or principles that I have worked through cognitively using a reason presumed to be detached from empirical history. Rather they are about the attempt to further the building of ideals of radical democracy and equality as that attempt confronts and is confronted by the forces of everyday existence at this moment of history. They are about thinking and living as a radical, and they concern my efforts to redo my own life as I try to work with others to imagine and to construct a different world.

This kind of writing is situated between rationalist discourse and imaginative fiction. If the rational logic of justice can become a reality only as a rhetoric of social forms, then the theory of justice must also be crucially about the point of crossing between those two realms, a point where the abstractions of theory and the anecdotes of experience meet. There, at that point, how we live and organize and form ourselves together become as important as our ideas, and those ideas have no validity outside of those processes.

At the intersection of science and imagination, the logic of a future just society comes to hinge as well on the rhetorical ability to create possible models of another world. The relation between logic and rhetoric, whereby the latter was thought secondary to the former, is recomputed in this undertaking. Thinking the content of a new world, fashioning the rational logic of its equations, comes to be seen as much as a matter of drama and fiction, of fabricating new ways of being and acting, as of scientific hypotheses or logical propositions. We must imagine before we can create, and what we create – a new world after a revolution – must allow us to develop not only new structures and ground rules, but also new forms of life for ourselves and between ourselves. It entails crossing certain boundaries.

* * *

We move away from the cold of Connecticut and toward the border with Mexico, down from Del Mar Heights, north of San Diego, where Jim and Laurie have just moved into their new home, toward the other world that has, at least in the parts we see, no new shopping centre or school or pool with cool blue water and a long view.

'Mexico *is* the Third World'. Doug will say later on the phone, but as we move from the white hills of the professional class paradise to the brown hills beyond Tijuana, we already see his point.

'How the landscape changes meaning', you say. 'An open field is not the same here as up there, over the border. It means something else. It isn't valuable land to be developed for real estate. Look at it, strewn with our garbage', you say, directing my attention to the heaps of used cars.

'It's funny how a border changes things', I say. 'And yet it's only an imaginary line really.'

In Ensenada, as the young boy helps us retrieve the keys from our locked car, you say again, how the frame changes the meaning. If he were doing this alone, the police would think him a thief, but put two lost looking tourists next to him, and his action takes on a different significance.

We travel further south, and in San Felipe, on the sands of the Sea of Cortez, we contemplate the turquoise water trying to ignore the beery American boys under the veranda down from Texas for the spring break, their hard redneck faces staring out of the shadows, and I say that I imagine an irony of history, whereby all the northerners, the whites like us, would be obliged by some catastrophe to move south to live, and this land that is now the dumping ground of America would become suddenly valuable, and the people on it, suddenly powerful.

'Imagine these Americans then', you say. 'Having to be polite to people they now insult.'

As we make our way north again, across the Sonora desert to a point where the sea beach, the green agricultural plain, and the desert mountains meet at an exact point in the land, we feel as if we are fleeing ourselves, the frames we have given our existence as white north-erners. In the small store in La Rumorosa at the top of the steep escarpment from whose point we can see out over the desert toward the huge blue lake of the Laguna Salada and beyond up into North America for what must be a hundred miles, the set-faced Indian woman charges us two bucks for a Pepsi, and you say you'd do the same thing to people like ourselves if you were her.

* * *

Power is fear and silence, not knowledge. Foucault was wrong to that extent, even though he was right to privilege power as a primary concern of our work. Power is fear and silence because it makes people fearful of speaking against it, and in that fear of speech, power is born.

The left has not escaped the feudalism of power. We organize together as if liberalism had not yet happened, huddled in tribes, with fetishized leaders, silent about power. I want to talk about this with you.

The emotional bonds that seal people together or fling them apart seem so important in what we think of as public life, especially within the public life of revolutionary organizations. And yet we hardly ever discuss such private things. I suspect we fear discussing emotion because it is so contingent as well as so dangerous; it is a place where we can lose our boundaries. In this we resemble conservatives, who fear losing the unity of power, the identity of the nation or the leader, the boundary of property, the sheltered security of the self – all things that interrelate and that are at stake here. Is this why conservatism continues to haunt the left – from Stalin to Brezhnev to Pol Pot – because we haven't figured out how to solve these dilemmas in our own lives, not just as supposedly private selves but also between ourselves in our organizations? Is it possible to organize in ways, to stipulate rules of organizations, that would prevent conservatism from ever taking power again? From ever turning the function of organizational unity – the party, the nation – into power? Or is such stipulation itself a form of conservatism, an attempt to quell democratic contingency? Half of me wants to say, 'of course', but something in me also wants to go for rules, but rules that formalize the first possibility, the democratic one: all organizational forms must be contingent and revisable, but they can only be revised in keeping with standards of greater democratization, equalization, and effectiveness in bringing about greater democratization and equalization. And this would include the state, so that the rules would implicitly hold off the conservative desire to annul contingency, close government, destroy democracy, eliminate equality.

The National Planners' Network was put together democratically, and the National Socialist Feminist Organization seemed to survive without power. It's not impossible, in other words, though the friendly flexibility of the latter was marked as well by the querulousness of the pro-leninists, fearful of 'too much' democracy.

I realize this isn't very coherent, but that's part of it too. Why fear incoherency?

*   *   *

At a certain point, a boundary of some kind, the personal loses the quality that make it personal and becomes instead the mark left by someone else, or it becomes feelings for or from someone else, or it becomes a materiality that is impersonal. Rethink how that happens, how one's self is other people in a certain sense. How that makes us recompute the hierarchies that place 'important' things like the displacement of economic and political and sexual and racial power before lesser things like remaking family violence or remaking the power relations between people in organizations.

Yet in the 'scientific' socialist and communist traditions, the practical forms, the materiality of personal interaction, are suborned, even though they show through in something like Stalin's murderous rage, his personal feelings of buffoonish rural resentment for the more urbane and intellectual Trotsky, or in the populist, peasant revenge against urban cosmopolitanism that was Cambodia. We are all mad in some way, formed neurotically by a world that is far from being one that would nurture healthy psychological forms of being. If we leave the rectification of that problem off our list of priorities, we will once again see the old forms of projection return – murderous rage, resentment, authoritarianism, intolerance: it's a familiar enough list.

I have a personal stake in all of this.

It fascinates me and it horrifies me – how violence gets transmitted by contact, as it were – from my grandfather, for example, a policeman on the wrong side of the first Irish rebellion, who singled out my mother from amongst her three brothers for brutal beating, to me and to my siblings whom she beat, and to Ginny, who I pushed over a chair once, translating a shame I must have contracted from those beatings into a rage that testified to a need for a comforting fusion as much as it pushed away its possibility.

Revictimization.

I fear how it might, this contagion of violence, be passed on to children of my own, through a relay of negativity that spreads it further. But I wonder too if perhaps the process of revictimization will end when the psychologies like my own that it produces, whose boundaries are fluid, constantly endangered, and perennially in search of a reduction of over-imagined as well as real threats of harm, succeed in transmuting its negative effects into reconstructive ideals, transforming what it causes – a need to protect oneself and a compensatory interest in non-violent practices of thought – into realized values and new institutionalized ways of being. Into a new self, but also, necessarily and implicitly, into new social relations and new social rules, so that the family, rather than being a site of 'privacy' threatened by 'bureaucracy' becomes a public social field where legislated equality and legal protections must 'intrude'.

I hear my sister say over the phone how her son has turned out 'just like me', and I become apprehensive. He is, I learn, a quiet boy who she no longer beats. Devoted to his school work, he seems to have learned the avoidance skill, the way of escaping the family into books, activities, anything. And he seems to have learned how to pacify his environment, soothing my sister through her hang-overs, which are regular and probably potentially violent, despite her denial. I see it happening again, the formation of a fearful and defensive self, genial and kind for the sake of survival, yet fearful of what can come at it, like a hand across the face, blindsiding.

* * *

I take these things to be more than personal concerns; they lead to, they are, public issues, just as the great public issues come back to personal lives eventually. Power stretches from the family to the corporation to the state, and the chain of fathers can't be broken until we find ways of being ourselves without fathers, without the instance of violence or threatened violence that quietens us. Power silences. This is why we have to take seriously something like family violence, because it is, in a way, a version of state violence or class violence or the implicit violence of organizations based on power. And it is the beginning of the chain, the first father.

This is why I cannot accept the freudian-lacanian position on the law of the father and the necessity of a threat of castration to social organization, a threat that separates child from mother and institutes the internalization of social laws. So much bullshit. (Sorry, but it makes me rather angry.) One must always take the side of the victims or of those without or with less power. (This is the counter-optimal logic of radicalism.) The last lacanian I heard speak suggested that children who claim to be abused can't always be believed. Children do lie, you know. But they don't physically abuse adults. Nor do they force themselves on them sexually. Why do we excuse power? Is it to safeguard our own?

* * *

Conservatism at first seems like a psychological contradiction. It espouses radical individualism, a kind of stark boundariedness that is strikingly unempathetic, even cruel, yet it also is oriented toward a fusion that dissolves identity into a boundary-less and frequently sentimental whole. That whole is nevertheless rigorously disciplined, itself defined as an identity that is privileged in some way – the Reich, for example – with its own boundary exclusions, its own violent assertion of a national self. It's as if the strong oppositional identities of the traditional conservative family – sterning father and caring mother, boundary-individualized male and fusion-oriented female – were replicated as political postulates [In this regard, see Blatt and Schichman's important 'Two Primary Configurations of Psychopathology' in *Psychoanalysis and Contemporary Thought*.]

One can understand conservative violence, I think, as an aggression that separates others from oneself and that radically institutes a distance that safeguards one's outlines. One thus preserves one's interiority, one's sense of an identity apart from others. That would explain conservative arrogance, the tendency of conservatives to dictate others' lives, as well as the conservative sense of ordination or exceptionalism, the myth of the unique self.

Does the solution to conservative violence reside then in the construction of a different sense of boundaries, in a different mode of identity that is secure enough in itself to be open to otherness without fear of a shaming derision, one whose boundaries are recognized as connectors to an outside at the same time that they designate an interiority that is secure without needing violently to assert or protect itself? And does that in part mean seeing ourselves – we radicals, that is – as involved in the same world as conservatives, sharing the same dispositions, partaking of and being driven by some of the same material psychological concerns – but attempting to draw our outlines differently?

* * *

At the moment of trauma, what must have been the trauma, the images of my memory become confused and overlapping, as if the trauma also produced a disturbance or wound of representation. My mother has beaten us, the two brothers who share the bed, and then what? The huddling together, a pubescent boy and a much younger one. Was it sexual? A comfort, you say, that had something sexual about it. The wetness against my back. And now the feeling of physical nausea in recalling it with you. Is this the origin of my own incest fantasies – displaced from my grandmother with whom I also occasionally had to share a bed, to my mother who, in so small a row house, had to dress in front of us, to my sister, to a potential imagined daughter? The family situation made such contact seem normal you say.

Linda Gordon, a historian of family violence, wondered in a talk recently if abuse is more common in working class homes.

My other siblings making fun of Don and me, the sharers of the bed, shaming us, exercising their bonded violence, brother and sister, who also had to share a bed. Was it their only protection against my mother's madness, her rageful beatings?

But I'm avoiding the topic, mispelling all these words even as I write them and having to go back over them, correcting. Can it be worked on, this problem – the incest fantasies? You say at least it's in front of us now, and I at least understand how they form: I get angry without realizing it at being unmet emotionally, at rushing home to see you, to find you out all evening, and the fantasy substitutes for anger, repressing it and replacing it with an image of greater care, filling in for your not being there. And there it is, the lack or absence, and the image or representation that take its place, securing my separation from you as a comforting one, but also being itself a compensatory image of a fusion denied. The problem is needing such fusion in the first place, not being able to be alone.

The night they left me in the back room to go off to midnight mass, a piece of cardboard over the bulb so half the room was cast in darkness. The light on the door. The fear. Is that when it all started?

I see the room where the beatings occured, no doubt larger in my memory than it is in life. It is still, as if the air couldn't move, and nothing is happening, as if nothing could happen. But I know this is the cover, the seal on the trauma. The attempt to make things stay still, be quiet, since it was the noise, our children's play, that brought on our mother's rage. And the image also stills the violence, makes it go away, as I had made go away all memory of her over us, her hand falling again and again, for years.

* * *

We live within forms and molds that are given to us by the very society we critique. The idea of a political party, for example, is one of the most anti-democratic inventions of republican capitalist liberalism. It presupposes structures of representation and personal identification that dilute popular and equal participation in governance. Yet in order to operate successfully politically, we must have recourse to them.

In organizations I've worked in or with like the Citizens' Party, an experiment in American Green-ery from the late 1970s and early 1980s, the New American Movement, a 1970s spin-off from SDS, the Progressive Labour Party, a communist group, and the National Socialist Feminist Organization, a network of activists, the comparative advantages and disadvantages of organizational forms were striking. In the Citizens' Party, the power of candidacy to disable collective participation was evident, and that seems endemic to the political party model, rather than being an accident of personality. It was instructive to compare the party model to other forms in which I also worked at the time such as the Charlottesville Activists' Coalition or the Socialist Feminist Alliance, which I organized. These other groups operated according to egalitarian procedures; responsibility rotated; people did what they felt motivated to do without being commanded; and there was a certain flexible contingency of action. We did what seemed appropriate to the moment – from teach-ins on El Salvador in the fall of 1979, to protests against racism on campus (the University of Virginia), to screening educational political films.

The political party model on the other hand was dominated by the candidate for office, and this led to strained relations around loyalty as well as to an egotism of control over campaign activities that made more painful the already difficult task of staging a losing campaign in a geographical location that was not accommodating to progressivism. I felt I didn't have strong enough ego boundaries to engage in the fights that the male-dominated campaign required (or to defend myself against the vituperative wife of the candidate – something I mention so that male-female doesn't get transformed into a natural or moral difference), and I ended up withdrawing from the campaign. But I took with me a sense that there was something wrong with an organizational form that let power become interpersonal violence in this way.

When I attended the party's national meeting as a delegate from Virginia, my sense of the problems of the political party form and of the model of candidacy deepened. At the convention, in the midst of debate, Barry Commoner, the founder of the party, strode to the head of the long line of people waiting to speak at the microphone and began to talk about an alliance he had just worked out with the German Green Party in the hallway. The proposal wasn't discussed, nor was it voted on. And it was clear that the party was a one-man show. After having spent days democratizing, I didn't know whether I should feel disheartened or enlightened.

But I also began to feel that the theoretical issues of representation and personal identification raised in rather abstract ways by post-structuralism had very real political implications. Some other way than the structure of representational substitution whereby one stands in for many has to be found. And the same can be said for the ideal of a personal identity that somehow 'leads' a mass of followers and is the locus of its collective identification.

The Citizens' Party was at least available for participation, an open organization into which anyone, especially on the local level, could come. The point was to create a base and to work up from there, and that ideal still strikes me as valid. It certainly seems better than the Progressive Labor Party model, which consisted of brown paper envelopes distributed to select members at front organization meetings, a selective distribution that created a noticeable difference between an in-group of cadres and an out-group of sometimes duped workers. But PLP remains, while the Citizens' Party and the other more democratic organizations like the National Socialist Feminist Organization are gone. All that's left of the Charlottesville SFA are the teeshirts. But perhaps in that impermanent malleability of formats (most of the former NSFO people are now in the Jesse Jackson campaign) there is something more positive than the permanence and the redundancy of the leninist communist party formations.

What we have to ask ourselves, it seems to me, is this: is a national, an international, new left organization possible, still possible, given everything, one that would overcome the tendency of our local, grassroots efforts to resist transformation into larger organizational levels, or will we have to continue working within the frameworks that mainstream politics gives us, especially the electoral framework? And if that is the case, can we do it in a way that points beyond the ideological implications of accepting such formats?

If we are to work within electoral politics, can we do so in a way that neutralizes the ideal of representational substitution and that limits the centring of personal identity in candidacy? Can we find ways of making the general become particular without there being a preemption of the general welfare by a particular interest? More immediately, how can we work for candidates while yet furthering the idea that the candidate is a multiplicity of people to whom she is connected, of whom she is part? Is it possible, in place of representational substitution, to construct a more metonymic or partial, multiple, and differential democratic process that connects candidates materially to their constituents? Invite constituents to Congress or to Parliament to stand in for their stand-ins?

Liberalism has given us much that is of value regarding the doctrine of rights, the need for constitutional universals such as freedom of speech, equality of access, and fairness of treatment. But it presupposes an individual model of reason and of social identity that is being surpassed by the new social philosophies. Can we work those into our own political practices or are we bound to the compromises I've described, for the time being at least?

* * *

One can't, I suspect, rehearse new forms of organization, of being unbounded from the limits of identity and from the delusions of representational substitutes that ideologically redeem the problematic and contingent messiness of things, unless one is also willing to talk about oneself in a way that is not limited by the need for ego identity or security, by the defensiveness of boundaries of privacy or by the self-embellishing images of purged public self-presentation. One only needs to protect something if it is hidden, if it stands behind walls; only then is power necessary to secure boundaries of exclusion whose crossing will otherwise seem threatening.

In this sense, power is keeping things hidden from others; it's how the bosses operate, fearing disclosure.

But one can only take such risks on the basis of an insight into a common condition, something without boundaries that constitutes all of our senses of bounded identity, a common materiality between us that one might call the realm of ethics. With men particularly, this means being able to tolerate shame, the feeling of not being addressed positively or held in esteem by others, of disclosing without embarrassment.

And what would the lessons of this new way of representing and constructing oneself be for our political work?

In our own organizing, it might mean creating an atmosphere of validating interaction in which the power of feelings of shame, ego-defensiveness, fear, embarrassment, anger, and the like can be addressed or foregrounded as objects of discussion without ridicule and recrimination. When was the last time any of us talked about shame and the real origins of anger in boundary dynamics at a political meeting?

* * *

Another instance. Some of us in the Marxist Literary Group put together a meeting in 1980 to start an organization called the Marxist Union, which was meant to bring together all the different academic leftist organizations from economics and law to literature and sciences, into an umbrella organization and to make connections with extra-academic leftist politics. Hence the title of the first meeting – 'Intellectual Labor and Class Struggle'. We tried to organize democratically, and we decided not to go into the meeting with anything other than a very general agenda. We wanted the organization to be self-determining, and we were particuarly worried about any one group taking over the new organization. What we didn't count on was the intrusion of a group that had an entirely different idea of what the organization as a whole should be. We wanted something like a rallying-ground for politically active academics; the group we found ourselves confronting wanted a traditional trade union that offered services. It was a curious misreading of the word 'union' in the name we gave the group.

I think now that we were naive in not setting the agenda of the organization ahead of time. And we were naive about how fair those desirous of power in left organizations are willing to be. What resulted were fights and shouting and a lot of male chest thumping. We eventually prevailed on the other group to go for mediation, and we handed the organization over to an intermediate organizing committee. But they let the process fizzle out, and eventually the other group took over the idea and continued it as the Socialists' Scholars Conference. The interdisciplinary meeting is now a front organization for the Democratic Socialists of America.

I tell the story because it puzzles me still – why democracy was so violent at the organizing meeting. We could rack it up to overweening personalities, but it also has to do with how radical men come together, with the contending senses of right and prerogative that seem inevitably to arise in such encounters. But why should it not be possible to relinquish the right-to-determine-things that is power in such organizations? We tried that, the initial organizing group from the MLG. Our ideal was to formulate a site where others could self-organize along certain general lines – coming together as radical academics, doing so with an eye to developing extra-academic possibilities for common work. I still think that is a good ideal. But what are we to make of the other group's attempt to impose more moderate general lines and their refusal to let the process of self-organization go forward without interference – without taking over the entire organization and determining it themselves? Egotism? Or is self-organization always going to be characterized by this kind of violence and difference and power-struggling? And if that is the case, what are we to do with the ideal of self-organizing? Make certain it is around shared principles from the outset? Make certain only the right people are at the meeting? And who are the right people?

Even as I read this over I notice a potential contradiction between my desire to have the organization be democratic and my desire to make certain it developed along certain general lines of commitment. I wanted control, yes, but I did so in order to prevent a coup, to make certain the organization remained open and democratic. Is that a contradiction? I could look at it psychoanalytically as abreactive to my desire to secure my environment, to remove the blindsiding of contingency. But also to remove the possibility of violence and power by trying to make certain that the more radical ideals, the ones in favour of equality of participation and democratic openness of form, not greater force or greater bureaucratic power, would prevail. I see my attempt to prevent the organization from congealing into a trade union model lorded over by the other group as an attempt to keep the principles of formation open.

To a certain extent, the MU was an experiment in a new kind of organizing that was sabotaged by an old kind of organizing. But that worries me. Are we doomed to repeat the difference between Trotsky and Stalin, between the revolutionary ideal and the bureaucratic imperative, between the radical desire to create open, democratic organizational forms and the conservative impulse to reduce the indeterminacy of democracy through power? Or are there organizational forms that we have not yet thought of, that we cannot yet begin to imagine, that would guarantee a consistency of organizational identity while yet preserving a democratic openness of participation? Does this require that we remake our own selves to a certain extent, so that we don't equate progressive political work with a hankering for power, or so that we don't confuse organizing with control?

* * *

Power reproduces itself representationally. How could my mother have thought of herself as anything but what she 'was' since there were no other representations for her to model herself on. And my brother Don? His sense of shame was equally representational, a certain degraded image of himself projected onto him by others' representation of him as someone foolish and deridable. He at least was able to compensate for this by living out a playboy fantasy, drugged out in fast cars. More representations.

It's important, this problem, because we think and exist only through representations. How we live and come together – so much of it depends on how we image ourselves and others. How much fear or openness there is in those interactions will depend on how we see each other, what pictures we paint in our minds.

I look at the leaders on the news, and it feels like a telescope, looking from the small end to the big. How we need to level these patterns of representation, look the other way through the glass. The great political filmmakers do this – Mizoguchi in *The Life of Oharu*, for example, the story of a prostitute in Japan, a long, woeful tale told from the ground level.

Aesthetics cannot be placed outside politics, then. And it isn't simply a matter of developing good or better forms, new modes of representation. We need an entirely new optics of the constitution of psychological and social being through representation.

*   *   *

As my sense of strength improves, my boundaries become more visible; the fantasies of incestual or sexual fusion disappear altogether; and I look back on it all as a hungry time, one prolonged in its privacy by the fear of disclosure itself. One has to put it before one, constitute it as an object, oneself as an object in a certain sense, that can be known and understood. I have a growing fondness for science, perhaps for this reason: that knowledge is therapy and empowerment, a move from the passivity of fatedness, of being weighted by history, including family history, to some understanding that permits one to imagine oneself acting differently and that is itself at that very moment an act of acting differently. Describe, and describe again, until everything is described – without fear. End secrecy altogether. And that, I think, is how science and ethics become one. Because if everything is described, everything about oneself that one feared or was ashamed about and didn't understand, then a point is reached where one becomes social, one becomes the transpersonal situation that produced one. Everything then is understandable, as a product of one's history, and everything then becomes something to be chosen or not chosen, as the case may be. But it isn't merely a matter of being free; it is also a matter of being before others fully disclosed. Science is ethics as the full description, full public description, of what one is, which is to say, what a particular formation of need and desire is in a certain situation and context – an Irish working class family, for example, in a small house, abandoned by a father, supported by church handouts, headed by a mother who beat her children and who slipped in and out of depression until she killed herself.

*   *   *

The post-structuralist critique of representation and of identity (the psychological illusion of being a person subtracted from relations and contextual determinants or the cognitive illusion that things exist on their own in a selfsame fashion, figures without grounds) posits an alternative world that emerges from the rubble of the one under critique. Representation, the act of cognitive imagining, no longer seems a matter of the right rendering of facts or of truths; rather, it becomes a work of projection, of making alternatives. Utopianism must be given new credit in this undertaking, and it can be allied with science, conceived as one mode of cognitive representation among other possible modes that aim at the creation of new worlds, the enabling of new possibilities. The project of a scientific utopianism is as necessary to the left's political work as the practical activity of organizing. Without goals we will continue to allow our activities to be defined by the prevailing, limited conditions. And such goals can themselves be arguments in organizing.

As we walk along the cliff above Newport Beach in California you ask what would become of all these beautiful homes in the kind of society I keep talking about. I offered that they might be raffled off on a rotating basis, so that all could benefit from the beautiful experience of living there or in a place like it at least once in their lives. In other words, the identity of person and of place would be dissolved so that one would have a multiplicity of possible existences, all equally distributed or equally accessible.

[Gloss: 'But what of the other desire for rootedness, for a place that is home? (What we're feeling these days with the desire to purchase another half acre, plant trees, and so on)']

*   *   *

Can one make oneself an object for others' analysis, defusing one's defences and opening oneself out onto that neutral space that is the terrain of the common materiality, the shared history of people? Can I take the violence done to me, the abuse, the beating, the derision and turn it into something else that ends it and keeps it from going any further? Is the answer to the issue of taking others as objects not the treating of them as subjects but rather the turning of oneself into an object for others? Linda Gordon noted that men particularly don't talk to case workers in abuse inquiries. Can we begin to talk, we men? As perpetrators as well as victims (the two always being linked, since every perpetration merely signifies a previous victimization). And what would such discussion mean for our ability to organize together without violence?

*   *   *

Political representations pretends to give forth an undifferentiated whole, but in a race, class, and gender plural society, there are only parts in connection. The post-structuralist assumption that modes of representation determine the reality they supposedly represent is at work in politics, since the reality of social life changes considerably depending on what mode of political representation is adopted to 'reflect' what social life supposedly already is. And a different reality of American political life (and of American society) would be created if representation addressed the multiplicity of contiguous social parts instead of pretending to give a substitute for an imaginary whole.

The make-up of the Congress (the US parliament), for example, could be determined by assigning representatives to each sector of the population, according to race, gender (or sexual preference), and income, rather than to each state or region by population alone. In other words, within a state, the number of representatives would still be determined by population, but rather than being assumed to be formal or neutral entities that are indifferent to the kinds of people they represent, those representative would be given a specific metonymic designation, a specific part to represent.

In states half of whose population is black, half the representatives from that state would either be black or be chosen exclusively by blacks. The same would of course be true of women, with the result that at least half of the representatives from any given state would probably be women chosen by women alone. [Fred Pfeil in the margin: 'Makes me want to ask about women who are also black: do they get two votes?] Similarly, each class sector in a state would choose its own representatives from its own ranks. Those making less than $20 000 would be given a certain number of representatives according to the proportion in which they stand in relation to other class sectors. Millionaires could no longer stand as representatives of the totality the 'people' because candidates would need to make less than $20 000 in order to qualify to represent that sector.

Regional distribution could still be a determinant, but the same rules would apply to regions. Districts in San Francisco, in other words, that are predominantly gay would be allowed to choose predominantly gay representatives if they wished. And, of course, regions that want to elect conservative microcephaloids would still be free to do so.

These changes would do much to alleviate the unfairness of representation that now occurs when formal equality is permitted to blunt substantive differences. A white male millionaire cannot represent the interests and desire of blacks or working class people or women. Neither should such people be permitted to legislate laws for people who are radically different from themselves. One consequence of these changes would be that men would no longer legislate for women, or whites for blacks, or rich people for the poor.

This system of representation is deconstructive to the extent that it calls for a respect for differences that are usually ignored or suppressed in metaphysical models of truth considered as an identity or totality and in metaphysical models of political representation. And it promotes the idea of the precedence of material connections between parts over the ideal of substitution, whereby a representative supposedly stands in for a unity, a social whole that is given entire in a single emblem.

The trouble with this reformulation of the forms of democracy, of course, is that it would lead to a disturbance, even a reformulation, of the very ground that made it necessary, that is, the reality of substantive inequality that creates significant differences of power, differences that in turn make differences of gender or choice or ethnicity as acute as they are. And that suggests to me at least why the maintaining of a particular form of political representation is esssential to the content of our particular kind of camp.

* * *

Over the past several years, I confined my work to a collaborative book project and to a collaboratively edited journal that was put together by a group of radical autonomists. Both experiences taught me something about my own limitations, but they also were theoretical lessons of sorts.

I discovered that my own psychology was obsessional and oriented toward control, at least over its own products, and that I was quite intolerant of other people crossing the boundaries of my work. It felt like a violation, and I found myself in the end of the collaborative book project simply going ahead with my revisions of my parts of the book without consulting my collaborator. But while all of this felt justified by the imperatives of my disposition, it also made me wonder about the value of ownership and especially the value of the possession of one's own thoughts and one's own work. To what extent was my unwilling-less to have my writerly will thwarted a sympton of my childhood treatment at the hands of not altogether kind older siblings and a depressive and violent mother? To what extent was it a justified sense of rights? Is the ideal of a post-capitalist, egalitarian world one that gives us all our due or is it one in which we sacrifice a sense of 'ownership' for the commonality?

The ideal of common work, of collaboration or of collective endeavour, implies that such rights find their mediation, that the self and the other come to terms, as we say. Why was this possible ultimately only as an exercise of power on my part over my collaborator, Doug Kellner, regarding what I considered to be 'my' part of our work? And why did I feel it necessary to put my name first on the title page simply because I felt I had done most of the writing? How can we mediate between the demands of anonymity implied by an ideal of equality and the urges of the ego toward recognition and acclaim? Can the differences and the inequalities of energy and capacity be reconciled with the ideal of non-exploitation? Should I feel ashamed about these things, or are they things that we all need to talk about, things that are important precisely because we never talk about them?

In working with the autonomist group, I realized that feelings between men run stronger precisely because they are so denied. In this case, the issue was the boundary of the group. Its identity was formed around a common endeavour – getting the journal out –, and that identity was like a shell that amplified the distortions of personality. One member's infexibility played negatively off my own urgency to be in flexible, controllable environments, and when I took up a position on the margins of the small community, this attempt at difference, a drawing of a boundary of safety, merely magnetized aggression, since the move was perceived to be an act against the others, an offense to that identity that was the collective.

I tried talking about these things once with one of them, but he seemed uncomfortable with so personal a mode of address that asked him to talk about his own anger. And when I raised the issue of authority, the attempt led nowhere. Groups bond around familiarity not flexibility; the characters were already formed; and jokes defused the tensions enough to allow them not to be addressed. When I look at my own character and realize that trying to rewrite personal history is like trying to wrestle free of a straitjacket, I understand how difficult these things are. Since then, I've withdrawn from the group even more, though I see them occasionally. Talk doesn't always work. Or perhaps it simply has to be more patient and persistent than mine was capable of being.

It seems a form of collaboration, that we think certain things cannot be talked about, either personal things or the interpersonal dynamics of our groups. It has to do with power, of course, and with fear, the complement to power, and both are always a function of scarcity – of support systems, of available options, of alternatives to having to put up with power. We fear losing something – prestige, goods, advance, gain in general, but also basic needs for companionship, significance, real belonging. Power takes root in the ability to satisfy those needs at a price – submission of some kind.

But why the fear of raising the issues of our own feelings in processes or political organization instead of acting them out? The possibility of violence perhaps, or of derision and ridicule, that reliable form of interpersonal policing that allows the cynicism of even left conservatism to succeed without seeming to be an exercise of violence.

And that violence succeeds to the extent that by necessity . . .

Can one write in a book like this – I'm confronted with a problem, and I'm uncertain about what to say – instead of writing – here's what's wrong and what's true, and here's the solution? If we were all able to cross that barrier of shame and unstatedness and apparent insolubility, what then? Would we organize together in better ways, without fear or power, since we wouldn't have to feel the need to be the hero of the narrative of our ongoing endeavour, the one who never fails, or stumbles, or falls?

* * *

The word 'utopia' is used with a certain abandon by liberals and conservatives to characterize radical descriptions of alternative social arrangements. It is a dismissive term, reflecting a violence and superciliousness characteristic of people determined to hold onto what they possess, tenaciously gripping the present and bundling it against their chest, their eyes red from watchfulness, their knuckles white, as much afraid of the future as without hope for what it contains.

And they are that way for good reason – because they are people around saying that things can be different. Getting there, however, is as much a matter of rupturing so-called 'mainstream' discourse, which claims such things simply can't be done, as of actually installing alternative institutions.

It is important, therefore, to rethink the way we characterize descriptions of alternative futures. I prefer to think of it scientifically as a matter of hypothesizing and theorizing about possibilities and probabilities. Experimental scientists arrive at determinations of truth by trying out different hypotheses, different maps of what might possibly be the result of certain events or experimental scenarios. The construction of the future will be the result of such theoretical mapping and experimentation based on an assessment of current possibilities. For example, it is easy to determine that now the world produces enough food to feed everyone and to maintain health. Why is this not the case, and how would a scientist map a solution to this problem?

First, she would determine what prevents the solution from being realized; then, she would prescribe ways of removing those barriers. And she would probably say that as long as food distribution is tied to a capitalist market system and to production for profit, a solution will never be realized. What if she projected a model of a world in which food was distributed equally? Would this be utopian? Not really, because one needs such models to be able to measure accurately the inadequacies of what exists and to determine what steps must be taken in order to realize the solution to those inadequacies.

So one could say that so-called utopian thinking is in fact a form of scientific hypothesizing, the projection of a theoretical solution to a problem that must be tested and proven. It is important to think in this way, to recast the 'mainstream' description of things and to make clear that the imagination of the future is a rational, even a scientific, procedure.

* * *

I remember my sense of embarrassment when my brother Don came to visit the upperclass southern school where I taught. He was already deep into it by then, and as we flew down together from Chicago, he put away ten or so shots of bourbon. I went off to teach the next day, leaving him on his own, and later that evening, he came back sodden, having found the local watering holes and talked to students about me and my classes. I wasn't quite appalled, but I was shocked enough to know I'd made a mistake by inviting him. We were in different worlds now from the time ten years earlier when he'd come out to school at Iowa and picked me up after my motorcycle accident and took me home. Or rather, he was in a different world – as indeed I was from him. His body had already begun to waste away, and he smelled of too strong cologne.

It's probably appropriate that I felt the difference as I did – between the abstraction of professional academic life and the messy materiality of my working class brother. I can't reconcile those things because they remain for me a conundrum. Family dramas get staged in certain ways, and it's as if bone tissue forms, they become so hard to bend without breaking. I've broken free and left it all behind, but that doesn't help matters really, other than as an idiosyncratic example of the exigencies of class mobile opportunism. When my sister calls, and I hear the slur in her voice, I feel it all again, and when I'm there and too much drink leads to a hot argument or hard words, I realize how far we have to go, how many areas need our work and our attention and our care. If there's to be what we call a revolution, it will have to be a very big one and a very wide-reaching one, and it will have to take a long time before we can say it's fulfilled its purpose.

* * *

The boundaries that differentiate persons or groups, or insides from outsides in general, motivate power and violence for the sake of protecting boundaries, and it is these things that worry me. If the attainment of identity is by definition the exclusion of the other, then should we not interrogate the possibility of alternative ways of constituting those positive things – rights, for example, or separatist movements – that now derive from the positing of identities.

And should we not also ask into the nature of those rights – ownership of the products of one's labour, for example? If what we are is derived from the structures we inhabit and life histories that lie behind us, then the idea of something 'own' is spurious except as a momentary fleck of spume on the surface of a rather large ocean. Why then though do we attach [it's probably significant, given what psychologists say about aggression establishing boundaries, that I typed 'attack' instead of 'attach'] such strong feelings to it. Perhaps it is because the structures of commonality do not yet exist, structures that would secure identity through the contextual and external apparatuses of society without requiring a violent fixing of boundaries.

Or is that, Doug, an excuse?

*   *   *

When I see the row house now, I can't imagine how so many people fit into it. No wonder we felt so crammed together, our bodies up against each other in the night, like bodies in a mass grave.

In the cemetery in Youghal at the end of town, we look around for the missing markers of my siblings and talk to the old men in suitcoats digging a grave with shovels. Despite the fact that 30 years have passed, they recall my father, 'the one in the army who lived up on the Town Walls', one of them says.

They all remember because memory is a way of resisting erosions. The Youghal carpet factory where my father worked is closed now, and the men are on the hand-out line. The long fishing boats are gone to the greater claims of efficiency, and the harbour now is filled with the leisure boats of the gentry. The real estate man who takes us about to show us houses we imagine buying says the old stone Elizabethan slaughterhouse on the quay must be torn down because there are too many old buildings and we must move forward.

And we move forward too finally, driving west, away from the place that almost itself seems set in stone, like a bad memory.

How would a revolution touch this place, and what would it bring? Get rid of the priests who beat the children? Train the adults not to abuse each other and their children? Give the men something to do besides drink and stand on the quayside looking out at the Blackwater? Tear down the row houses and build homes with large rooms in which each would have a bed and in which children could play far into the night if they wished, without being beaten?

*   *   *

When I try to think the consequences of supposedly personal concerns, of the project of self-reconstruction, I see a relationship between these psychological issues and social politics. A closed government, the ideal of the conservative republican state that 'leads' and is not accountable to the people of democratically run through direct participation, is boundaried in a way that the self is supposed to be bounded and undisclosed in the individualist model of unethical freedom that permits us to victimize, appropriating and acquiring power or wealth behind our boundaries, without disclosing and assuming relational responsibility (the fight against investment disclosures on the part of conservatives, for example). My ideal of a boundary-fluid government, which is no longer a government really, since its operations are entirely public and its decisions are made by all the members of society, seems predictable given everything I've said. It's as if victims of violence can only imagine a political form that would guarantee an end to victimization.

Such an ideal government requires different psychological dispositions, ones that are less modelled by the ideal of boundedness, of privacy and self-identity. This is why conservatism is not simply one political option among others. It is the denial of politics understood as negotiation, deliberation, and common, democratic decision-making. It is the coup as a legitimate governmental form.

* * *

But how are we to come to an understanding of positive power, of the capacity to reshape our world in accordance with the ideal of full democracy and equality? We need standards and rules that are compelling but that do not constitute a mathematical formalism that merely enforces inequality through a spurious claim to formal autonomy. Is there a formalism that is also substantive or that is normed by substantive criteria like equality and full democracy? Can we specify a rule of distribution, for example, that is not normed by the merely abstract freedom of the market but that is guided by formulae that guarantee balance, symmetry, proportion, and commutability?

We can then begin to formulate a different calculus of rights, not as located in a 'subject', but as relations of possibilities and limitations, minimal standards and maximal boundaries. Assuming a society in which the right of the individual subject to accumulate infinitely without regard for others is eliminated, how would such things as housing, income, power to determine things, and the like be distributed? I have already mentioned housing and democracy in regard to the splintering of identity and the differentiating of representation. We can now go further and formulate those two problems as optimality statements.

First, housing. Make a livable home a universal guarantee. But one can own only one home. All extra housing will be given to elected public trusts for rotating distribution. Dwellings in highly valued locations shall be available to everyone on a rotating basis over and above their minimal dwellings for set periods of time.

Similarly, in regard to power: power should be formalized as a right that is distributed proportionally. There are no non-electoral positions of power, nor is there any 'ownership' of power. Bureaucracies are replaced by a universality of electoral positions. Power is communally constructed, temporary and assigned, not assumed. The right to designate actions in others for common ends is made a function of situation, and it is limited by context, reversible, and never the property of a subject. The rights of power are formalized and specified according to the needs or ends to be addressed by its function – making sure everyone's minimal material and social needs are met, guaranteeing that no one's rights are being abused, policing the elimination of exploitation and violence in all arenas of life, and so on. One might be granted power in one realm in order to help facilitate the attainment of certain ends, not in another, but the granting is always electoral, temporary and limited by situation.

Is it possible to model or construct a non-accumulative, deindividualized, non-ownership economy that is not a market economy but that does preserve the dynamism of invention and modernization made possible by an exchange value economy? Consider:

There is a basic dividend share for need maintenance combined with some variable of income factored according to differences in work, time, and effort expended. Money is a common measure that helps facilitate distribution, but it is not in itself a bearer of value. People can choose to be given their surplus dividend in various forms – time tokens to allow them not to work, investment tokens that allow them to place their earnings in production units, or consumption tokens that can buy goods. Rather than determining the shape of economic life through a market, the entire system of price and wages is subject to voting. Prices and wages are set through referenda; the entire economy is made participatory and democratic.

Equality is guaranteed through compensation and adjustments, through balances against accepting non-optimal living conditions or disproportions in the distribution of power. Inverse proportionality guarantees that those who make do with less in one arena get more proportionally in another.

No one shall have the right to accumulate in a way that exceeds the optimal standards of living of everyone else until those standards are met. In the mean time, you can still obtain additional income in the form of time off tokens or extra rights of access to housing on Newport Beach. Money cannot become a power in itself, since it must take the form of time, or investment, or consumption tokens. If one invests well, the most one can accumulate, so long as general standards of optimal living are not yet met, would be more free time or more goods. Power – economic or political – is broken off into another, non-monetarized realm of democratic and symmetric distribution, so it cannot become an instrument of wealth. Indeed, one could formalize a rule that would make the right of access to power inversely proportional to one's investment income.[1]

If the idea of the autonomous subject is preserved as community-owned and managed productive units that compete with each other in the post-need realm, the idea of an iterrelational self is maintained in the ideal of a sharing of any surplus beyond the reward for innovation, or craftmanship, or extra work. This idea only seems to involve sacrifice under our current regime of enforced sectoral scarcity and maldistribution. Like the self, which is most capable of generosity when its own basic needs are met and when its boundaries are assured, inhabitants of this world engage more readily in dividend sharing and mutual, combined redistributive investment decisions for having their needs guaranteed and for creating possibilities for having their inventiveness rewarded because they already have assured levels of need satisfaction.

* * *

Power in my family was a matter of silence. My father never disclosed himself when he escaped to America and stopped sending money. My mother kept everything that drove her mad secret and as a result she imagined children were her enemies, their distracting noise the thing that she had to swat into submissive sleep. My older siblings kept the whole story from me, protecting the younger one, but also keeping him out of the negotiations. It was the unconscious as a social principle, as a family matter. So the unconscious is not the 'Other', something big and overwhelming. Rather, it is what isn't said. *Ça ne parle pas*.

And as I say this, I see that I do so by turning myself into a third person, narrating as if I were someone else – 'the younger one'. I've lived outside of myself for all of these years. My gift for abstraction. For such gifts . . . When I see it happening, when I have the strength to venture near the trauma again, it is happening to someone else. I am there looking on; it isn't happening to me. I wanted to be elsewhere, you say. It's understandable.

And that kind of event, I realize, not some narcissistic hankering for a unity with the mother, is the origin of utopic desire. It is not a need to e one with a neonatal totality, a unity of bliss. It is a transmutative and therapeutic desire to be outside pain and victimization. It is utopian because it has to be elsewhere to avoid pain and nowhere to avoid power; it has to slip free, always be other than the person who is being beaten. The utopian is nothing more than a good story, a better one, than that experienced by the victim, in the third person.

*   *   *

There are a number of lessons, then, that can be derived from post-structuralist thinking for reformulating our political and economic strategies. The first is the idea of non-ownership. No one owns beyond their needs – house, transportation, daily life instruments, food, clothing, and so forth. The economy is run as trusts are now run; they belong to no one, and they are managed by elected boards who oversee their operation and the preservation of the funds, but the boards do not own, nor do they derive profit. The second is the idea of multiple democracies. No public subject is given out to represent the totality of society. Twenty-six per cent of the population can no longer claim to stand in for the whole society. Voting is sectoral. Only those directly affected by an issue can vote; only women, for example, can vote on such issues as abortion. Democracies are also multiplied as direct determination of so-called 'public' life. Direct referenda – tele-referenda of the kind now used in popular culture – give access to decision-making to people without having to go through substitute representatives. What is needed is not more 'leadership', the great republican ideal that still haunts the left, but more access to and more accessibility of power. Which, of course, ceases to be 'power' once it is made public, no longer kept as the reserve of 'representatives'.

*   *   *

By now, two questions may have come to your mind. First, can I take seriously the economic and political proposals of a man who admits in public to having, or having had, incest fantasies? Second, can I trust the proposals of a man who doesn't make such public disclosures?

*   *   *

But how can we imagine things to be different within the limits of thought – not to say the limits of power – imposed by our situation? What we say we are capable of attaining is so often a repositing of effects of our common victimization. Dedetermination? Seeing the structures as personal and the personal as a structure. At the end point of reference, I am boundary with the social history of schizophrenia in west Ireland that shaped my grandparents and my mother. But I am also the possibility of being more than that, of rewriting my history as my future.

It's necessary, from within the framework of the existing social regime, to locate points where the interiority guaranteed by its self-replication melds with a possible exteriority, points where its boundary breaks down but also breaks open, toward something else. It's as frightening, that, as losing one's own boundary security, one's own sense of being a self sealed off from an outside, frozen within one's private, which is to say, shared but untold thoughts. Yet why can I not conceive of those breaks as violence, even revolutionary violence? Perhaps it is because I see revolutions, even supposedly violent ones, as always putting an end to violence, and victimization, even the 'private' victimization of child abuse. And this, the combined breaking through of social boundaries and breaking out of the 'self' that will be our next revolution will necessarily be violent, a breaking of a certain hold on power that plays itself out as our shared fear, but that will also, by that very token, mark an end to violence, the violence that is our 'civil' society and the violence that is our family life. It will be a lesson in overcoming derision, abuse, and shame as much as in ending inequality and exploitation.

* * *

When Don died, in part as a victim of family history, in part as a victim of the Vietnam War, I felt relieved for his sake. Drugs and drink over many years had left him pitiful and wasted. And behind it there seemed some great pain, his wetting of our common bed perhaps, the derision of Sean and Anne, or my mother's beatings. He never quite got over it all, I think. He always seemed ashamed and subdued by the world.

A week before they found his body, he called, and I refused to talk to him. He was drunk again, and I wanted nothing to do with it. I was still trying to struggle free of it all, as I strove to get away from him in the bed in Ireland. It was the worst feature of my temperament speaking – the moralizing, stern judge – the person created by the same accumulation of silence that created him as he was at that moment. Revictimizing.

I wonder how it can all be changed, how the revictimization can be stopped. I imagine it as an act of mourning, a taking in of the feared past, of what has been thrown out and repressed, that stills it while yet acknowledging one's material connection to it, as one lets go of a dead person by holding on to his image. The boundaries of what is one's 'own' make no sense in such an endeavour, because someone else is in one, yet also outside, purely outside, in the blank materiality of things. The disruption that is the death of someone like that, someone 'close' as we say, makes the dust of the grave settle on us, burying us as well. When my hands reach into the dirt of the flower beds behind the house, I think I am reaching toward him, that somehow my hand is touching what remains of his body.

What protects us from emotion, from the crossing of boundaries, is abstraction from materiality. Only in abstraction can there be identity. Perhaps this is why the great abstract idealist, liberal thinkers like Kant and Habermas are so unemotional. Do we need, then, we radicals interested in going beyond the collaborationist silence of such liberalism, to connect with a certain personal materiality as much as with the materiality of social life?

*   *   *

The division between materialism and rationalism is played out as the difference between empirical and theoretical work, between political work within existing situations and political work that aspires toward a fundamental reconstruction of the structuring presuppositions of society. Can we do both at once, accepting the incommensurability? I can imagine two possibilities. On the utopian register: propose new constitutions that argue the placing of issues of economic power on referenda that would make them a matter of national choice. On the realist register: take the conservative ideal of freedom beyond itself and argue for the expansion of private rights of ownership to include workers' rights of management over all firms that employ people, for the limitation of single-person ownership to 1 per cent of a company, and for an expansion of the privatization of public property as the redistribution to the larger public of rights of ownership of stock in all companies that make goods in any way associated with the satisfaction of general public needs.

And for myself, here and now? I'm struck by how thick radical politics gets in urban areas and how thin it gets out here in less populated areas like the one where I've just moved, areas where defence corporations have a certain greater freedom of action as a result. I want to put ads in the local newspaper, try to find out if there are any other radicals around (call Fred when he gets back to Hartford), but I'm not certain I have it in me any longer to go through the process of organizing meetings, reserving halls, staging protests, running candidates, posting flyers, holding teach-ins, and the like. I will go look over the local Democratic Party because that, it seems to me, will for us in America, be a site of work as the generation of 1968 comes of age. And I want to try to contribute to the making of that change of period by trying to start a left version of conservative William Buckley's television talk show, *Firing Line*, which has helped place the right-wing agenda before the American public over the past few decades. We need to do something similar.

And beyond that? The Communist Party? Just to be on the winning side of our moment in history with my black revolutionary friends? Or the Democratic Socialists of America, just to be with my more fastidious white new left friends? Or both at once? And what does this dilemma, this real material difference mean for my ideal of a connective, multiple politics? Is it really possible? Fred again: the story about marching with minorities one day in downtown Hartford, an economic demilitarized zone, and being on a strike line with white workers the next, hearing them hurl racist abuse at the black strike breakers. Up in your face, as he puts it. Is there a way through these 'hard realities' other than through the hard organizations – such accurate reproductions of the world they represent – that Raymond Williams touts – the trade unions and the professional organizations? That may be for us to decide, and that's why our own bad practices worry me so much, our own questionable ideals – leadership, for example. Rather than leadership, whose negativites I've felt too patently in my own work, what we need is another altogether more complicated process of organizing, building, empowering, and binding together. Our own sense of moral righteousness must stop being an excuse for what we think of as justified violence against each other. Otherwise, we have no right to be involved in the organization of a new society.

* * *

If we continue to think of the private negatively as a realm of ego imaginaries, we lose much of value politically in the process. If the private is a precipitate of interpersonal relations, shot through with mediations that tie it to public structures, it is also a gateway to that world, a way of refiguring its supposedly systemic laws.

Something similar must be said of the public world, which in this perspective is seen as a congeries of private interests, a series of discrete, personal acts whose repitition creates the appearance of a structure. Work on the private and the public cannot, therefore, be thought of as disconnected, but for that reason, their relation must be reconceived.

The public, in the form of its instrument the state, has been successfully attacked by conservatives over the past decade and a half in the name of private interest. And the left will be tempted upon retaking power to reassert the ideal of the public state as a response to the reactionaries. Yet in the conservative victories, there may be a critique of the old left ideal of representational substitution – the public standing in for the private, the state for the democratic electorate – that the left would do well to heed. And by this I do not mean an acceptance of privacy and 'free' self-interest as a standard. Rather, what I have in mind is a deconstruction of the structuring of social life as a polarization of the private and the public, the free self and the unfree state.

We have to imagine a refiguration that would create greater connections between people and the public institutions that bear on their lives. One result of such connection would be that the state could no longer be the emblem of a separate 'public' that stands juxtaposed to a disconnected 'private' self. This is why we have to argue for the real possibility of more direct forms of democracy – referenda on all major social issues, referenda that are sectorally differentiated so that certain classes of people vote on their own lives, while matters of general welfare are addressed by all. We must argue for the making of distribution decisions not by representational substitutes but by those whose lives are at stake in (which is to say materially or metonymically connected to) those decisions.

What this presupposes as well is a successful refiguration of what privacy means, of what it means to hold privately wealth that is produced through common endeavour. Any possibility of a democratic encroachment on that right will mean delegitimizing the boundary that separates the public from the private, sealing off private accumulation from public, communal decision-making. That crossing cannot occur legitimately so long as the public is conceived as a substitute state representative in no way connected to and bound up with people's lives, in no way a material extension of their own 'private' activities.

The model of a non-participatory state merely reaffirms the public as a detached, impersonal instance that stands in opposition to and exclusion from private subjects, and it thereby also reaffirms the figure of the private self as something whose boundaries cannot be crossed by that external public instance. If the state must be reconnected with those it supposedly represents, the self must be reconceived as a precipitate of object relations that create boundaries which are elastic and contingent and that make social relations and contextual situations internal to subjectivity. As much as it is subject to laws, therefore, the self must become subject to democratically arrived at decisions regarding wealth distribution, decisions that are the result of direct referenda.

This democratization would be one answer to the question of how we prevent the republican coups of recent years from happening again, how we keep conservatism from repeating the damage it has done. We must constitutionalize the deconstruction of the public and the private so that a separate instance of state power cannot ever again become detached from direct referenda on all issues, including economic issues.

In this way, moreover (and the result, I suspect, would be guaranteed), democratic participation becomes the means of a material reconfiguration, the instrument eventually of an economic revolution whose popular appeal and structural consequences would far exceed anything state representatives, secure in their substitutional power and with their own self desires camouflaged behind the imagery of public life, could accomplish.

* * *

I remain angry at the beatings and the derision and the war that made Don as he was, a waste sustained by life-support systems in a hospital the last time I saw him alive, and I remain afraid of the violence.

He was proud of the purple colour his leg had turned, of the fact that he was holding up so well under such bad conditions, and I feel pity still to think of it – the paltry rewards that are eked out to the victims, the delusion of being someone, the brief glad flash of the bulb, one's illumination, then retraction into darkness. If I could hold him again, I would. Even if I could feel him crying on my back, forcing me to squirm away toward the cool of the row house wall, I'd have that too, painful as it was. Anything but this sense of loss. I'd hold him and have him dream of nights without nightmares and of worlds without pain. No more victims.

At his funeral, the coffin was closed, and I felt immobilized by its impersonality, just as I felt immobilized by the sheer angry force of the beatings we endured together, prone before a physical power as well as a power of madness that was greater than anything we two together could ever match. I think of his funeral as bringing to a sum a bad history I want to end, almost as one tries to end a strain of virus by not allowing it to reproduce. His death for me was the culmination of a line of victimization. For though my mother was for us the source of it all, she was, as much as Don, a victim, herself an endpoint of another, probably much worse history of violence.

She seemed, like Don, desperate for death. And when the first bottle of pills didn't work, she tried again, walking off into the night so that they couldn't find her a second time. I still don't know whether such determination is admirable. I can only feel its weight, like the slamming of a door in anger. I want it not to have happened. Just as I want the beatings not to have happened.

That, I think, is the real source of utopian desire. Wanting the pain to end, wanting there to be no more victims.

*   *   *

The committee met again today.

Notes

INTRODUCTION

1. Portions of the introduction consist of a revised version of papers presented in the 'Feminism/Marxism/Psychoanalysis' panel at the Modern Language Association convention in 1981 and in the 'Politics and Ideology' panel, sponsored by the Marxist Literary Group, at the 1982 MLA convention. A portion was published under the title 'Literary Criticism and Cultural Science: Transformations in the Dominant Paradigm of Literary Study', *The North Dakota Quarterly*, Vol. 51 (Winter 1983) pp. 100–12.

2. *Marxism and Deconstruction: A Critical Articulation* (Baltimore: Johns Hopkins University Press, 1982).

3. On plasticity, see R. M. Unger *False Necessity: Anti-Necessitarian Social Theory in the Service of Radical Democracy* (Cambridge: Cambridge University Press, 1987).

4. M.Harris, *Cultural Materialism: The Struggle for a Science* (New York: Vintage, 1980) p. 47.

5. P. Bourdieu and A. Passeron, *Reproduction* (Los Angeles: Sage, 1977); P. Bourdieu, *Distinction* (Cambridge: Harvard Unversity Press, 1985).

6. C. Geertz, *The Interpretation of Culture* (Princeton: Princeton University Press, 1972); V. Turner, *Drama, Fields, and Metaphors* (Ithaca: Cornell Unversity Press, 1974) and *From Ritual to Theater* 'New York: Performing Arts Journal Publications 1982).

7. See especially 'Ideology and Ideological State Apparatuses', in *Lenin and Philosophy* (London: New Left Books, 1971) pp. 127–88.

8. See below note 16.

9. J. Lotman, *et al.*, Theses for the Semiotic Study of Culture (Lisse: DeRitter, 1975) p. 7; J. Lotman and B. Uspensky, 'On the Semiotic Mechanism of Culture', *New Literary History*, Vol. 9 (Winter 1978) no. 2, pp. 211–32.

10. T. Kogawa, *The Electronic State and the Emperor System* (Tokyo: Kawadeshoboshinsha, 1986).

11. I am thinking of deconstruction as it can be applied to culture, although included under the rubric of post-structuralism here would also have to be work of Foucault, Baudrillard, and Deleuze/Guattari. Some work along these lines is already underway within the discipline of anthropology. See J. Clifford and G. Marcus *Writing Culture*, (eds) (Berkeley: University of California Press, 1986).

12. See M. Mann, *The Sources of Social Power* (New York: Cambridge University Press, 1986) p. 462.

13. R. Williams, *The Sociology of Culture* (New York: Shocken, 1982) pp. 207–11.

14. P. Bourdieu, *Outline of a Theory of Practice* (New York: Cambridge University Press, 1977).

15. It would be unfair to Williams not to note that in later work, he himself elaborates conclusions similar to the ones I offer here. See particularly *The Year 2000* (New York: Pantheon, 1983), where he speaks of the 'intricate interdependence' of 'life forms and land forms' (p. 260).

16. S. Hall, 'Cultural Studies and the Centre: some problems and problematics', in *Culture, Media, Society* (London: Hutchinson, 1980) p. 27. The bibliography of the Birmingham School is too extensive to cite entirely. The salient collective works are *On Ideology, Resistance Through Rituals, Policing the Crisis*, and *The Empire Strikes Back*. See also the individual works by Hebdige (*Sub-Culture: The Meaning of Style*), Frith (*Sound Effects*), and Chambers (*Popular Culture*).

17. I am referring to Hall's lectures at the 'Marxism and Culture' conference held at the Unversity of Illinois, Urbana, in the summer of 1983. See L. Grossberg and C. Nelson *Marxism and the Interpretation of Culture* (eds), (Urbana: University of Illinois Press, 1987).

18. Hall, *et al.*, *Resistance Through Rituals: Youth Sub-Cultures in Post-War Britain* (Birmingham: Centre for Contemporary Cultural Studies, 1975) p. 41.

19. See Williams' remarks about 'interactive observation' as a necessity of even basic agriculture. *The Year 2000*, p. 265.

20. For a discussion of the problems entailed in the interpretation of these social events, see P. Willis, *Learning to Labour* (New York: Columbia University Press, 1981).

1. THE JOKER'S NOT WILD: CRITICAL THEORY AND SOCIAL POLICING

1. J. Habermas, *Theory of Communicative Action: Reason and the Rationalization of Society*, Vol. 1 (Boston: Beacon Press, 1984), and *Theorie des Kommunikativen Handelns: Handlungsrationalität und gesellschaftliche Rationalisierung*, Band II (Frankfurt: Suhrkamp Verlag, 1981). All subsequent references will be in the text. For critical assessments of this work, see the special issue of *New German Critique* devoted to Habermas (No. 35, Spring-Summer 1985), especially the essays by McCarthy and Mitgeld, and S. Benhabib, *Critique, Norm, and Utopia: A Study of the Foundations of Critical Theory* (New York: Columbia University Press, 1986). This is an excellent critical assessment of Habermas that points toward a mediation between critical theory and post-structuralism. See also the essays by N. Fraser, and I. Young in S. Benhabib and D. Cornell (eds) *Feminism as Critique* (London: Blackwell, 1987) For a feminist assessment. For a critical summary of recent work, see D. Ingram, *Habermas and the Dialectic of Reason* (New Haven: Yale University Press, 1987), especially pp. 169–71.

2. Habermas is concerned with defending a metaphysical, romantic and naturalist notion of interiority. The real danger from capitalism is not the expanded exploitation of people's energies in the making of the

social factory, but rather the 'colonization of the lifeworld' by 'systems' of money and power. Already in an earlier work like *Theory and Practice*, this metaphysical and logocentric tendency was evident, especially in the nostalgic privileging of an earlier age when theory and practice were joined, before being sundered in the modern age. In his most current work, that romantic mataphysics reappears as the ideal of a life world, threatened by systemic instances deemed to be external to it. This romanticism is surprising in a philosopher who wears his rationalist credentials like medal bars on a general's chest. But it really should not be (Kant, the godfather of Habermas' rationalism, was, after all, one major father of romanticism). The boundary that separates validity from the process of communicative interaction that it norms is replicated in the boundary between life world and system. In each instance, something secure and self-identical, not defined by articulation, differ-ence, alterity, or a referentiality that opens it beyond itself constitutively to an outside, is privileged and protected by that boundary. So also, the norm of validity is a purely internal norm. Not surprisingly, social negativity for Habermas does not consist of the oppressive manipulation of people's bodies in work (that trouble was dispensed with long ago by building a boundary securing a metaphysical distinction between communication and labour), but rather of the encroachments by bureaucracy on so-called private family life and on freedom defined in neo-subjective terms.

3. J. Habermas, *Die Philosophische Diskurs der Moderne* (Frankfurt: Suhrkamp, 1986) pp. 191–247. I have concentrated exclusively on that part of Habermas' book that touches on my own work here, the section on Derrida, which is based almost entirely on Culler's *On Deconstruc-tion* (Ithaca: Cornell University Press, 1982). Culler's book is a clear exposition of Derrida's ideas, and Habermas has a hard time finding anything to criticize. What he does ultimately criticize is not Derrida but Culler's thoughts about Derrida. Habermas especially latches onto those statements of Culler's where he argues for an understanding of philosophy as 'literature'. This is an interesting idea, one elaborated on by Richard Rorty, for example, but Derrida himself does not make this argument. The one time Culler cites Derrida directly on the topic the word 'literary' is in quotes. Derrida does argue that philosophical conceptuality is inseparable from representation, rhetorical tropism, syntax, the polysemousness of language, and the spatial inscription usually associated with writing. But he carefully avoids identifying these representational processes that undermine the idealist pretensions of philosophy with a social institution like literature or with the idea of fiction, which belongs to a conceptual system, differentiating fiction from truth, that itself would no doubt be seen by Derrida as deconstruc-tible. In his transposition of Derrida's critique of metaphysics into the literary critical frame of reference, Culler often replaces Derrida's rhetorical and philosophical categories with literary ones – archi-literature' instead of Derrida's 'archi-writing' or 'fictive' instead of 'scriptural', 'metaphoric', or 'representational'. And precisely these

transposed terms become the target of Habermas' most scathing attacks. I will not attempt here to deal with the debate between Habermas and Culler over whether or not philosophy is a literary genre.

Habermas' second major critique of Derrida focuses on a statement attributable to Culler but not to Derrida: 'If a text can be understood, it can in principle be understood repeatedly, by different readers . . . These acts of reading or understanding are not, of course, identical. They invoke modifications and differences . . . We can thus say . . . that understanding is a special case of misunderstanding' (*On Deconstruction*, p. 176). This is a problematic rendering of Derrida's idea that all understanding can never be purely purged of the possibility of misunderstanding, so that the latter cannot be declared external to the former. Culler's wording is more his own than Derrida's. Derrida argues that all understanding is necessarily structured by the possibility of misunderstanding because all understanding, the communication of meaning from one subject to another, is necessarily mediated by representation and language, and representation holds no guarantee that it will not go astray and betray the intended meaning it carries by giving rise to other meanings, other understandings. It is in the very nature of representation, signification, and language to be open to this possibility, a possibility that cannot be closed off. Now, this does not mean that all understanding is a special case of misunderstanding. It means that understanding relies on an instrument that is plagued constitutionally by indeterminacy, and therefore, knowledge or understanding can never fully rid itself of the possibility of a plurality of understandings that 'miss' the mark of the intended one. Consequently, the possibility of misunderstanding is a permanent and irreducible part of the structure of all understanding. The claim that 'understanding is a special case of misunderstanding' owes more to literary critics like Harold Bloom and Paul de Man than it does to Derrida.

Consequently, Habermas (with the exception of his neo-idealist rebuttal of Derrida's critique of Husserl's theory of meaning) for the most part takes up the ideas of an interpreter of Derrida. And the fact that Habermas engages in such a radical misreading is perhaps an indicator of whose side in the debate carries the greater weight of truth.

For a more balanced account that nonetheless is somewhat prejudiced against Derrida, see P. Dews, *Logics of Disintegration: Post-Structuralist Thought and the Claims of Critical Theory* (London: Verso, 1987).

4.   Jurgen Habermas, *Autonomy and Solidarity, Interviews*, ed. P. Dews (London: Verso, 1986) pp. 67–9. These are, of course, the traditional excuses of social democracy and of liberalism everywhere – the fear of democracy as the fear of the fragmentation of the social unities upon which liberal psychology depends, unities whose excuse for lasting is that they are too 'complex' for the 'simple' imperatives of democratic management.

Habermas in *Communication and the Evolution of Society*: 'I can imagine the attempt to arrange a society democratically only as a self-controlled learning process [As, in other words, a correlate of the individual's cognitive development toward greater ego universality and individuation, greater formal abstractness – greater, if you will, male socialization.] It is a question of finding arrangements which can ground the presumption that the basic institutions of the society and the basic political decisions would meet with the unforced agreement of all those involved, if they could participate, as free and equal, in discursive will-formation. [This is the rationalist poll tax of validity, I think.] Democratization cannot mean an a priori preference for a specific type of organization, for example, for so-called direct democracy' (Boston: Beacon, 1979), tr. T. McCarthy, p. 186). But how is so-called democracy distinguished from 'so-called direct' democracy, if democracy means rule by people over their own lives?

What a republican rationalist like Habermas fears is the messiness of material democracy, the struggle for truth as the rhetorical struggle for particular material constructions of reality. And it is feared that the right to decide such matters should reside with the mass of people and be based on their needs and desires because that would entail a significant material change in the order of society, an order that is, as a modernization attaining ever more formal differentiation, merely a mirror of 'mature' reason. The order Habermas sees as so 'complex' that it needs to be preserved under the tutelage of an 'extraordinarily intelligent' party is in fact a structure of material deprivation and domination that would not be tolerated were the possibility of deciding on its preservation or destruction in the hands of those who lose in the bargain that it offers. Although the terms 'rationalism' and 'materialism' are assumed to be already deconstructed in this analysis, so that we can think of what they used to signify only as figural arrangements of terms whose identity is given by those figural arrangements themselves, I will continue to use materialism as a sign for the outside of what rationalism seeks to preserve as pure inside, a realm of rational decision making exempt from worldly concerns or deprived of a constitutive connection to a social world. On the materialities of power in actual decision bargaining, see H. Van Den Doel, *Democracy and Welfare Economics* (Cambridge: Cambridge University Press, 1979).

In the next chapter, I will look at an alternative pro-democratic radical theory in the work of Negri. A theory of 'autonomy' is not alien to Germany. See Karl-Heinz Roth, *Die 'andere' Arbeiterbewegung* (Munich: 1974) as well as the German issue of *Semiotext*, for an account of the alternative movements.

5.   My description of Habermas' position on validity is not a recapitulation of what he himself claims. It is rather a critical analytic description. Habermas claims validity is what will be arrived at through communicative action oriented toward mutual understanding. In other words, in order for such communication to take place, the participants must agree to speak in certain ways, to offer justifications for their positions, and so on. What will be accepted as valid will be a matter of discussion, and it will emerge from the debate itself. Habermas would no doubt claim that

this does not consitute a prenorm to discussion or a foundation in the old sense he rejects. But by already positing validity as what communicative interaction will arrive at, he assumes it as a norm. Why should validity be what people assume as the norm or goal of their communicative interaction? Why not difference or multiplicity or creativity or what will in experimental situations prove to be the most substantively just or, worst of all, what feels best?

I also counter-textually suggest that Habermas' norm of validity cannot but be an individual subject (despite his assumption of a more pragmatist position that focuses on intersubjectivity in Volume 2) because of his emphasis on validity. A norm really based in discussion between two or more subjects would be open and contingent. Validity implies a closure of certainty that can only be (and then in deluded fashion) the possession of a single subjectivity. A discussion not normed by something like validity is determined more as an interaction of forces whose direction is not always predictable. It is more dialogic, and its creative potential resides precisely in its capacity to take and build, give and receive. Validity is one possible norm for such discussion, and it is one possible ideal of the supposed 'rationalization of society'. But it is not the only one.

Finally, Habermas's choice of logical debate – the exchange of arguments and reasons – as a model for communicative interaction is itself shaped by the adversarial tradition of philosophic discussion. What matters is who wins by giving better reasons. This is a model he inherits from Plato; hence, his frequent reference to someone else's 'vulnerability' to attack. If the style is adversarial, the goal is power, greater cognitive mastery and the domination of one's opponent. Habermas would no doubt argue that since all communicatively arrived at norms must be mutually agreed upon, I'm being unfair. But from the outset, one can only enter into debate on terms Habermas has already determined – the assumption, for example, that rationalization (defined as greater and greater formalization) is a good thing, that Eurocapitalist modernization consists of rationalization, and that reason and validity should be the norms of interaction. What if you believe none of the above? That contingency, that possibility of difference is not permitted in the republic of left kantianism.

The idea of validity is most clearly elaborated in *Communication and the Evolution of Society*, and that discussion is presupposed in the *Theory*. Behind the idea lies Apel's notion of a 'transcendental constraint', the presupposition of a communicative community. (See K. O. Apel, *Towards a Transformation of Philosophy*, tr. G. Adey and D. Frisby (London: Routledge & Kegan Paul, 1980). The idea of a transcendental constraint must be supplemented with the idea of an immanent constraint, the material universe of material needs and contextual forces that shape both the form and the possibility of validity. There is no purely internal criterion of validity. Speech acts do not only work because of cognitively testable validity claims. They also very crucially are a matter of power. Austin's example of the naming a ship by the Queen presupposes both an appropriate context and a power to engage in such a speech act that will compel acceptance.

The idea of a purely internal norm of validity also exempts validity from being socially negotiated and from being differentially defined, so that it might vary from context to context. It is an anti-democratic concept. Essential to the elaboration of a more democratic concept that would fulfill the same function of guaranteeing a common ground of discussion while yet leaving open the possibility of differential inflections and mutual negotiation of terms is a different concept of language. Such a concept would see social setting as a crucial feature of meaning. For a critique of language that moves beyond Habermas by describing how social context and power relations inhere in speech acts, see P. Bourdieu, *Ce que parler veut dire* (Paris: Payot, 1980) and M. Bakhtin, *The Dialogic Imagination* (Austin: University Texas Press, 1981)

Habermas reacts with hostility and dismissiveness to other theorists who encroach on the sacrosanctness of reason by proposing that it might be anchored in the social, yet interestingly, his argumentation at such points becomes anything but rational. In response to Pitkin's claim (in *Wittgenstein and Justice*) that our concepts are shaped by 'our forms of life', Habermas answers: 'That may well be. But who guarantees that the grammar of these forms of life not only regulates customs but gives expression to reason. It is only a small step from this conservative appropriation of the great traditions in terms of language games to the traditionalism of a Michael Oakshott' (*Communication*, p. 204). This is a rhetorical move, disparagement by association, and a very contiguous or metonymic association at that. I thought reason was supposed to be metaphoric, a way of substituting higher, more formal and abstract concepts for exercises of mere rhetorical force or for mere empirical observations?

All of this makes understandable Habermas' claim, when he examines the problems entailed by welfare state bureaucratic intervention in people's lives, that this kind of problem would be a paradox for Marx, while also claiming there is no specific class character to the life world of late capitalism (II, 517). Such lack of distinction is probably only possible in this kind of metaphysical thinking, which mistakes its own 'rational' and 'modern' social surroundings (I suppose the Turkish guestworkers in West Germany, because they are a race, don't constitute a class) for a norm that is not differentially constituted through the exercise of force against Third World peoples. (Where are Third World theorists of underdevelopment such as Amin, Frank, and Rodney in Habermas' understanding? Nowhere because they're radicals?) Habermas forgets that problems of bureaucracy arise in a context in which many First World corporations merely shift production to the Third World, maintaining the nineteenth century of raw industrial exploitation in other places, out of view. Should we really accept then that capitalism has entered a new, higher phase, when it seemingly must continue as it was elsewhere? The Third World of exploited labour is an external internality of the capitalist system, something it must keep out, but on which it depends, and that is the specific class character of the life world of late capitalism.

6.　Agnes Heller addresses some of these issues from within the sphere of German critical theory, though Habermas reacts negatively to her critique. See 'Habermas and Marxism', in J. B. Thompson and D. Held (eds), *Habermas: Critical Debates*, (Cambridge: MIT Press, 1982), pp. 21–41. Habermas' response is in the same volume, 'Reply to my Critics', pp. 219-83. See also Heller's critique of Habermas 'universal pragmatics' in *Beyond Justice* (London: Basil Blackwell, 1987) pp. 234–42.

7.　At the end of the second volume, Habermas does come around to a more radical position, after seeming to opt for potentially anti-radical theories (wallowing in liberal sociologists like Weber and Parsons, while ignoring radicals like Bourdieu and Foucault; describing the new autonomous social movements as generational 'pathologies'). Even more surprising is the way he promotes a viewpoint that brings him close to the French thinkers I have been using as a criterion for criticizing his position. He argues for the inmixture of practical reason with theoretical reason in an ideal of a formal pragmatics akin to what develops out of post-structuralism. He speaks of the necessary inclusion of the non-objective viewpoint in science, of the practical in art, of hedonist criteria in moral theory, and so on (II, 586). His goal is a communicative version of what Marx called a 'real abstraction' when describing the generality of labour, its indifference to its specific forms under fully developed capitalism (II, 591). Habermas' version is to say that communicative action becomes practically true as the background knowledge of the life world. One can take it for granted. Thus, social development itself becomes a way to generalize the structure of the life world, to reduce the power of the systems of money and power over against it (II, 593). His celebration of the multiplicity of social movements resembles what Negri and Guattari do in their work.

　　But the import of the words materiality, historicity, alterity, and rhetoricity remains obscure for Habermas. It is the very historical character of the life world that prevents it from being a guarantee of reason; it is always shaped by domination and inequality. By dissociating himself from a materialist position, he sacrifices insight into the ways the colonization of culture and the life world are materially connected to economic and social domination (by gender, race and so on), not as reflexes of an economy deemed external to culture, but as extensions of material power through empirical connectors that relay domination from one domain to another. When reason becomes the fulfillment, the fabrication of the abstract ideal of substantive equality, in economics, culture, politics, aesthetics, and so forth, then only will it be possible to call it a real abstraction or the realization of reason.

2.　THE THEORY OF AUTONOMY

1.　Negri's two early works on legal theory were published by Cedam in

Padua. All of his later works were published by Feltrinelli in Milan. Several of his works have been translated into English, and Red notes in England has published an anthology entitled *Revolutionary Writings*. The works published in English so far are *Domination and Sabotage* in *Working Class Autonomy and the Crisis* (London: Red Notes, 1979), and *Marx Beyond Marx* (Amherst: Bergin & Garvey, 1984). The latter book contains an excellent bibliography on Negri and the autonomy movement by Harry Cleaver (see pp. 222–9). The theory of autonomy derives from the work of Reniero Panzieri and Mario Tronti in *Quaderni Rossi* in the early 1960s. Panzieri first advanced the idea that workers possessed a political power within the sphere of production that would determine points of struggle based on the contradictions inherent in the attempt in state planning to manage the labour process. In later works – *On the Capitalist Use of the Machine in Neo-Capitalism* and *Surplus Value and Planning* – Panzieri advances arguments found also in Negri: that capitalist planning merely spreads the antagonism of the capitalist labour relation throughout society and that the unification of the factory and of society becomes the tendency of capitalist development. Panzieri also analyzed the role of unions in the exercise of capitalist political control, and he perceived that the struggle for the reappropriation of the productive forces, between workers and the state, was the fundamental problem of radical politics. Tronti's *Operai e Capitale* [*Workers and Capital*] (1966) is to some extent a proto-autonomous theory. There, Tronti argues that the working class should be seen as external to the project of capitalist economic development, that it can become autonomous from capital, that the more the capitalist system is perfected, the more the class becomes a contradiction within it, that marxism requires an autonomous organization of the working class, that capitalist production becomes identified with the social relations of the factory, which spread over society, and thereby becomes inherently political, that all society comes to function as a moment in production, that state planning is simply a higher level of capitalist organization, that with the socialization of capitalist relation, workers' control over the social process becomes more possible, that the purpose of struggle is to decompose capital on the basis of its own organic composition from within production, that the more capital grows, the more it needs to control the labour force, which is the dynamic of capital, that the capitalist process of production is already revolutionary because it compresses the productive force of workers, that all capitalist contradictions refer to the fundamental one between workers and owners, that capital can be made a moment in the development of workers' self-government because workers can destroy capital but capital cannot do without workers, that to stop work is to refuse capital's command as the organizer of production, that economic crises are always political, produced by the subjective movements of the organized working class, and that autonomous working class power is the only thing that can break the capitalist relation of production through a political organization modelled on what the class already is. Negri and Tronti share the idea that the sphere of production is a common terrain between labour and capital, and control moves back and forth between the two. Wage demands are countered by inflationary prices, but ultimately, for both thinkers, power resides on the side of workers, especially in their ability to make themselves autonomous from capital. Negri differs from Tronti, who concentrates on workers in the sphere of production, by emphasizing the larger proletariat – 'the party of the new social strata'.

2. For an example of contemporary autonomy analysis in the United States, see 'The Left Today', in *Midnight Notes*, no. 7 (June 1984) pp. 6–8 (P.O. Box 204, Jamaica Plain, MA 02130). See also the first issue of *Copyright*.

3. THE POLITICS OF DECONSTRUCTION

1. Review, *The New York Review of Books* (27 October, 1983).
2. J. Derrida, 'Limited Inc', *Glyph*. Vol. 2 (1977).
3. 'La question du style' in *Nietzsche auhourd'hui?* (Paris: Livres de poche, 1975). The essay has been subsequently republished under the title 'Eperons'. The section of this chapter on Derrida on Nietzsche was first written for Michelle Le Doeuff's 'Women and Philosophy' seminar at the Ecole Normale Superieure at Fontenay-aux-Roses in 1976–77. It was presented as a paper at the Radical Philosophy Festival at Bristol, England, in spring, 1977.
4. Derrida writes: 'In *Ecce Homo*, two paragraphs follow each other in which Nietzsche advances successively that he has 'a large number of possible styles', or that there is no 'style as such', because he 'knows woman well' (269).
5. *The Gay Science*, tr. W. Kaufmann (New York: Vintage, 1974) p. 122; *Nietzsche Werke* (Berlin: DeGruyter, 1968) Vol. V, pt. 2, p. 20.
6. *Ibid.*, 128; 105.
7. *The Will to Power*, tr. W. Kaufmann (New York: Vintage, 1967) pp. 318, 528, 545; *Nietzsche Werke*, Vol. VIII, pt. 2, pp. 30, 119; Vol. VII, pt. 2, p. 223.
8. *Gay Science*, p. 38; p. 20.
9. *Beyond Good and Evil*, tr. W. Kaufman (New York: Penguin, 1966) p. 2; *Nietzsche Werke* (Berlin: DeGruyter, 1968) Vol. VI, pt. 2, p. 3.
10. F. Nietzsche, *Ecce Homo, Werke*, ed. G. Colli and M. Montinari (Berlin: DeGruyter, 1960) Bd. 6, pt. 3: 267. On the outtakes, see Montinari, 'Ein neuer Abschnitt in Nietzsches *Ecce Homo*', *Nietzsche Studien*, 1 (1972) pp. 380–418. On this issue further, see M. Ryan, 'The Act: *Ecce Homo*', *Glyph*, 2 (1977) pp. 64–87, and M. Meskel and M. Ryan, 'Pas de deux: Esquisse d'un (non)-rapport', in *Qui a peur de la philosophie*, ed GREPH (Paris: Flammarion, 1977).
11. *Will*, p. 257: *NW*, Vol. VIII, pt. 3, p. 402.
12. *Ecce Homo*, tr. W. Kaufmann (New York : Vintage, 1969) pp. 332, 334; *Nietzsche Werke* (Berlin: DeGruyter, 1969) Vol. VI, pt. 3 pp. 369–72; *Beyond*, p. 209; *NW*, p. 224.

13. *Nietzsche Werke* (Berlin: DeGruyter, 1969), Vol. VI, pt. 3, p. 74: Vol. VI, pt. 3, p. 74.
14. *Will*, pp. 292–3; *NW*, VIII, pt. 2, p. 216.
15. *Ibid.*, p. 292: *NW*, VIII, pt. 2 pp. 296–7.
16. *Beyond*, p. 161; *NW* p. 175.
17. *Will*, pp. 443–4; *NW*, VIII, pt. 3. pp. 38–9.
18. *Ecce* p. 267; *NW*, p. 304: *Nietzsche Werke* (Berlin: DeGruyter, 1977), Vol. VII, pt. 1, p. 120: *Ecce*, p. 308; *NW*, p. 346. My italics.
19. *Ecce*, p. 265; *NW*, p. 302.
20. *Science*, p. 343; *NW*, p. 316.
21. *Nietzsche Werke* (Berlin: DeGruyter, 1969), Vol. VI, pt. 3, p. 399.
22. *Beyond*, p. 161; *NW, p. 175.*

4. POST-MODERN POLITICS

1. F. Jameson, 'Post-Modernism' or the Cultural Logic of Late Capitalism', *New Left Review* (July 1984) Vol. 146, pp. 53–92. There are a number of excellent sympathetic accounts of post-modernism. See especially B. Wallis (ed.), *Art After Modernism: Rethinking Representation* (New York: New Museum of Contemporary Art, 1984), H. Foster *Recodings: Art, Spectacle, Cultural Politics* (Port Townsend: Bay Press, 1985), and the special number of post-modernism published by the London Institute of Contemporary Art.
2. J-F. Lyotard, *Driftworks* (New York: Semiotexte, 1982).
3. J. Baudrillard, *Simulations* (New York: Semiotexte, 1983) and *In the Shadow of the Silent Majorities* (New York: Semiotexte, 1984). Baudrillard's position in his political pamphlets combines strands of autonomy with a somewhat more conservative polemic. See especially *La gauche divine: chronique des annees '77-'84* (Paris: Grasset, 1985). His most recent work seems more influenced by the Marquis de Sade than Marx, and he seems, as Doug Kellner notes in his forthcoming book on Baudrillard's politics (with Blackwell), to have capitulated to an aristocratic outlook that seeks pleasure somewhat cynically in the derision of others and of all political idealism.
4. A. Fuentes and B. Ehrenreich, *Women in the Global Factory* (Boston: South End Press, 1985).
5. A. Kroker and D. Cook, *The Post Modern Scene: Excremental Culture and Hyper-Aesthetics* (New York: St. Martin's Press, 1987).
6. F. Guattari and A. Negri, *Communists Like Us* (New York: Semiotexte, 1987).

6. RHETORIC AND IDEOLOGY

1. L. Althusser, 'Ideology and Ideological State Apparatuses', *Lenin and Philosophy, op.cit.*
2. See chapter 2.

3. Essential to this strain of psychoanalysis is the idea that a sense of self boundaries is constructed through the internalization of representations of others, especially of primary caretakers. It is a theory of the social and rhetorical formation of self identity. See N. Chodorow, *The Reproductions of Mothering* (Berkeley: University of California Press, 1977), and more specifically G. Platte and F. Weinstein, *Psychaonalytic Sociology* (Baltimore: Johns Hopkins University Press, 1972), as well as R. Schafer, *Aspects of Internalization* (New York: International Universities Press, 1968); D. Beres and E. Joseph, 'The Concept of Mental Representation in Psychoanalysis', *International Journal of Psychoanalysis* (1970), no. 51, pp. 1–9; S. J. Blatt and S. Schichman, 'Two Primary Configurations of Psychopathology', *Psychoanalysis and Contemporary Thought* Vol. 6 (1983), no. 2, pp. 187–254.
4. For a study of the contradictory impulses present in popular thinking around popular issues, see C. Reinarman, *American States of Mind* (New Haven: Yale University Press, 1987).
5. I am grateful to one of my students, Eric Reed, for an excellent paper that drew my attention to this way of thinking about the difference between metaphor and metonymy.
6. See Ryan and Kellner, *Camera Politica* (Bloomington: Indiana University Press, 1988), especially the appendix.

7. THE RHETORIC OF LIBERALISM

1. By 'liberalism' I mean the social theory of individualism. On liberalism in general, see R. M. Unger, *Knowledge and Politics* (New York: The Free Press, 1975), and T. Spragens, *The Irony of Liberal Reason* (Chicago: University of Chicago Press, 1981). Spragens characterizes what he calls 'Liberal Reason' in the following way. It assumes that 'human understanding, guided by the "natural light" of reason, can and should be autonomous. Moreover, it constitutes the norm and the means by reference to which all else is measured. It is possible and necessary to begin the search for knowledge with a clean slate. It is possible and necessary to base knowledge claims on a clear and distinct, indubitable, self-evident foundation. This foundation is to be composed of simple, unambiguous ideas or perceptions . . . The entire body of valid human knowledge is a unity, both in method and in substance . . . Genuine knowledge is in some sense certain, "verifiable", and capable of being made wholly explicit'.
2. T. Paine, *The Rights of Man* (London: Penguin, 1979) p. 187.
3. J. Locke, *Two Treatises of Government* (New York: Cambridge University Press, 1980) p. 324.
4. This is clear in Hayek's *Law, Legislation, and Liberty: The Mirage of Social Justice* (London: Routledge & Kegan Paul, 1976), which reasserts liberal doctrine. Nature, for Hayek, is not a pre-historical category, but the name for post-liberal, anti-capitalist socialist experiments: 'The demand for "social justice" is indeed an expression of revolt of the tribal

spirit against the abstract requirements of the coherence of the Great Society with no such visible common purpose' (p.144). Don't ask me to try to make sense of this passage.

5. See S. Federici and L. Fortunati, *Il grande Calibano: storia del corpo sociale ribelle nella prima fase del capitale* (Milan: Angeli, 1984) for an account of the primary accumulation of capital in Europe as an accumulation of women's power of species reproduction.

6. T. Hobbes, *Leviathan* (London: Macmillan, 1962) p. 113.

7. See C. B. MacPherson, *The Political Theory of Possessive Individualism* (Oxford: Clarendon Press, 1962). 'The agreement to enter civil society does not create any new rights; it simply *transfers* to civil authority the powers men [sic] had in the state of nature to protect t ieir natural rights' (p. 218).

8. Locke, *Treatises*, p. 460.

9. B. de Montesquieu, *The Spirit of Laws* (New York: Hafner, 1949) p. 109.

10. M. Wollstonecraft, *The Vindication of the Rights of Woman* (London: Penguin, 1978) p. 319.

11. J. S. Mill, 'An Essay on the Subjection of Women', in A Rossi (ed.) *Essays in Sexual Equality* (Chicago: University of Chicago Press, 1970) p. 222.

12. Paine, *Rights*, p. 265.

13. Charles Darwin, *The Origin of the Species* (New York: Collier, 1962) p. 27.

8. THE LAW OF THE SUBJECT

1. See M. Minow 'Interpreting Rights', *Yale Law Journal*, 96 (July 1987) 1860; J. W. Singer, 'The Legal Rights Debate in Analytical Jurisprudence from Bentham to Hohfeld', *Wisconsin Law Review* (1982) 975; and M. Tushnet, 'An Essay on Rights', *Texas Law Review*, 62 (May 1984) 1313.

2. Q. Skinner, *The Origins of Political Theory* (New York: Cambridge University Press, 1980).

3. See P. Bierne and R. Quinney (eds), *Marxism and Law* (New York: Wiley, 1982).

4. See L. Fuller, *Legal Fictions* (Stanford: Stanford University Press, 1967).

5. The relation between formal abstraction, the denial of substantive and practical determination in the name of ideal universality, and the social power of property and of the sexual institutions of patriarchal capitalism is particularly clear in Kant: 'The proposition concerning the possibility of possessing a thing outside myself after abstracting from all the conditions of empirical possession in space and time . . . does extend beyond the aforementioned conditions. It is a synthetic proposition, for it postulates as necessary to the concept of what is externally yours or mine a kind of possession not involving detention. Now, it is the task of

reason to show how such a proposition that extends beyond the concept of empirical possession is a priori possible' (*The Metaphysical Elements of Justice* (Indianapolis: Bobbs-Merrill, 1965) p. 571). Possession without empirical detention is, of course, crucial to capitalism: 'Thus I can say: I possess a field even though it is located at a place completely different from the one in which I now actually find myself. For we are concerned here only with an intellectual relationship to the object, namely, so far as it is subject to my authority (the concept of possession as a concept of the understanding, which is independent of spatial determinations)' (pp. 61–2). To elevate a rational subject, capable of abstraction, over the objective world is also, it would seem, to elevate men over their 'objects': 'Again, the same thing holds for the concept of the *de jure* possession of a person so far as he belongs to the subject (for example, his wife, child, servant)' (p. 63).

6. P. Lejeune, *Le pacte autobiographique* (Paris: Seuil, 1977).

7. For a discussion of related issues, see M. Sandel (ed), *Liberalism and its Critics*, (New York: New York University Press, 1984).

8. The economist Amartya Sen's idea of 'capabilities' relates to what I am describing as exercisable rights. See *The Standard of Living* (Cambridge: Cambridge University Press, 1987).

9. POST-STRUCTURALISM AND LAW

1. I wish to thank my students in my Philosophy of Law courses at Northeastern University Law School for all of their help, explicit and implicit, in thinking through the ideas in this essay. To John Willshire, Nancy Kelly, and Karl Klare I also owe a special debt of gratitude for their help in preparing the courses. Clare Dalton, Mary Jo Frug, Morton Horowitz, Duncan Kennedy, and David Trubek also gave generously with their time and minds to the courses. I am grateful to Dan Givelber for making them institutionally possible.

2. See R. Posner, *The Economic Analysis of Law* (Boston: Little, Brown, 1977).

3. See M. Kelman, 'Trashing', *Stanford Law Review* (1984), Vol. 36 (1984) pp. 293–348.

4. See Posner, *Economic Analysis*, pp. 34–9. The other classic examples are also rural in character. The famous Coase Theorem, for example, is based on an interaction between a cattle rancher and a corn farmer. See R. Coase, 'The Problem of Social Cost', *Journal of Law and Economics*, Vol. 3 (1960) pp. 1–44.

5. R. Dworkin, *Taking Rights Seriously* (Cambridge: Harvard University Press, 1977).

6. R. Dworkin, *A Matter of Principle* (Cambridge: Harvard University Press, 1985).

7. R. Dworkin, *Law's Empire* (Cambridge: Harvard University Press, 1986).

8. See *The Politics of Law* (ed.), D. Kairys (New York: Pantheon, 1982); the special issue of the *Stanford Law Review* devoted to Critical Legal

Studies; R. Unger, 'The Critical Legal Studies Movement', *Harvard Law Review*, Vol. 96, no. 3 (1983) pp. 562–680 (reprinted as a monograph by Harvard University Press and in *Essays on Critical Legal Studies* (Cambridge: Harvard Law Review Association, 1986); D. Kennedy, 'Form and Substance in Private Law Adjudication', *Harvard Law Review*, Vol. 89 (1976) pp. 203–38: 'The Role of Law in Economic Thought: Essays on the Fetishism of Commodities', *American University Law Journal*, Vol. 34 (1986) pp. 939–1001; M. Minow, 'Law Turning Outward', *Telos* (Autumn 1987), Vol. 73, pp. 79–100; and J. W. Singer, 'The Player and the Cards: Nihilism and Legal Theory', *Yale Law Review*, Vol. 94 (1984) p. 1. On the relationship between CLS and deconstruction, see G. Peller, 'The Metaphysics of American Law', *California Law Review* (1986), Vol. 75, pp. 1151–1290 and C. Dalton, 'An Essay in the Deconstruction of Contract Doctrine', *Yale Law Journal*, Vol. 94, no. 5 (1985) pp. 999–1040; J. M. Balkin, 'Deconstructive Practice and Legal Theory', *Yale Law Journal* (1987), Vol. 96, pp. 743–86. See also J. Malkan, ' "Against Theory", Pragmatism and Deconstruction', *Telos* (Autumn 1987) pp. 129–54, who mistakenly identifies the work of Stanley Fish with deconstruction. In recent years, Fish has incorporated some deconstructive insights, and he sometimes cites Derrida as one of his 'forefathers'. Fish began as a sceptic, writing on Milton using the philosophy of David Hume, which claims that the mind makes sense out of empirical data, but that the data themselves have no inherent meaning or essence. Using this model, Fish argued that readers create the meaning of a literary text in their own minds. Later, he would argue that they do this together in interpretive communities. With this move, Fish recapitulates the intellectual history of the sceptical critique of natural law as it evolved from the strategy of cognitive doubt (Hume) to the programme of legal positivism (the idea that no legal entities exist apart from acts of legal positing or legislation– another way of saying an interpretive community). Fish never interrogates the actual powers of so-called communities, and the goal of the critique, like that of the sceptical attack on natural law in the eighteenth century, seems to be to disable any attempt to change those powers. See 'Consequences', in W. T. J. Mitchell, *Against Theory* (Chicago: University of Chicago Press, 1985); 'Working on the Chain Gang', *Texas Law Review* 60 (1982) p. 551; 'Fish vs. Fiss', *Stanford Law Review* 36 (1984) p. 1325.

9.   R. M. Unger, *Politics* (Cambridge: Cambridge University Press, 1987).
10.   *Federal Reporter*, Second Series, Vol. 828 (1987), pp. 936–40.
11.   Much CLS writing can be said to be prefigurative in this way. See especially, Singer, 'The Reliance Interest in Property', *Stanford Law Review*, Vol. 40, no 3 (February 1988) pp. 611–751.

10. WORKING HYPOTHESES FOR A POST-REVOLUTIONARY SOCIETY

1.   The literature on the economic modelling of equality is summed up

rather nicely by Sen in *On Economic Inequality* (New York: Norton, 1973). I am grateful to Alan Dyar of the Economics Department at Northeastern University and to Donald Peppard of the Economics Department at Connecticut College for suggesting readings related to these issues.

Logic of mass prodn — e.g TV.

Logic of mass prodn — e.g TV.

For it seems to be confusing the logic of capitalist mass prodn, which
   is the centralised prodn + distribn (broadcast) of a 'mass' product,
with the potential socialist use of a technology such
   as it TV — of participation in the production of
audio-visual cultural products.

→ Glenn Gould — Nigel Kennedy — v. Eno — the techn
                                            brought on by the technics
                                            now the medium of music

→ V. Dethier — Thoughts on why Derrida
                  misinterprets.

_____

→ For it seems to be points to Ryan's area of contested signs.
                        but does not make this explicit!

problem surrounds
→ Product + the system of distribution + consumption
— mass produce a product by all means — it is
   democratic access of product.

but — to get away from everybody has passive 'universal'
not have equal access to and control over
the means of production: those who are
now the consumer may also be able to 'produce'
products for mass distribution. [related to Erik above